ROYAL HISTORICAL SOCIETY

STUDIES IN HISTORY

New Series

SCOTTISH PUBLIC OPINION AND THE ANGLO-SCOTTISH UNION 1699–1707

SCOTTISH PUBLIC OPINION AND THE ANGLO-SCOTTISH UNION 1699–1707

Karin Bowie

THE ROYAL HISTORICAL SOCIETY
THE BOYDELL PRESS

First published 2007

A Royal Historical Society publication
Published by The Boydell Press
an imprint of Boydell & Brewer Ltd
PO Box 9, Woodbridge, Suffolk IP12 3DF, UK
and of Boydell & Brewer Inc.
668 Mt Hope Avenue, Rochester, NY 14620, USA
website: www.boydellandbrewer.com

ISBN 0 86193 289 7
ISBN 978 086193 289 4

ISSN 0269–2244

A CIP catalogue record for this book is available
from the British Library

This publication is printed on acid-free paper

Printed in Great Britain by
Antony Rowe Ltd, Chippenham, Wiltshire

Contents

Acknowledgements

For their help and encouragement with this book and its predecessor, my 2004 University of Glasgow doctoral thesis, I would like to thank Ted Cowan, Clare Jackson, Lionel Glassey, Chris Black, John Robertson, Chris Whatley, Douglas Watt, Lynn Abrams, Don Spaeth, Thomas Munck, Alison Peden, Dorothy Mallon, Amanda Epperson, Linda Fleming and Ruth Johnston. I owe much to John Morrill for supporting the publication of this book. Above all, I thank Colin Kidd for his outstanding generosity of spirit and unwaveringly high expectations. I am grateful to the former Student Awards Agency for Scotland for their PhD studentship. I thank the librarians and archivists at the University of Glasgow Special Collections, the National Library of Scotland, the National Archives of Scotland, the Mitchell Library and local archives in Dumfries and Motherwell for all their help. It has been a pleasure working with Christine Linehan and the Royal Historical Society. Lastly, I thank my husband Jonathan for his steadfast support, and my daughter Emily for not arriving before the thesis was finished.

Karin Bowie
January 2007

Abbreviations

NAS   National Archives of Scotland
NLS   National Library of Scotland

APS   *Acts of the parliaments of Scotland*, ed. Thomas Thomson, [Edinburgh] 1824–70
HJ   *Historical Journal*
JMH   *Journal of Modern History*
P&P   *Past & Present*
SHR   *Scottish Historical Review*

Note on the Text

All dates have been provided in Old Style, with the year beginning in January. Original spelling in primary sources has been maintained in quotations, but manuscript contractions have been expanded and printed italics have been omitted. Initial capitals have been retained in quotations but not in pamphlet titles.

Pounds Scots and sterling have been identified as such where this is clear from the sources. £1 sterling = £12 Scots.

Introduction

In the early modern period, increasing numbers of ordinary subjects became involved in national politics through the emerging phenomenon of public opinion, with a demonstrable effect on political outcomes. This book seeks to understand the formation and power of public opinion at this historically specific moment. It begins with the premise that the early modern public sphere will not be found in particular spaces or media, such as coffeehouses or newspapers, but in the encouragement of popular political participation by oppositional political groups. In periods of intense conflict, oppositional leaders sought to develop a power base in public opinion. They took advantage of expanding print markets and distribution networks to communicate with widening audiences and they adapted traditional practices of consultation and complaint to advance forms of collective opinion as an authority through which to demand change. This process generated the willing participation of many subjects through successful persuasion and mobilisation, producing statements of opinion that claimed to speak in the name of a public interest. Often these statements have been interpreted, as their makers intended, as the collective and consensual voice of the people. In recognising these representations as constructed artefacts of a political process, this study suggests that their deconstruction can offer significant insights into the nature of the early modern public sphere.

Public opinion existed at two levels: first as the actual opinions of individuals created through the interaction of prior experience and attitudes with current events, news and political rhetoric; and second as representations of opinion created to influence political authorities. To be effective, such representations had to appear to represent the consensual views of the relevant public, whether a parish, burgh, shire or nation, even though they may not have reflected the actual range of views held by the individuals concerned. The moral power of public opinion arose from the representation of consensual grievance, reinforced by an implicit threat of violent resistance by members of the aggrieved body. To understand the actual opinions held at the grass roots and how these opinions were expressed in the political process, we need to consider how political communications and events interacted with local conditions to influence individual opinions; how these opinions were mobilised and projected upwards to put pressure upon the authorities; and how authorities reacted to these activities. This chain of opinion formation, expression and impact defines the scope of early modern opinion politics.

Opinion politics allowed an increasing number of subjects to participate in a widening public sphere. This was a major change arising over time through complex, iterative processes that rested on equally complex political, social and economic conditions. The development of opinion politics was not smoothly continuous, for the idea and influence of public opinion was resisted as it evolved. Not surprisingly, this process of change has attracted significant scholarly attention from a variety of perspectives, particularly in the historiography of early modern England. Those taking a high-level view have sought to trace the development of notions of egalitarian democracy, 'the public' and the public sphere.[1] Others have examined the development of popular participation in politics through printed, written or spoken communications.[2] Some have analysed political communication and popular political activity in order to explain particular events or periods within national history.[3] Still others have sought to identify the pathways by which ordinary

[1] J. A. W. Gunn, *Politics and the public interest in the seventeenth century*, London 1969; Jürgen Habermas, *The structural transformation of the public sphere*, trans. Thomas Burger and Frederick Lawrence, Cambridge, MA 1989; Margaret R. Somers, 'Citizenship and the place of the public sphere: law, community and political culture in the transition to democracy', *American Sociological Review* lviii (1993), 587–620; David Zaret, *Origins of democratic culture: printing, petitions and the public sphere in early modern England*, Princeton 2000; Geoff Baldwin, 'The "public" as a rhetorical community in early modern England', in Alexandra Shepard and Phil Withington (eds), *Communities in early modern England*, Manchester 2000, 199–215; Mihoko Suzuki, *Subordinate subjects: gender, the political nation, and literary form in England, 1588–1688*, Aldershot 2003.

[2] F. J. Levy, 'How information spread among the gentry, 1550–1640', *Journal of British Studies* xxi/2 (1982), 11–34; Richard Cust, 'News and politics in early seventeenth-century England', *P&P* cxii (1986), 60–90; J. A. Downie, 'The development of the political press', in Clyve Jones (ed.), *Britain in the first age of party*, London 1987, 111–28; Tessa Watt, *Cheap print and popular piety, 1550–1640*, Cambridge 1991; Harold Love, *Scribal publication in seventeenth-century England*, Oxford 1993; Pauline Croft, 'Libels, popular literacy and public opinion in early modern England', *Historical Research* lxviii (1995), 266–85; Joad Raymond, *The invention of the newspaper: English newsbooks, 1641–1649*, Oxford 1996; Adam Fox, 'Rumour, news and popular political opinion in Elizabethan and early Stuart England', *HJ* xl (1997), 597–620; Sabrina A. Baron, 'The guises of dissemination in early seventeenth-century England: news in manuscript and print', in Brendan Dooley and Sabrina A. Baron (eds), *The politics of information in early modern Europe*, London 2001, 41–56.

[3] J. A. Downie, *Robert Harley and the press: propaganda and public opinion in the age of Swift and Defoe*, Cambridge 1979; Gary S. DeKrey, *A fractured society: the politics of London in the first age of party, 1689–1715*, Oxford 1985; David Stevenson, 'A revolutionary regime and the press: the Scottish Covenanters and their press, 1638–51', *The Library* vii (1985), 315–37; Tim Harris, *London crowds in the reign of Charles II: propaganda and politics from the Restoration until the Exclusion Crisis*, Cambridge 1987, and 'London crowds and the revolution of 1688', in Eveline Cruickshanks (ed.), *By force or by default? The revolution of 1688–1689*, Edinburgh 1989, 44–64; Pauline Croft, 'The reputation of Robert Cecil: libels, political opinion and popular awareness in the early seventeenth-century', *Transactions of the Royal Historical Society* 6th ser. i (1991), 43–69; Mark Knights, *Politics and opinion in crisis, 1678–81*, Cambridge 1994; John Miller, 'Public opinion in Charles II's England', *History* lxxx (1995), 359–81; Paul Monod, 'The Jacobite press and English censorship, 1689–95', in Eveline Cruickshanks and Edward Corp (eds), *The Stuart court in exile and the Jacobites*, London 1995, 125–42; John Walter, *Understanding popular violence in the English revolution: the Colchester plunderers*, Cambridge 1999; Richard Cust, 'Charles I and popularity', in Thomas Cogswell, Richard Cust and Peter Lake (eds), *Politics, religion*

subjects engaged with political affairs at the local level.[4] Taken together, this work provides an increasingly cohesive view of the operation of public opinion in seventeenth- and early eighteenth-century England, allowing historians to take greater account of the importance of public opinion in national political narratives.[5]

The focus on popular participation and the public sphere in English historiography reflects both a general turn towards cultural and popular history and the more specific influence of Jürgen Habermas's identification of England as the birthplace of the modern public sphere.[6] England, however, was not the only early modern state with what might be called a public sphere. Studies of political communication and popular politics have provided insights into the development of public opinion and the public sphere right across early modern western Europe.[7] This book offers a study of Scotland as a contribution to this larger historiography and as a point of comparison with the archetypal English experience. Though the national trajectories of Scotland and England increasingly intertwined after the 1603 union of the Scottish and English crowns, Scotland retained distinct political institutions and cultures that influenced the forms and practices of its public sphere. The Scottish case therefore represents a unique moment of development with relevance in a European and British context.

In order to capture the complex processes by which public opinion was shaped, generated and applied to political events in the early modern period,

---

and popularity in early Stuart Britain, Cambridge 2002, 235–58; Gary S. DeKrey, *London and the Restoration, 1659–1683*, Cambridge 2005.

4   Keith Wrightson, 'The politics of the parish in early modern England', in Paul Griffiths, Adam Fox and Steve Hindle (eds), *The experience of authority in early modern England*, Basingstoke 1996, 10–46; Mark Goldie, 'The unacknowledged republic: office holding in early modern England', and Steve Hindle, 'The political culture of the middling sort in English rural communities, c. 1550–1700', in Tim Harris (ed.), *The politics of the excluded, c. 1500–1800*, Basingstoke 2001, 153–94, 125–52; Peter Lake, 'Puritans, popularity and petitions: local politics in national context, Cheshire, 1641', in Cogswell, Cust and Lake, *Politics, religion and popularity*, 259–89.

5   Tim Harris, *Restoration: Charles II and his kingdoms, 1660–1685*, London 2005.

6   Habermas, *Structural transformation*, 57.

7   For example, Christian Jouhaud, 'Readability and persuasion: political handbills', in Roger Chartier (ed.), *The culture of print: power and the uses of print in early modern Europe*, Cambridge 1989; Jeffrey K. Sawyer, *Printed poison: pamphlet propaganda, faction politics, and the public sphere in early seventeenth-century France*, Berkeley 1990; J. A. W. Gunn, *Queen of the world: opinion in the public life of France from the Renaissance to the Revolution*, Oxford 1995; Hans Speier, 'The rise of public opinion', in Robert Jackall (ed.), *Propaganda*, Basingstoke 1995, 26–46; Bob Harris, *Politics and the rise of the press: Britain and France, 1620–1800*, London 1996; William Beik, *Urban protest in seventeenth-century France*, Cambridge 1997; Wayne te Brake, *Shaping history: ordinary people in European politics, 1500–1700*, Berkeley 1998; Jon Cowans, 'Habermas and French history: the public sphere and the problem of political legitimacy', *French History* xiii/2 (June 1999), 134–60; Dooley and Baron, *Politics of information*; and Brendan Dooley, 'The public sphere and the organisation of knowledge', in John Marino (ed.), *Early modern Italy, 1550–1796*, Oxford 2002.

this book will focus on the 1699–1707 union crisis in Scotland. This upheaval in Anglo-Scottish relations culminated in the passage of acts of union in the Scottish and English parliaments that created a new united kingdom and parliament of Great Britain in 1707. This significant shift in Scotland's constitutional status was strongly linked to the development of opinion politics in Scotland from the late 1690s, providing an ideal case study of the emergence of public opinion in national politics. The union crisis also captures the episodic nature of the development of the early modern public sphere as high levels of conflict motivated change in political practices and expressions of public opinion became increasingly prominent and influential in political discourse and events. In providing a picture of the developing public sphere in Scotland, this book seeks to contribute to the study of popular political participation and to our understanding of the union of 1707. Though not a comprehensive study of the making of the union, it aims to provide fresh insights into this significant question in Scottish and British historiography through an understanding of the workings of opinion politics in 1699–1707.

Early modern public opinion

Public opinion has been called a 'sociologically complex phenomenon'.[8] No single factor, such as urbanisation, literacy, printing or social change, can adequately explain public opinion in an era when the growing middling sort was important but still small and when barriers of censorship, illiteracy, poor distribution and high costs could still contain print culture within distinct limits. If any factor will be emphasised here, it will be the politico-religious commitments created by the Reformation and early modern state formation that connected subjects ideologically across social levels and geographies.[9] These ideological differences made the medieval ideal of consensus politics unrealisable, leading to the development of adversarial politics and loosely organised oppositional groups operating in a partisan fashion within political institutions.[10] These groups sought to use popular pressure to achieve political control through the authority of a claimed consensus of opinion, backed up with the threat of popular disorder. This was not an immediate response to ongoing conflict: traditions of consensus politics and the control of politics by a small elite militated against the casual publication of dissenting opinions, while conventions against disorder and the irrational mob discouraged the overt organisation of crowd activities. Under the strain of intractable

8   Bob Harris, 'Historians, public opinion and the "public sphere"', *Journal of Early Modern History* i (1997), 377.
9   Tim Harris, 'The problem of "popular political culture"', *History of European Ideas* x (1989), 43–58.
10 Mark Kishlansky, 'The emergence of adversary politics in the Long Parliament', *JMH* xlix (Dec. 1977), 617–40; Paul D. Halliday, *Dismembering the body politic: partisan politics in England's towns, 1650–1730*, Cambridge 1998.

religious and political differences, however, these conventions began to bend and to be broken. The public sphere began not simply in the newspaper or a growing bourgeoisie but in a failure of consensus politics and the emergence of new strategies to oppose authority on the grounds of a public interest.[11]

Drawing on traditional ideas of consultation and remonstrance, oppositional leaders found a deep, if dangerous, source of power in the engagement of ordinary subjects in the expression of public opinion. The medieval petition, for example, could be modified from a vehicle for the humble expression of grievances into a populist weapon with the organised collection of thousands of signatures on aggressively worded documents. Its power could be strengthened further by the gathering of crowds of supporters to accompany formal presentations to governmental bodies.[12] As adversarial leaders pursued old communicative practices with new belligerence, governments had to decide how to respond: would they maintain restrictions on the publicity of government or participate in an emerging politics of public opinion? Though early modern governments had long been concerned with the development and maintenance of popular support in a general sense, their active participation in opinion politics occurred under duress.[13] Resistance to new practices gave way to reciprocal participation in order to secure short-term gains. In the longer term, state acceptance of innovative activities tended to elevate the legitimacy of public opinion and contribute to the transformation of the political process. As a result, the degree to which a state accepted, controlled or countered the claims of public opinion can be read as an indicator of the level of development and legitimacy of public opinion in a given polity.

A number of preconceptions about the public sphere need to be set aside before embarking on the study of opinion formation, expression and impact in the early modern period. Jürgen Habermas's work on seventeenth-century England has encouraged a focus on newspapers and coffeehouses as the signature media of the emerging public sphere.[14] The present study suggests that the particular means by which oppositional leaders engaged popular opinion varied according to the institutions and traditional practices of individual states and political cultures. Research into the public sphere therefore needs to embrace whatever methods were in use to inform, influence and represent public opinion in a given place and time, interpreted within the context of contemporary political culture and experience. These might include

11 Zaret, *Origins of democratic culture*, ch. iii; Cust, 'Charles I and popularity'; Gunn, *Politics and the public interest*, ch. i.

12 Geoffrey Koziol, *Begging pardon and favor: ritual and political order in early medieval France*, Ithaca 1992; Zaret, *Origins of democratic culture*, 81–99, ch. viii.

13 Miller, 'Public opinion'; Raymond, *Invention of the newspaper*; Tim Harris, '"Venerating the honesty of a tinker": the king's friends and the battle for the allegiance of the common people in Restoration England', in Harris, *Politics of the excluded*, 195–232.

14 Steve Pincus, '"Coffee politicians does create": coffeehouses and Restoration political culture', *JMH* lxvii (Dec. 1995), 807–34; Bob Harris, 'Scotland's newspapers, the French Revolution and domestic radicalism (c.1789–1794)', *SHR* lxxxiv (Apr. 2005), 39–45.

the public and private channels by which news and argument spread, from printed pamphlets and newspapers to meetings, sermons, letters and coffee-house conversations; and the methods by which opinion was organised and expressed upwards, whether by oaths, petitions, instructions, crowd protests, riots or otherwise.

A further Habermasian legacy can be seen in the conception of the public sphere as a place of rational debate that produces a unitary view of the public interest.[15] This overlaps with the desire of some social historians to hear the voice of the people in popular political activity.[16] If factions sought to influence outcomes with expressions of public opinion legitimated by a rhetoric of consensus, then surviving expressions must be interpreted with caution. The dynamics of opinion politics suggest that representations of opinion more often emerged from conflict than unanimity as partisan leaders mobilised support to win local control or convince the centre of a local consensus.[17] Representations of opinion may have spoken for a wide constituency, perhaps a majority or even a large majority, but the historian cannot assume this without corroborating evidence. An amalgamation of various forms of representation, stretching across geographies and social levels, could provide the grounds for conclusions on a majority view, but the opinions of those not represented must always remain in question.

If representations of opinion should not be interpreted as the spontaneous voice of the people, then are they to be rejected as the product of elite manipulation? Such black-and-white distinctions hide the social complexity of early modern opinion politics.[18] Social hierarchies did influence political activities: the natural leadership of elites was presumed, allowing them to organise activities on the national political stage to which many commoners gave their willing support. Moreover, the nature of information dissemination in the early modern period meant that some commoners relied on local elites for the supply of political information, introducing a potential source of bias. Nevertheless, elite-sponsored messages still had to resonate with local grievances, attitudes and loyalties to be influential. Audiences received unintended as well as intended communications and interpreted this information through their own perceptual frameworks to produce unique meanings not necessarily identical to party discourse or printed argument.[19] Participation in political activity relied on grass-roots engagement and could include adaptations to reflect a non-elite agenda. In petitioning, for example, elites might

15 Cowans, 'Habermas and French history', 135.
16 E. P. Thompson, 'The moral economy of the English crowd in the eighteenth century', *P&P* 1 (1971), 76–136; more recently, Andy Wood, *Riot, rebellion and popular politics in early modern England*, Basingstoke 2002.
17 Halliday, *Dismembering the body politic*; Lake, 'Puritans, popularity and petitions'.
18 Harris, '"Popular political culture"'.
19 Fox, 'Rumour, news and popular political opinion'; Michael P. Hanagan, Leslie Page Moch and Wayne te Brake, *Challenging authority: the historical study of contentious politics*, Minneapolis 1998, p. xvi.

coordinate mass campaigns but texts often contained the specific concerns of a particular group or locality.[20] The manifestation of local or plebeian concerns within organised expressions of opinion can also be seen in crowds, where traditional crowd behaviours, such the purging and punishing of persons seen to present a danger to the community, could overtake collective demonstrations orchestrated by elites.[21]

Representations of opinion, therefore, in all their forms, contained a diversity of social perspectives and were unlikely to reflect a straightforward popular consensus. Having recognised this, we can begin to reconstruct the politics of public opinion from these sources with due attention to their complexities. Such a reconstruction would begin by examining the links between political messages, collective activities, political factions and the government. To what degree were oppositional leaders attempting to communicate with extra-institutional audiences? How successful were they in drawing on grassroots concerns to generate support for demands at the national level? How did they justify their attempts to influence the government with expressions of opinion? And how did governmental institutions react to the pressure of public opinion?

For the early modern period, such questions are most likely to be posed for periods of crisis, when controls on communication and political practices loosened under conditions of conflict. Crises drove deep levels of popular participation for periods of time in what scholars of collective action have called a 'cycle of protest'.[22] Through repeated crises, strategies for the use of public opinion increased in sophistication and aggression. Each episode set precedents for the next, contributing to the establishment of public opinion as a rhetorical entity with a contested and evolving role in national politics. Over time, political theory caught up with practice, justifying innovative practices with new philosophies of popular power.[23] We can begin to understand this tangled process by studying particular events that generated broad political participation and aggressive claims for the authority of public opinion.

From 1699 to 1707 popular participation in Scottish national affairs increased dramatically through a rising flood of pamphlets, adversarial mass petitioning and a variety of crowd protests and riots. The scale of popular involvement was remarkable for the time, whether assessed in a Scottish, British or European context, yet few historians have asked how this level of engagement came to be or considered in detail what effect it had on the making of the Anglo-Scottish union of 1707. Currently dominant interpretations assume a popular rejection of union in Scotland based on the manifesta-

---

20 Zaret, *Origins of democratic culture*, 231–9.
21 Natalie Zemon Davis, 'The rites of violence', in her *Society and culture in early modern France*, London 1975, 152–87; Beik, *Urban protest*.
22 Hanagan, *Challenging authority*, xvi.
23 Zaret, *Origins of democratic culture*, 266–70.

tion of anti-union opinion in petitions and riots in 1706. The passage of the treaty over the objections of the people has been attributed to English intimidation and crown management, including open bribery, making the union 'probably the greatest "political job" of the eighteenth century'.[24] Rooted in a transparent acceptance of representations of opinion as the voice of the people, as well as a rejection of the influence of public opinion in the political process, this approach threatens to reduce our understanding of this complex event to a simple story of coercion, betrayal and Scottish impotence.[25] A closer look at the dynamics of public opinion in the Scottish public sphere can suggest different conclusions.

Not all scholars have sustained a focus on political jobbery: some have pointed to the unionist implications of increasing Scottish trade with England in the seventeenth century while others have indicated the importance of the rise of religious moderation in post-Restoration Scotland and the growing acknowledgement in intellectual circles of the limited nature of Scottish sovereignty under the Anglo-Scottish union of crowns.[26] These studies acknowledge the flourishing print debates on union, particularly those of 1706–7, though none investigates the distribution, readership or popular impact of these pamphlets. A prosopographical study has evaluated a wide range of influences bearing on each member of parliament, including petitions from constituents as well as kinship connections, business interests and religious affiliations. Not finding a direct link between petitions and anti-union votes, this study concluded that these representations had little impact on the making of the union.[27] Other work, however, has noted a relationship between riots in Edinburgh and amendments to the economic provisions of

[24] William Ferguson, 'The making of the treaty of union of 1707', *SHR* xliii (Oct. 1964), 110.

[25] Idem, 'Recent interpretations of the making of the treaty of union of 1707', *Scottish Tradition* vii/viii (1977–8), 95–114; P. W. J. Riley, *The union of England and Scotland: a study in Anglo-Scottish politics of the eighteenth century*, Manchester 1978; Paul H. Scott, '"Bought and sold for English gold"', *Chapman* lxix–lxx (Autumn 1992), 161–6, and *Andrew Fletcher and the treaty of union*, Edinburgh 1994; William Ferguson, *Scotland's relations with England: a survey to 1707*, Edinburgh 1994.

[26] T. C. Smout, *Scottish trade on the eve of union, 1660–1707*, Edinburgh 1963; 'The Anglo-Scottish union of 1707: the economic background', *Economic History Review* xvi (1963–4), 455–67; and 'The road to union', in Geoffrey Holmes (ed.), *Britain after the Glorious Revolution*, London 1969, 176–96; Christopher A. Whatley, 'Salt, coal and the union of 1707: a revision article', *SHR* lxvi (Apr. 1987), 26–45, and 'Economic causes and consequences of the union of 1707: a survey', *SHR* lxviii (1989), 150–81; Colin Kidd, 'Religious realignment between the Revolution and the union', and John Robertson, 'An elusive sovereignty: the course of the union debate in Scotland, 1698–1707', in John Robertson (ed.), *A union for empire: political thought and the British union of 1707*, Cambridge 1995, 145–68, 198–227; Christopher A. Whatley, 'Scotland, England and "the golden ball": putting economics back into the union of 1707', *Historian* li (Autumn 1996), 9–13.

[27] Allan I. Macinnes, 'Influencing the vote: the Scottish estates and the treaty of union, 1706–7', *History Microcomputer Review* (Fall 1990), 11–25.

the union treaty.[28] Historians have begun to follow this lead by considering the question of extra-parliamentary pressure in more recent studies, though there is still a tendency to see representations of opinion as uncomplicated barometers of popular opinion.[29]

New interest in the making of Britain has reopened the union question from a fresh direction.[30] Coming largely from an English historiographical background, the new British historians have tended to pay more attention to public opinion and to reject the 'political job' explanation for the making of union as reductionist.[31] Their conclusions, however, often rest on a reinterpretation of previous scholarship. One recent study has offered a new analysis of voting patterns in the 1703 and 1706 parliaments, observing from this a correlation between petitioning in 1706 and oppositional voting in 1703 and 1706. Noting that petitions may indicate the presence of 'an organised opposition', this study reveals a continuing need for more research in this area.[32]

This book seeks to fill this gap with a two-part analysis of Scottish politics and communications during the union crisis. The first section will examine the early years of the crisis to show how the public sphere in Scotland developed rapidly between 1699 and 1705 as oppositional groups marshalled public opinion against the government. Chapter 1 begins by providing a contextual explanation of Scottish politics at the end of the 1690s. The necessary conditions for an explosion in political participation are described in the deep political divisions present in Scottish society and politics; the establishment of regular channels of political communication between Edinburgh and Lowland localities; and growth in literacy and the book trade. These circumstances provided grounds for the development of adversarial opinion politics orchestrated by an emerging Country party. Chapter 2 shows how forms of popular participation and representation evolved in the period 1699–1705 through a series of specific events: the failure in 1699–1700 of the Central American colony established by the Scottish Company Trading to Africa and the Indies; the questionable legality of Queen Anne's 1702 parliament;

---

28 Whatley, 'Economic causes and consequences', 160–2.
29 J. R. Young, 'The parliamentary incorporating union of 1707: political management, anti-unionism and foreign policy', in T. M. Devine and J. R. Young (eds), *Eighteenth-century Scotland: new perspectives*, East Linton 1999, 29–37; Christopher A. Whatley, *Bought and sold for English gold? Explaining the union of 1707*, East Linton 2001, 77–80, appendix 5; Jeffrey Stephen, 'The Kirk and the union, 1706–07: a reappraisal', *Records of the Scottish Church History Society* xxxi (2002), 83–9.
30 Geoffrey Holmes, *The making of a great power: late Stuart and early Georgian Britain*, London 1993; Mark Goldie, 'Divergence and union: Scotland and England, 1660–1707', in Brendan Bradshaw and John Morrill (eds), *The British problem c. 1534–1707: state formation in the Atlantic archipelago*, Basingstoke 1996, 220–45; W. A. Speck, *The birth of Britain: a new nation, 1700–1710*, Oxford 1994; Jim Smyth, *The making of the United Kingdom, 1660–1800*, Harlow 2001; Iain McLean and Alistair McMillan, *State of the union*, Oxford 2005.
31 Smyth, *Making of the United Kingdom*, 95–102.
32 McLean and McMillan, *State of the union*, 33.

proposals for a toleration of Episcopalian worship in Scotland in 1703; anti-Catholicism in Dumfries in 1704 during a Jacobite scare; and the trial in 1705 of an English captain and his crew for their alleged piracy of a Scottish African Company ship. This chapter identifies pamphlets, mass petitioning and organised crowds as the primary means used to shape and express opinion in the Scottish public sphere at this time. Chapter 3 reviews the government's response to these developments in opinion politics and assesses the degree to which it chose to counter, control or concede to public opinion, providing a view of the power and legitimacy of public opinion at this early modern moment.

Working within the context established in part I, part II considers the generation and expression of public opinion on the union treaty and its impact on the final form of the union. This begins in chapter 4 with a study of public communication on the union question from 1699 to 1705. This shows the critique of the 1603 union of crowns advanced by oppositional writers and their development of a vision of a federal union secured by a treaty with England in return for Scottish acceptance of the Hanoverian succession. The impact of these communications is evaluated within the context of the Court party's response to the rising publicity of politics in Scotland. The contours of public opinion on union are further traced in chapter 5 with a review of the intense print exchanges seen in 1706–7 before and during the debates on the treaty of union in the Scottish parliament. This evaluates the impact of discourse on opinion as oppositional writings became more radical and the number of communications in favour of an incorporating union increased sharply. Chapter 6 expands the scope of the public sphere beyond print discourse to consider the dozens of addresses sent to parliament from national and local bodies in the 1706–7 session. This demonstrates the opposition's deliberate pressuring of parliament with anti-treaty opinion, following precedents set since 1699. Reactions to the addressing campaign are assessed, showing the degree to which opinion politics could influence outcomes. Chapter 7 further expands the analysis to incorporate crowd activities. This chapter explains the role of crowds in oppositional strategies and assesses the impact of collective action on the treaty debates. The book concludes with observations on what the Scottish public sphere can tell us about the making of the union, and what the making of the union can tell us about the early modern public sphere.

PART I

THE PUBLIC SPHERE IN SCOTLAND, 1699–1705

1

Politics and Communications in Post-Revolution Scotland

The Revolution settlement of 1689–90 created conditions for the growth of adversarial parliamentary politics in Scotland. The politics of the Reformation and the 1603 union of crowns had created longstanding divisions in Scottish society over the government of the reformed Church and the legitimacy of resistance to the monarch. After the Revolution, this translated into divisions between Presbyterians and Episcopalians; and Revolution Whigs, Tories and Jacobites. In addition, ongoing conflicts of interest between England and Scotland in the union of crowns fuelled a Court–Country split in a parliament that met more frequently and exercised greater liberty of speech. Histories of Scotland have recognised these conditions and the resulting inability of the crown to manage parliament; less well recognised is the degree to which the new parliamentary debates began to include a wider public.[1] Improving literacy and communication networks increasingly allowed political news and information to spread beyond Edinburgh and its elites, involving many ordinary Scots in the affairs of the day. As the next chapters will show, these trends made it possible for the Country party to pursue increasingly populist strategies from the late 1690s as the collapse of the Scottish colony of Darien in central America led to a crisis in Anglo-Scottish relations.

Early modern Scotland has been described as a 'deeply and bitterly divided nation', split over incompatible notions of the government of Church and State.[2] Struggle over the extent of the monarch's spiritual powers dated from the Reformation, while developments in state formation, particularly the 1603 personal union of the English and Scottish crowns, created conflict over the extent of the king's temporal powers. Would the king control the Church through an erastian episcopalian hierarchy or would the Church govern itself through presbyterian assemblies? Was the king's power over Church and State absolute or was sovereignty shared with parliament? Was the Scottish kingship elective and subject to the collective censure of the aristocracy or was the (mythical) unbroken succession of the Scottish kingship over 2,000 years to be maintained at all costs? How could the Scottish king in London govern both Scotland and England in their best interests when those interests

---

[1]   P. W. J. Riley, *King William and the Scottish politicians*, Edinburgh 1979, represents the accepted view. This has been challenged by Derek John Patrick, 'People and parliament in Scotland, 1689–1702', unpubl. PhD diss. St Andrews 2002.
[2]   Gordon Donaldson, *Scotland: James V to James VII*, Edinburgh 1971, 360.

clashed? These fundamental problems fuelled significant levels of disruption in the seventeenth century as church government changed from episcopalian to presbyterian in the Covenanting Revolution, back to episcopalian at the Restoration and again to presbyterian at the Revolution of 1688–9; similarly, parliament took powers from the king in the Covenanting Revolution, gave them back at the Restoration and took some back again at the Revolution of 1688–9.

By the end of the century, these revolutions in Church and State had ensured that there was little possible basis for a national political consensus. The Revolution settlement of 1689–90 maintained grounds for adversarial politics in Scotland with the forfeiting of James VII and the reinstatement of presbyterian church government. Although oaths excluded the most extreme Episcopalians and Jacobites from public office, and the most extreme Presbyterians excluded themselves from an uncovenanted polity, this left a volatile mix of religious and political interests vying for advantage in parliament: Covenanting and mainstream Presbyterians and conformist Episcopalians; radical and Revolution Whigs and royalist Tories. The political picture was further complicated by the personal ties and rivalries that were threaded through these ideological differences.

Though the post-Revolution government relied on the support of Revolution Whigs, William and Anne both attempted to build broad ministries that drew in Whig and Tory elements. As a result, parliamentary parties emerged not on a Whig/Presbyterian and Tory/Episcopalian axis, but on a Court–Country axis with moderates gravitating to the Court. In the Restoration period the Court party had been made up of royalist Episcopalians, while a nascent Country opposition contained those of 'the interest for liberty and privileges' and those of 'the interest of religion and presbytery'.[3] With the establishment of Presbytery in 1690, this polarity reversed as Revolution supporters and Presbyterians identified with the court. They were joined by conformist Episcopalians who chose to adhere to the crown for the sake of stability or advantage.

These court followers were managed by the crown's royal commissioner to parliament, aided by other state officers. By the late 1690s this was usually James Douglas, 2nd duke of Queensberry. The realignment of allegiances at the Revolution left a disparate assortment of those unwilling or unable to work with the Revolution regime for political, religious or personal reasons to make up the Country opposition. This grouping lacked a common ideological base and a clear leader until 1699 when a more cohesive Country party began to emerge as James Hamilton, 4th duke of Hamilton, led a more assertive opposition which claimed to represent a patriotic interest. The Court and Country parties thus forming around the figures of Queensberry and Hamilton in the late 1690s should not be confused with modern parliamentary parties.

---

[3] Quoted in Clare Jackson, *Restoration Scotland, 1660–1690: royalist politics, religion and ideas*, Woodbridge 2003, 74.

These early modern groupings did not have distinct political philosophies or elected leaders. They are better understood as loose coalitions of factions differentiated by the degrees of support or opposition they offered to royal policies and containing a range of political and religious interests.

The unicameral nature of the Scottish parliament meant that nobles acted as heads of the parliamentary parties, using social status, territorial influence, kinship links, ideological affinity, patronage and interpersonal persuasion to draw together followers from the three estates of nobles, shires and burghs. Some of these followers acted as organising lieutenants, such as the Jacobite George Lockhart of Carnwath, commissioner for Midlothian from 1702 and associate of the duke of Hamilton, or as leaders of opinion, such as Andrew Fletcher of Saltoun, a radical Whig associated with a group of young Whig nobles.[4] Although shire and burgh commissioners followed in the lead of their social superiors in political factions and were often linked to them by patronage or kinship, they also defended the interests of their estates. The burgh commissioners developed clear objectives as an estate through their annual national assembly, the Convention of Royal Burghs, focusing on matters of trade and economic development. The shire commissioners lacked the central organisation of the burghs but their political clout increased in the early modern period as land ownership expanded and shire representation increased. By the time of the union crisis, the shire estate was the largest in parliament.[5]

To some degree, noble leaders of the Court and Country factions managed to coordinate party strategy, contest open elections and marshall followers for votes. With Scotland's infrequent elections and small electorates, there was little public electioneering, but Court and Country leaders used their local influence to support preferred candidates for the shires and burghs. The Court party had the advantage of royal patronage to achieve these ends, while Country factions had to use ideological persuasion to a greater extent, tapping grass-roots discontent to generate support. One of the measures of the growing influence of the Country party during the union crisis was its ability to win over local opinion and seats, as seen in the by-elections for the May 1700 parliamentary session, when the Country party secured ten out of fourteen open seats.[6]

In leading the Court party, the royal commissioner relied on the assistance of other crown servants to rally factional followings. Queensberry was associated with the powerful Dalrymple family of advocates, judges and officers, including the brothers John Dalrymple (2nd viscount of Stair and from 1703 earl of Stair, who had served as a secretary of state under William in the early

---

4 Daniel Szechi, *George Lockhart of Carnwath, 1689–1727: a study in Jacobitism*, East Linton 2002, ch. iv; Andrew Fletcher, *Political works*, ed. John Robertson, Cambridge 1997, pp. xvi–xvii.

5 In the 1706–7 session there were 69 nobles (excluding officers of state), 82 shire commissioners and 66 burgh representatives: *APS* xi. 300–2.

6 Patrick, 'People and parliament', 249.

1690s), Sir Hew Dalrymple (Lord President of the Court of Session from 1698 and a commissioner to the 1702 union talks) and Sir David Dalrymple (solicitor-general to Queen Anne). Also important within the Court party was James Ogilvy, a younger son of the earl of Findlater made viscount of Seafield in 1698 and earl of Seafield in 1701 for his dedication to the crown. A diligent and loyal adminstrator, who maintained a wide network of supporters in Scotland, Seafield held office from 1696, surviving multiple changes in ministries. Among the committed Presbyterian Revolution men in the Court party, Patrick Hume, raised to the peerage for his services by William as Lord Polwarth in 1690 and earl of Marchmont in 1697, and Archibald and John Campbell, first (d.1703) and second dukes of Argyll, were prominent. In the union parliament, a key supporter of Queensberry was John Erskine, 6th earl of Mar, who replaced William Johnstone, 1st marquis of Annandale, as secretary of state in 1705.[7]

In 1703 it seemed that the Court party might expand to include the Cavaliers, a group of Jacobites elected or attending after taking the oaths of loyalty to the Stewart Queen Anne, daughter of the forfeited James VII, who came to the throne in 1702. These Episcopalian Jacobites formed a significant faction within Anne's parliaments from 1703 to 1707, led initially by the earl of Home. Anne's Episcopalian sympathies and Stewart credentials suggested the possibility of a Court–Cavalier alliance, but disagreements between the Cavaliers and Court Presbyterians on toleration for Episcopalian dissenters meant that the queen's ministers could not retain the Cavaliers in coalition. To the government's dismay, the Cavaliers joined with the Country party thus creating an oppositional majority in Anne's parliament. [8]

The opposition had been gaining in strength since 1699 under the leadership of the duke of Hamilton, together with his brother-in-law the crypto-Jacobite John Murray, earl of Tullibardine and from 1703 duke of Atholl. Entering parliament as the union crisis began, Hamilton drew on his status as the highest-ranking Scottish peer, his personal Jacobitism at the Revolution and his parents' strong Presbyterian and Revolution credentials to establish himself as the leader of the diverse interests contained in the Country party, though some Jacobite nobles doubted his sincerity. His key lieutenants included his brother Lord Basil Hamilton, Robert Wylie, the zealous Presbyterian minister of Hamilton parish and George Lockhart of Carnwath, the Jacobite Cavalier. Hamilton also capitalised on his family's heavy involvement in the African Company and its Darien colony as the failure of this venture in 1699–1700 sparked the first phase of the union crisis.[9]

While Hamilton provided continuity as a leader of the Country party, other nobles and their followers moved in and out of the opposition during

7   Riley, *King William*, and *Union of England and Scotland*.
8   'Scotland's ruine': *Lockhart of Carnwath's memoirs of the union*, ed. Daniel Szechi, Aberdeen 1995, chs i–ii.
9   John Gibson, *Playing the Scottish card: the Franco-Jacobite invasion of 1708*, Edinburgh 1988, 45; 'Scotland's ruine', 20–2.

the crisis. The Country opposition contained a Whig grouping led by John Hay, 2nd marquis of Tweeddale, whose father lost office after giving the royal assent to the act creating the African Company in 1695. This Whig faction included the young nobles John Leslie, 9th earl of Rothes and Robert Ker, 5th earl of Roxburgh. Andrew Fletcher of Saltoun provided an ideological lead for this group's oppositional activities, particularly in 1703. Nevertheless, the inherent sympathy of these Whig lords for the Revolution and the Protestant succession, as well as their interest in office, caused them to break away from the Country party to form a new government for the queen in 1704. Joining the London-based Whig James Johnston, a former secretary of state under William, this group became known as the New Party. After returning to the opposition in 1705, it joined the Court party in 1706, earning it the name *squadrone volante*. (Fletcher remained in the opposition, cooperating with the duke of Atholl in 1705–7.) In turn, the creation of the New Party ministry in 1704 caused the friends of the duke of Queensberry to move into opposition to undermine their new rivals for power. Loss of office brought John Murray into opposition at key moments as earl of Tullibardine in 1698–1702 and duke of Atholl in 1705–7. Though related to Hamilton, Murray maintained a separate faction within the Country party. Lastly, the dropping of the marquis of Annandale from office brought this Whig lord into the Country party for the 1706–7 session.[10]

The winning or losing of office by leading nobles was not the only factor driving membership of the opposition. The composition of the Country party also shifted as its leaders won over Court followers on policy grounds. Identifying the Court party with an absentee, Anglocentric monarch and a compliant ministry, the Country party highlighted the negative effects of royal policy and demanded change in the name of an aggrieved public. With this approach, the diverse collection of interests making up the Country party found a new ideological coherence in claiming to represent Scotland's national interests. The pursuit of this powerful rhetorical and political strategy initiated the union crisis as the party succeeded in shifting a substantial number of votes to the opposition in 1700–1.

The emergence of Court and Country parties was facilitated by the establishment of regular meetings of parliament and the lifting of restrictions on debate under the Revolution settlement. In the Restoration period the government had controlled parliament's agenda through a committee known as the Lords of the Articles. Since all overtures had to pass through this committee before being presented to parliament, and the committee's election process favoured the crown, the crown could restrict the subjects brought forwards for debate in parliament. When acts came to the house, the crown exerted further control through the generally loyal voting of the estate of bishops. When parliament proved difficult to manage even with these measures, the

---

[10] Riley, *Union of England and Scotland*, ch. iii; '*Scotland's ruine*', ch. iv.

crown could dispense with regular meetings and use smaller Conventions of Estates to vote taxes.

In reaction to these restrictions, many members pressed for changes in parliamentary procedures as part of the Revolution. As a result, the 1689 Claim of Right asserted that 'Parliaments ought to be frequently called, and allowed to sit, and the freedom of speech & debate secured to the members.'[11] Under William, the estates met ten times in twelve years with only one Convention (that of the Revolution), while parliamentary meetings under Anne were annual.[12] In addition, the 1689 Articles of Grievances declared that 'the Committee of Parliament called the Articles is a great grievance to the Nation' and an act of 1690 abolished it.[13] As a result, overtures and motions could be introduced into the house without advance notice, allowing oppositional interests to disrupt proceedings with unwelcome proposals backed by a roster of prepared speakers. Committees continued to be used by the House on occasion to review overtures, but new election procedures for these committees reduced the likelihood of crown control. The removal of the estate of bishops through the Presbyterian Church settlement further weakened crown control of proceedings in parliament, with a similar effect in the General Assembly.

The re-establishment of regular meetings of the General Assembly provided a further impetus to the development of public politics in Scotland. Having not met between 1649 and 1690, the General Assembly convened in 1690, 1694 and annually thereafter. A smaller number of nominated ministers also met in an executive committee, the Commission of the General Assembly, between these annual sessions. As meetings of the assembly did not necessarily coincide with those of parliament, the commission provided an ongoing forum for leading ministers to discuss political developments and engage with parliamentary politics. Members of the commission came from the regional presbyteries, providing a direct link between centre and locality.

Like parliament, the General Assembly experienced a loosening of its agenda after the Revolution. A Committee of Overtures maintained some control over the assembly's business, but presbyteries could instruct their representatives to introduce motions to the entire house. In 1703, for example, the presbytery of Innerkeithen directed its representative to 'be very carefull that thir instructions be read & considered by the Committee of overtures, & if they shall not be considered by that Committee. ... Then they are ordered to table them in open Assemblie'.[14]

As in parliament, internal disagreements over royal policy led to the development of Court and Country factions within the Church. Church culture

---

[11] APS ix. 40.

[12] In contrast, Charles II called just eight parliamentary sessions, plus three brief conventions, in a reign of over twenty years: APS vi–vii.

[13] APS ix. 45, 133.

[14] NAS, CH 1/2/23/3 (186).

placed a premium on consensus and the avoidance of schism, but differences on the Covenants and erastianism provided ample grounds for dissent in the post-Revolution Kirk. Though the presbytery of Humbie instructed its representative to the General Assembly to prevent 'any appearance of faction and division in this national church', others were less scrupulous.[15] Ministers like Robert Wylie regularly called upon the General Assembly to assert the Church's intrinsic right to call its own meetings. Since the Church's moderate leadership sought to avoid open confrontation with the monarch over his erastian powers, by 1701 this annual battle had taken on 'the odiouse names of Court and Country party'.[16] These struggles in the assembly were linked to parliamentary politics with the submission of overtures to parliament containing similar assertions of the Church's intrinsic rights.[17] Through this and other issues, the sphere of adversarial politics was extended to the General Assembly.

As well as providing an ongoing forum for debate, the regular meetings of parliament and General Assembly improved political communications between the centre and localities. These meetings, along with the continuing annual meetings of the Convention of Royal Burghs, allowed elites and middling sorts from the localities to engage in national political affairs. Representatives brought provincial concerns to the national stage, often through formal written instructions, and sent back news and printed material from the capital.[18] Surviving presbyterial instructions show that, alongside parochial problems like disputed calls, ministers raised issues of national scope, from the problem of Episcopal intruders to requests for the renewal of the National Covenant. Some also urged the assembly to apply to parliament or privy council for civil authorisation of fasts or the prosecution of Catholics.[19] Similarly, parliamentary instructions aired grievances with national policy alongside requests for local concessions.

Longer-term growth trends in Scottish literacy, the book trade and transport provided an infrastructure for the increasing political communication associated with regular national assemblies. Burgh and parish schools, along with private schools and home schooling, produced literacy rates in Scotland on a par with those of other early modern western European kingdoms.[20] Education provision and occupational demands in the burghs created high literacy levels in urban areas for those in crafts and trade, with somewhat lower literacy in the country. A growing print market supplied this reader-

---

15 NAS, CH 1/2/22/2 (162).
16 *Early letters of Robert Wodrow, 1698–1709*, ed. L.W. Sharp, Edinburgh 1937, 155.
17 Sir David Hume of Crossrigg, *A diary of the proceedings of the parliament and privy council of Scotland, May 21, 1700–March 7, 1707*, Edinburgh 1823, 12.
18 *Seafield correspondence from 1685 to 1708*, ed. James Grant, Edinburgh 1912, 427.
19 For example, from 1702 General Assembly instructions: NAS, CH 1/2/22/2 (149, 157); CH 1/2/22/3 (258).
20 R. A. Houston, *Scottish literacy and Scottish identity: illiteracy and society in Scotland and northern England, 1600–1800*, Cambridge 1985, 22.

ship through Lowland distribution networks of booksellers, postal deliveries and private carriers. By the early eighteenth century, many ordinary subjects in the Lowlands could access news and information on matters of national scope, though greater access to print material and news among the middling to upper sorts allowed these groups to enjoy a more detailed understanding of the national situation.

Encouraged by a series of acts of parliament and privy council, by 1700 schools had been established in the burghs and many rural parishes in the Scottish Lowlands. Schools were more likely to be established in burghs, where urban jobs more often required literacy and the burgh council controlled the funding of schools. Towns allocated income from public assets to schools, as in Lanark where in 1691 the town paid its schoolmaster from income earned on the roup (auction) of its customs and milling privileges.[21] Burgh grammar schools served the sons of burgesses and local lairds, and some charity students, with some towns having dedicated schools for the daughters of burgesses.[22] Private schools (known as vulgar or English schools), charity schools and dame schools for younger children all supplemented the burgh grammar school, helping to provide at least reading literacy to a broad section of society. In 1672 Glasgow boasted fourteen private schools, including eight dame schools.[23] In Edinburgh a charity school established in 1699 taught reading and writing in English plus arithmetic, music and spinning.[24]

Outside the towns, the provision of schools in rural parishes was patchy. Funding could be difficult to obtain where nonresident or uncooperative heritors resisted their statutory obligation to provide a school. After long experience of helping parishes mount legal cases against recalcitrant heritors, John Dundas, advocate and clerk to the General Assembly, published a manual in 1709 containing the procedures and legal forms needed to force landowners to pay up.[25] Some parishes came to rely on bequests or kirk collections to fund their schools; others, especially in remote areas, did not manage to create schools before 1700. Of twenty-five parishes in the stewartry of Kirkcudbright, only five had parish schools established by 1700.[26] This situation in the rural

[21] *Extracts from the records of the royal burgh of Lanark*, ed. Robert Renwick, Glasgow 1893, iv. 240–1.

[22] In recognition of 'how necessarie and advantageous it is and will be for this place that ane qualified school misteris were incouradged to come and recide heir for teaching and educating of burgessis daughteris', Stirling offered a house plus expenses or fifty marks a year in 1694 to any gentlewoman interested in the post: *Extracts from the records of the royal burgh of Stirling, 1667–1752*, ed. Robert Renwick, Glasgow 1889, ii. 73.

[23] James Scotland, *The history of Scottish education*, London 1969, i. 106.

[24] *Extracts from the records of the burgh of Edinburgh, 1689–1701*, ed. Helen Armet, Edinburgh 1962, 243.

[25] John Dundas, *The method of procedure by presbyteries in setting of schools in every parish*, Edinburgh 1709.

[26] James Anderson Russell, *History of education in the stewartry of Kirkcudbright*, Newton-Stewart 1951.

south-west contrasts with the parishes surrounding the city of Edinburgh, all of which had schools by 1700.[27]

Driven by burgh schooling, the strongest literacy gains in the early modern period occurred among urban middling sorts. Scotland's pattern of urbanisation in the seventeenth century, with relatively high proportions of town dwellers in the shires around Edinburgh, created a large pool of literate subjects within a short distance of the capital. Of the inhabitants of the shire of Midlothian, where Edinburgh was located, 55 per cent were urban-dwellers in 1691; the figure for nearby East Lothian was 47 per cent; 50 per cent for West Lothian; 30 per cent for Stirlingshire; 51 per cent for Clackmannanshire; 26–39 per cent for southern Fife; and 47 per cent for the East Neuk of Fife.[28] Edinburgh itself contained a high proportion of literate citizens, with 95 per cent signature literacy among craftsmen and tradesmen in the first decade of the eighteenth century. Literacy followed socio-economic opportunity and trade requirements, with nearly all merchants and professionals being literate. Male signature literacy among crafts and trades fell in outlying areas but was still fairly high at 77 per cent in towns and 69 per cent in villages.[29] As reading was taught before writing, and to girls as well as boys, it is probable that these measures understate actual reading ability in the population.

As numbers of readers rose in Scotland, so the book trade grew, especially after the Restoration as the Scottish economy recovered from the devastations of the British civil wars. By the time of the union, book sales had quadrupled from their average levels in 1600. Printing was established in Glasgow and Aberdeen as well as Edinburgh, though most political prints came from Edinburgh presses. Unlike English booktraders in the Stationers Company, Scottish printers and booksellers did not face gild-based restrictions on their trade. Low taxes on paper and book imports favoured booksellers and printers alike. The recession of the 1690s reduced book trade volumes and drove marginal players out of business, but book sales and numbers of traders rose again in the late 1690s and early 1700s. Printed parliamentary overtures and political tracts contributed to growth while newspapers swelled outputs with the licensing of the twice-weekly *Edinburgh Gazette* in 1699, followed by the *Edinburgh Courant* in 1705.[30]

The new Scottish newspapers contributed to the distribution of political information to the burghs. In the 1690s, before the establishment of the *Edinburgh Gazette*, London papers and newsletters were a regular source of news in Scotland. The London papers, however, were expensive, the English price

---

[27] Alexander Law, *Education in Edinburgh in the eighteenth century*, London 1965, 61.

[28] Michael Lynch, 'Urbanisation and urban networks in seventeenth century Scotland: some further thoughts', *Scottish Economic and Social History* xii (1992), 36.

[29] Houston, *Scottish literacy*, 47.

[30] Alistair J. Mann, *The Scottish book trade, 1500–1720: print commerce and print control in early modern Scotland*, East Linton 2000.

of 2d. sterling being equivalent to 2s. Scots. Edinburgh printers occasionally printed news broadsides for exceptional events, including reprints of London papers, as in September 1701 when the publishers of the *Edinburgh Gazette* reprinted a London news bulletin announcing Louis XIV's recognition of James Stewart, the son of James VII and II, as the rightful king of England and Scotland.[31] Nevertheless, affordable printed news remained a problem. As a result, the merchant community hailed the launch of the *Edinburgh Gazette* for its provision of an inexpensive digest of European, English and Scottish news. The Convention of Royal Burghs awarded £30 Scots to the editor in 1699 to support his venture and encouraged its burgh members to take the new paper 'by everie post'.[32] The town council of Stirling subscribed in May 1699, noting 'that they may be served with the weeklie newes by the Edinburgh Gazett, which contains both forraigne and domestick occurrences, at ane far more easie rate'.[33] At its launch, the paper sold at a discounted subscription price of 1d. Scots.[34]

When available, political pamphlets provided information and commentary at a range of prices. Shorter polemical tracts, copies of parliamentary overtures and broadside ballads cost just pennies. In 1700 6d. Scots would buy *A defence of the Scots settlement at Darien* while an overture on money and credit in 1705 cost 7d. The 1705 *Observator*, a Scottish periodical paper on current affairs, cost 9d. per issue.[35] More sophisticated or higher quality materials, including the government's printed speeches and letters and tracts by prominent politicians, were more expensive. In 1705 the queen's speech to parliament, speeches by Lord Belhaven and proposals from Dr Hugh Chamberlen for a land credit scheme each cost 1s. Scots, while a speech by Andrew Fletcher of Saltoun cost 2s. This higher price band included some London titles reprinted by Edinburgh printers, like Peter Paxton's *A scheme of union*, priced at 4s. Scots.[36] London-printed tracts sold in Edinburgh tended to fall into an even higher price bracket, including Viscount Tarbat's *Parainesis pacifica* (1702) at 7s. and George Ridpath's *The reducing of Scotland by arms* (1705) at more than £3.[37] Like the London newspapers, however, expensive works, whether English or Scottish, could be reprinted: in 1703 a Presbyterian editor reprinted Andrew Cant's *A sermon preached on the XXX day of January 1702/3* so that 'the meaner sort may have a view of the great Reflections and

31 NAS, PC 1/52/285.
32 W. J. Couper, *The Edinburgh periodical press*, Stirling 1908, i. 207.
33 *Stirling burgh extracts*, 90, 94.
34 *Edinburgh Gazette*, no. 3 (Mon. 6 Mar.–Fri. 10 Mar. 1699).
35 Ibid. no. 185 (Thur. 28 Nov.–Mon. 2 Dec. 1700); *Analecta scotica*, ed. James Maidment, Edinburgh 1834, ii. 73.
36 *Analecta scotica*, ii. 73–6.
37 *Edinburgh Gazette*, no. 185 (Thurs. 28 Nov.–Mon. 2 Dec. 1700); *Analecta scotica*, ii. 74.

Clamours he throws upon the present Church Government, the Price being so exorbitant as to take Fourteen Shil. Scots for Four Sheet of Paper'.[38]

Improving distribution networks helped to disseminate political print from Edinburgh to the localities. In the Scottish Lowlands there were many small market towns with trading links to Edinburgh.[39] Between 1689 and 1707 fifty-one new burghs of barony and regality were created, along with 246 markets or fairs, providing a network of smaller points of exchange.[40] Booksellers set up shop in regional centres like Stirling or Ayr, capitalising on the flow of people from landward areas to these towns for schooling, markets, church courts, legal services and news. By 1700 market towns with booksellers included Perth, Stirling, Dundee, Ayr, Dumfries, Lanark, Paisley, Peebles and Kelso. Larger burghs could support several booksellers, with at least eight appearing in Glasgow by 1657. Burgh fairs and chapmen supplemented established book traders, providing periodical injections of print and news to more remote areas. Booktraders in the Gaelic-speaking Highlands remained rare, with only Banff and Inverness supporting a local bookseller by 1707, though itinerant traders and private commissions produced a limited flow of print to the north.[41]

The growth of the book trade and the multiplication of fairs and markets in rural Scotland improved the reach of print despite an underdeveloped road system. Riding to Edinburgh in the summer of 1705, the Englishman Joseph Taylor found good quality roads near Edinburgh, but marvelled that the main road from Edinburgh to Carlisle was in places a mere track.[42] Nevertheless, road connections between Edinburgh and the larger Lowland towns could support a flow of news and print carried by political representatives, common carriers, merchants, chapmen and postmen, augmented by frequent sea traffic between coastal towns.

By the mid-seventeenth century, the king's post from London to Edinburgh had been incorporated into earlier private or burgh postal services in Edinburgh, Aberdeen, Glasgow and Dumfries to form a national postal system under the management of a postmaster-general in Edinburgh. The main postal routes followed the roads from Edinburgh north to Inverness via Dundee and Aberdeen; west to Stirling; west and south to Portpatrick via Glasgow and Ayr; south and west to Dumfries; and south to Berwick with ongoing carriage to London. By 1708 the post reached a total of thirty-four Scottish towns, most serviced by foot. London mail was scheduled to reach Edinburgh in five days; from there the post reached Glasgow in two days

---

38 [Andrew Cant], A sermon preached on the XXX day of January 1703 at Edinburgh, Edinburgh 1703, preface.
39 Ian D. Whyte, 'Urbanisation in eighteenth-century Scotland', in Devine and Young, Eighteenth-century Scotland, 176–94.
40 Theodora Pagan, The convention of the royal burghs of Scotland, Glasgow 1926, 139.
41 Mann, Scottish book trade, 223, 226.
42 Joseph Taylor, A journey to Edenborough in Scotland, ed. William Cowan, Edinburgh 1903, 98, 145.

and Aberdeen in three or four days. Larger destinations received mail three times a week while smaller towns were serviced once or twice a week. Mail volume on the major routes was substantial, with 67,000 letters carried on the Berwick road between May 1693 and April 1694.[43]

Although the Scottish post was not cheap, it was within the reach of the middling to upper sorts. An act of 1695 set prices for a single sheet sent within fifty miles of Edinburgh at 2s. Scots, 3s. for 100 miles and 4s. for over 100 miles. Cheaper rates could be had in private transactions with low-paid letter carriers, who might accept mail at less than the full rate. In addition, goods carriers took letters and parcels (though this broke the postmaster's monopoly) and private persons and servants carried letters for friends and masters.[44]

To reduce the cost of newspapers brought by post, town councils negotiated standing orders for the supply of papers to the magistrates and their friends. The towns of Montrose and Dundee both contracted with the Edinburgh post office from 1700 to supply the *Edinburgh Gazette*, the *London Gazette* (the official paper authorised by the English government) and the *Flying Post* (a Whig paper published in London by George Ridpath, an expatriate Scot) on a weekly basis for £6 sterling per year. The papers were placed in a shop in Dundee for wider public access while in Montrose they circulated amongst the councillors. The magistrates of Dumfries arranged for the supply of papers locally by placing them in the town clerk's office.[45]

Coffeehouses and taverns served as further nodes of communication. The smaller Scottish cities did not support large numbers of coffeehouses as could be found in London, but advertisements in the *Edinburgh Gazette* between 1699 and 1707 suggest the presence of at least six coffeehouses in Edinburgh: the Caledonian, the Royal, the Exchange, Donaldson's, McClurg's and the German coffeehouse; while Glasgow burgh records mention one coffeehouse in 1706.[46] In Scotland, taverns remained important social centres, with political clubs meeting in particular Edinburgh haunts like Patrick Steel's tavern. Like coffeehouses, taverns also supplied papers: in the early 1700s, the Three Crowns tavern in Burntisland advertised the availability of newspapers to patrons.[47]

Burgh subscriptions to London as well as Edinburgh newspapers indicate that London print continued to be an important source of political news and commentary even as the supply of domestic print increased. As communica-

[43] A. R. B. Haldane, *Three centuries of Scottish posts: an historical survey to 1836*, Edinburgh 1971, 26–7, 39–42.
[44] Ibid. 28, 48.
[45] Dumfries Archive Centre, RB 2/2/10; *Charters, writs and public documents of the royal burgh of Dundee, 1292–1880*, ed. William Hay, Dundee 1880, 175; Couper, *Edinburgh periodical press*, i. 75.
[46] *Extracts from the records of the burgh of Glasgow*, ed. Sir James D. Marwick, Glasgow 1908, 403.
[47] *Edinburgh Gazette*, no. 301 (Thurs. 29 Jan–Mon. 2 Feb. 1702).

tion networks in Scotland improved, greater quantities of English as well as Scottish materials dispersed across the Lowlands, driving awareness of English affairs and their implications for Scotland. Newspapers, including the Tory *Post Boy*, the pro-Scottish *Flying Post*, the government's *London Gazette* and the more neutral *Daily Courant*, all provided a different spin on the news from London. Essay periodicals provided a stronger party perspective, with Charles Leslie's *Rehearsal* giving a flavour of high-flying Anglican Toryism, John Tutchin's *Observator* providing a Whig point of view and Daniel Defoe's *Review* supplying a moderate (government-funded) stance. London pamphlets supplemented the papers with English views on Anglo-Scottish issues like the Scottish African Company, the succession, the Act of Security and the union. Scottish printers reprinted some of the more virulent English tracts, extending the domestic reach of these attacks on Scottish policy.[48]

The re-establishment of regular assemblies in Church and State and expansions in literacy, print and transport thus provided better political communication between London, Edinburgh and Lowland localities by the early eighteenth century. Many restrictions on communication remained, however, producing social differentiation in access to information. The supply of detailed, complex arguments in print tended to be limited to literate, affluent nobles, barons, burgesses, heritors, clergy and professionals. These local elites and middling sorts could develop a sophisticated understanding of national politics, enhanced by their personal experience of national markets, assemblies or government policy. Urban-dwellers could take advantage of the commercial concentration of print in their towns, while country gentry and parish ministers supplemented their visits to town with a flow of news provided by letters and social contacts.[49] Those at lower social levels had increasing access to political discourse, but their knowledge tended to lack the breadth and depth of those with more points of contact. Outside the burghs, ordinary subjects might rely on their social superiors, such as their minister or laird, for the supply of political information. Sermons, letters and conversation became more important sources of communication as information was converted from print to oral or manuscript forms. This process tended to provide summary information rather than detailed argument and could shade into rumour and distortion.[50] Deep reach of national news, therefore, was best at crisis points when large quantities of cheap print, plus sermons, letters and word of mouth, drove political communication to distant communities and lower social levels.

Despite these variations in the quality and quantity of political communication, post-Revolution circumstances in Scotland provided a foundation for

---

[48] In 1704, for example, during debates on the Act of Security the anonymous tract, *A manifesto, asserting and clearing the legal right of the Princess Sophia, and her issue, the Serene House of Hanover, to the succession of Scotland,* was reprinted in Edinburgh.
[49] As seen in England: Levy, 'How information spread', 11–34.
[50] Fox, 'Rumour, news and popular political opinion', 597–620.

the development of popular participation in national politics. The emergence of the Country party created a permanent opposition that could claim to represent a national interest. With regular political meetings and improving communications between centre and locality, elements in the Country party were able to engage popular opinion in adversarial politics and invoke the authority of public opinion to demand change. The next chapter will outline the activities between 1699 and 1705 through which the politics of public opinion began to develop.

2

Oppositional Opinion Politics

With improving communications linking localities with regular political assemblies in Edinburgh, leaders in the parliamentary opposition in Scotland in the late 1690s were able to encourage popular political activity to support demands for change. When events created a basis for widespread discontent, they shaped and mobilised this through pamphlets, petitions and crowd protests, portraying them as the voice of the people acting in a patriotic interest. This began with the failure of the African Company's Darien colony in 1699–1700, the last in a series of economic problems deriving in part from Anglocentric foreign and economic crown policy. In what became the Darien crisis of 1699–1701, the Country party demonstrated the potential power of organised opinion as it marshalled economic disaffection into assertive demands in the name of the nation.

The party leadership continued to put pressure on the crown, using what became known as 'country opinion', in protests against Anne's first parliament in 1702. From 1703 the Country party held a numerical majority in a newly-elected parliament, reducing their need to generate public expressions of support in addresses or crowds. Nevertheless, party elements continued to appeal to public opinion in print on the question of union, as will be discussed in chapter 4. In addition, leading Episcopalians began to adopt the Country party's methods when pressing the crown for toleration. Crowd activities erupted in Glasgow in response to the toleration campaign, demonstrating the degree to which ordinary individuals at the community level were willing to act to defend their interests against unwanted crown policy. Local protests on national affairs also emerged in Dumfries with demonstrations against the state's failure to pursue local Catholics during a Jacobite scare in 1704, and in Edinburgh in 1705 with rioting against a potential crown reprieve for an English crew convicted of piracy. Combined with the aggressive opinion politics practised by the Country party at the national level, these activities established a significant presence for public opinion in Scottish politics between 1699 and 1705.

In the late 1690s a combination of circumstances produced significant levels of discontent across many sectors of Scottish society. Scotland and England's monarch, William II and III, had taken his British kingdoms to war with France in the Nine Years War (1688–97), cutting off Scottish commerce with France, a key trading partner. French privateers attacked Scottish shipping while the crown raised taxes to fund troop levies. A series of crop failures and famine in the mid-1690s added to these economic woes. From 1695 a Scottish attempt to participate in overseas trade with a joint stock company, the Company of Scotland Trading to Africa and the Indies, found its ability to recruit foreign capital limited by a lack of royal support. The absence of royal backing, among other factors, also contributed to the collapse of an African Company colony at Darien on the isthmus of Panama in 1699–1700, sinking a significant proportion of Scotland's capital. Public comment on Scotland's situation had begun to emerge in the late 1690s, most notably in Andrew Fletcher of Saltoun's *Two discourses concerning the affairs of Scotland*, published in 1698. From 1699 a flurry of Country pamphlets blamed the Darien failure on malign English influence and accused the king of failing to defend Scottish interests. Led by the duke of Hamilton, the earl of Tullibardine and the marquis of Tweeddale, the Country party drew on widespread discontent to generate three mass petitions to the crown backed with hundreds of signatures. These aggressive petitioning practices, encouraged by pamphlets and reinforced by riots in Edinburgh, set new precedents for the engagement of public opinion in Scottish politics.

The colony at Darien was an ambitious attempt by the small kingdom of Scotland to build a colonial trade. Licensed by a 1695 act of parliament, the African Company invested in two expeditions, in 1698 and 1699, to establish a trading plantation at Darien. The company faced two formidable problems: the Spanish crown claimed Darien as its own territory, though it had no permanent settlements there, and the colony represented a competitive challenge to nearby English Caribbean settlements. Spanish resentment at this act of piracy, as they saw it, and the concerns of English trading interests, plus William's own delicate negotiations on the Spanish succession, combined to convince the king that he could not support the Scottish colony. When Spain attacked the settlement in 1699, William declined to defend it and ordered his English colonies to refuse all assistance to the Scots. Proclamations to this effect in the colonies caused consternation in Darien where provisions were running low, contributing to the abandonment of the colony on 19 June 1699 after the death of 400 settlers from disease and privation. A second expedition met a similar fate. Though a Spanish attempt to invade by land was defeated early in 1700, a Spanish blockade forced the final abandonment of the colony on 31 March 1700.[1]

The Darien troubles converted widespread enthusiasm for the African Company and its colonial venture into high levels of unhappiness in Scotland. When English opposition forced the company out of London capital markets early in 1696, indignation had fuelled investor interest in Scotland. Copies of an address by the English parliament to the king against the company had been printed in Scotland at the time of the opening of the company's books, alongside tracts advertising the new venture.[2] The company main-

[1] George P. Insh, *The Company of Scotland*, London 1932.
[2] Ibid. 62–5.

tained public support by publishing a series of petitions to the government in 1697–9 complaining of ongoing English interference.[3]

One of these petitions described the company's investors as including 'the most considerable of the Nobility, Gentry and the whole Body of the Royal Burrows'.[4] Investment in the company ranged from a maximum of £3,000 sterling per person to a minimum of £100. The 1,400 subscribers included royal burghs investing on the security of their common good, and landed families, with cumulative commitments of thousands of pounds, as well as more humble figures making smaller collective investments. In the small burgh of Brechin forty-one individuals together purchased £650 in stock, including a pledge of £5 by a shoemaker's widow.[5] Involvement, however, went beyond subscriptions as farmers, merchants and artisans provided trading goods and provisions to the colony and communities provided hundreds of men and women as settlers. The local significance of the colonial enterprise can be seen in Stirling, where the town fathers spent more than £13 Scots on elaborate birth certificates for twelve individuals emigrating to Darien from the town.[6]

Widespread support for the Darien venture can be seen in reports in the *Edinburgh Gazette* in April 1699 of public rejoicings in Glasgow, Perth, Cupar, Inverness, Aberdeen 'and several other places' on the receipt of news of the safe landing of the colony's first expedition.[7] Soon the paper reported word from a Glasgow merchant's son in Jamaica that people were 'flocking' to the colony from surrounding islands and paraphrased a letter from 'an intelligent gentleman' in London suggesting that the English 'who formerly dispised us, now begin to change thoughts of us'. Early in 1699 it seemed that the Scots' colony would be 'a key' to the East India trade.[8] Enthusiastic tracts on the colony, such as *The golden island* (1699), a poem by 'a Lady of Honour', praised the company, its directors and the king for the triumphal settlement of the Scottish colony. Other pamphlets described the colony's situation and provided maps of the area. *A letter, giving a description of the isthmus of Darian* (1699), dedicated to the African Company's leader, the marquis of Tweeddale, provided information on the colony for the relatively low price of 7d.

News of the abandonment of the colony caused widespread emotional and

3 For example, *To his grace his Majesties High Commissioner, and the right honourable the estates of parliament: the humble petition of the council-general of the Company of Scotland trading to Africa and the Indies*, [Edinburgh] 1698. For all the addresses see Company of Scotland Trading to Africa and the Indies, *A full and exact collection of all the considerable addresses … and other publick papers relating to the Company of Scotland trading to Africa and the Indies*, Edinburgh 1700.
4 *Edinburgh Gazette*, no. 328 (Mon. 4 May–Thurs. 7 May 1702).
5 John Stuart Shaw, *The political history of eighteenth-century Scotland*, Basingstoke 1999, 6.
6 Insh, *Company of Scotland*, 117.
7 *Edinburgh Gazette*, nos 11 (Mon. 3 Apr.–Thurs. 6 Apr. 1699), and 14 (Wed. 12 Apr.–Fri. 14 Apr. 1699).
8 Ibid. nos 3 (Mon. 6 Mar.–Fri. 10 Mar. 1699), and 6 (Thurs. 16 Mar.–Mon. 20 Mar. 1699).

financial shock in September 1699. Concern was reported among 'persons of all ranks, and even of the meaner people, who are not particularly interested, and have no shares in the stock'.[9] The failure caused a loss of national face as well as lives and money. As the earl of Tullibardine wrote in an October 1699 letter, the 'shame it brings on our Country is the worst thing in itt, for after we had made such a noise abroad & been the envie of Europe we will now become their scorn'.[10]

As the colony's situation worsened, news of the king's proclamation to his English colonies denying aid to the Scottish colonists provided ammunition for growing criticism of him.[11] The author of A short and impartial view of the manner and occasion of the Scots colony's coming away from Darien (1699) asked 'who could ever have imagined, that such Rigorous Proclamations, or indeed any at all, should be issued forth against us, in the Name of our own Sovereign, who gave our Company first a Being'.[12] Writing from London, the Scottish radical Whig Robert Ferguson also defended the colony and accused the English secretary of state, James Vernon, of funding a series of anti-Darien pamphlets written by Walter Herries or Harris, a surgeon from Dumbarton who sailed to Darien after serving in the English navy.[13] These tracts defended the legality of the Scottish colony against accusations of piracy, reinforcing this with reprints of memorials written to the king by the company.[14]

The noble leadership of the Country party and African Company saw an opportunity to petition the king for a meeting of parliament. The African Company asked the king in late October 1699 to call parliament while party leaders discussed the possibility of supporting this with a petition from the shires or an address from 'a meeting of the whole proprietors of the Company'. The earl of Tullibardine advocated the latter, but after speaking to some of the gentry, the marquis of Tweeddale felt that mass petitioning from the shires would be feasible 'if a right methode were fallen upon to goe about it'.[15] Lacking any significant precedent for mass petitioning since the supplications of 1637-8, the party's noble organisers began to invent new methods.

William's answer to the Company's October address, that parliament would remain adjourned until March 1700, made it even easier than Tweeddale had hoped to generate signatures for the chosen method of a national address. The arrival in Scotland in late November 1699 of surviving colonists from

---

9   State-papers and letters addressed to William Carstares, ed. Joseph McCormick, Edinburgh 1774, 511.

10   NAS, GD 406/1/4444.

11   Sir William Beeston, By the honourable Sir William Beeston Kt his majesties lieutenant, Edinburgh 1699.

12   Anon., A short and impartial view of the manner and occasion of the Scots colony's coming away from Darien, [Edinburgh] 1699, 24.

13   [Robert Ferguson], A just and modest vindication of the Scots design, for the having established a colony at Darien, [Edinburgh] 1699; Insh, Company of Scotland, 84.

14   [Company of Scotland Trading to Africa and the Indies], Scotland's right to Caledonia (formerly called Darien) and the legality of its settlement, asserted, [Edinburgh] 1700.

15   NAS, GD 406/1/4444, 4368.

the first abandonment kept the Darien issue at the forefront of public attention. The duke of Hamilton launched a national address in December 1699 in Edinburgh, beginning the process of collecting signatures from 'several Subscribing Noblemen, Barons and Gentlemen'.[16] Organisers in Edinburgh secured the support of a number of nobles, as well as the Faculty of Advocates, the Incorporation of Surgeons and the Merchant Company, while the duke of Hamilton, earl of Tullibardine and other gentlemen collected signatures in the provinces. Subscriptions took place at pre-existing meetings of heritors, burgh councils, court sessions or funerals, though special meetings were also arranged.[17] The party's efforts produced a reported 21,000 signatures, leading one correspondent to term the petition a new 'nationall covenant'.[18]

The Country party sought to engage the Presbyterian Church's communication networks to develop support for the Darien cause. The Church had been involved in the colonial venture, supplying three ministers to the second expedition to found a presbytery of New Caledonia. In October 1699 the African Company asked the Commission of the General Assembly for a national fast day for the colony. This appeal was supported by a letter to the commission from the synod of Glasgow and Ayr instigated by Robert Wylie after the duke of Hamilton had recommended a fast to the synod.[19] The commission did not petition the government for an official fast day, but on 8 December 1699 renewed an earlier recommendation to ministers to pray for the colony.[20] Letters from the time confirm that many clergy were active in leading prayers.[21]

Crown resistance to initial requests for a meeting of parliament gave its opponents time to organise further expressions of discontent. When parliament finally met in May 1700, the Country party presented eight addresses from shires and burghs outlining a platform of grievances of which the lack of crown support for the Darien colony was only one. These petitions came from the shires of East Lothian, Roxburgh, Lanark, Stirling and Perth and the burghs of Haddington, Coupar and Dunbar. As with the national address, Tullibardine and Hamilton had exerted their regional influence to encourage subscription.[22] Coordination of petitioning can also be seen in the use of East Lothian's text by the burghs of Haddington and Dunbar.[23]

Country party agitations produced a shift in allegiances, delivering control of parliament to the opposition.[24] As royal commissioner, the duke of Queensberry responded with a sudden adjournment after just nine days. Country

16 African Company, *A full and exact collection*, 105.
17 Insh, *Company of Scotland*, 205; Patrick, 'People and parliament', 230–8.
18 *Wodrow letters*, 59; NAS, PC 1/52 (67).
19 *Carstares papers*, 500–1.
20 *The Darien papers*, ed. John Hill Burton, Edinburgh 1849, 254.
21 *Carstares papers*, 490.
22 Patrick, 'People and parliament', 256.
23 *APS* x, appendix at pp. 36–41.
24 Riley, *King William*, appendix B.

leaders immediately organised a second address from members of parliament protesting at the adjournment as well as the king's failure to respond to a 1698 address from parliament on the African Company. This address did not elicit an immediate response from the king, spurring the party to initiate yet another national address demanding a meeting of parliament.[25] Canvassing in the provinces through the summer and early autumn of 1700 produced what Lord Yester, the son of the marquis of Tweeddale, described as the signatures of 'a great Number' of subjects.[26] Country leaders decided to present the address to the king in November even though parliament already had been called to meet, signalling the party's continuing resolve to use public opinion to put pressure on the crown.

Individual shire and burgh petitions again supported the opposition in the second parliamentary session of 1700. The Country party generated eighteen addresses from the shires of Midlothian, Wigtown, Ayr, Dumbarton, Renfrew, Inverness, Nairn, Fife, Banff, Elgin and Forres and Orkney; and the burghs of Perth, Dysart, Kirkaldy, Anstruther Easter, Crail, Inverness and Glasgow. Eight of the eighteen addresses used the East Lothian text from May, while the burgh of Perth used its shire's address from May as a template. In addition, two pairs of burghs in Fife shared texts.[27]

The Country party encouraged grass-roots engagement in all its addresses with the distribution of pamphlets and news. In January, two thousand copies of a tract on the Darien colony and the national address were circulated to targeted localities.[28] During the brief May 1700 parliament, prints of the minutes of parliament and overtures in favour of Darien provided news of parliamentary proceedings. Archibald Foyer, minister of Stonehouse parish in Lanarkshire, published a tract to support requests to the 1700 General Assembly for a fast for the colony while William Seton of Pitmedden and George Ridpath published polemical works advancing a parliamentary programme of Country reforms.[29] *The people of Scotland's groans and lamentable complaints, pour'd out before the high court of parliament* (1700) used patriotic rhetoric to speak to parliament in the voice of the people, 'humbly imploring, nay Conjuring You by all that is Sacred, and by the Honour of the SCOTTISH Name, that you would not suffer this Ancient and Gallant Nation to be so much Contemn'd and Injur'd'.[30] The unusual nature of this propaganda can

---

25 Insh, *Company of Scotland*, 219; African Company, *A full and exact collection*, 127–30.
26 African Company, *A full and exact collection*, 133–7.
27 APS x, appendix at pp. 73–86.
28 Patrick, 'People and parliament', 238.
29 [Archibald Foyer], *Scotland's present duty*, [Edinburgh] 1700; [George Ridpath], *Scotland's grievances relating to Darien*, [Edinburgh] 1700; [William Seton of Pitmedden], *Memorial to the members of parliament of the Court party*, [Edinburgh 1700], and *A short speech prepared to be spoken, by a worthy member of parliament, concerning the present state of the nation*, [Edinburgh] 1700.
30 NAS, PA 7/17/21A.

be seen in strong attempts by the state to punish the printers and distributors of these tracts, as will be discussed in chapter 3.

In its publications, the Country party outlined a wide range of issues for parliament to consider, from trade, taxation and the Darien colony to constitutional complaints on infrequent parliaments and arbitrary imprisonment. In contrast, the shire and burgh addresses displayed a more limited range of issues. Common to the locality addresses were economic complaints, including loss of trade and the failure of the Darien colony, and requests for a reduction in the standing army and therefore the cess (land tax) to pay for it.[31] To this shared agenda, shires and burghs added particular concerns. Perthshire, for example, complained of Highlander depredations and crop failures as reasons why its heritors could not continue to fund a standing army.[32] By accommodating local grievances within its national campaign, the Country party was able to generate support for its core demands for a meeting of parliament and a resolution of the Darien situation.

With each round of petitioning, organisers penetrated more deeply into society and generated greater popular involvement. The party's first address of December 1699 defined a relatively narrow constituency of noblemen, barons and gentlemen, with burgesses and lesser inhabitants not mentioned. This omission made some burgesses doubt the propriety of signing the first address, as the earl of Tullibardine found when he took it to a meeting of the Stirling burgh council. Other burgesses had no such reservations, though organisers tended to prefer the signatures of higher-ranking burgesses. In Glasgow, for example, merchants were preferred over tradesmen.[33] The first round of locality addresses also tended to involve relatively high social levels within the shires and burghs. Signatory lists were short, bearing the hands of a few dozen gentry or the town officers of a burgh. The party's second national address limited itself to members of parliament, but its third broadened its target to 'Noblemen, Barons, Gentlemen, Burgesses and other Subscribers'.[34] The accompanying burgh and shire petitions presented in January 1701 also contained a broader social constituency, with some shires including wadsetters and liferenters along with heritors, and a number of burgh councils claiming to speak 'in name of the Communitie'. The greatest shift towards popular participation appeared in the January address from Glasgow, which came not from the town council but from 474 'Inhabitants', including one illiterate. Though the Glasgow town council had refused to address, organisers had secured signatures in the town without the council's authority, representing the address as the voice of the city.[35]

---

[31] *A selection from the papers of the earl of Marchmont, 1685–1750*, ed. G. H. Rose, London 1831, 218.
[32] APS x, appendix at p 39.
[33] Patrick, 'People and parliament', 235, 237.
[34] African Company, *A full and exact collection*, 133.
[35] APS x, appendix at pp. 82, 84–6.

Country organisers also encouraged crowd activities in support of the colony and the Country party. Echoing pageantry organised by the state for the royal commissioner on his arrivals from London, a grand entry to Scotland was staged for the duke of Hamilton on his journey up to Edinburgh in October 1699. Seafield reported that 'there has been a great deal of pains taken to represent it here truly greater than it was', including a report on the reception in the *Edinburgh Gazette*.[36] As the court saw it, the opposition did not hesitate to 'take advantage and occasion to impose upon the multitude'.[37]

Significant levels of support in Edinburgh for the African Company manifested itself in a major riot in June 1700, preceded by several smaller altercations in 1699. In August 1699 a mob attacked a Frenchman in Edinburgh after mistaking him for a person believed to have plotted to betray the colony to the French.[38] In September, rumour blamed one of the company's directors, James Balfour, for delaying the departure of relief ships earlier in 1699, sparking a mob that was only with difficulty prevented from pulling down his house.[39] When news arrived in Edinburgh of the first withdrawal from the colony, sympathisers lit unauthorised bonfires in the street and fired pistols and squibs on 14 October, the birthday of the deposed James VII. It is likely that oppositional nobles influenced the choice of day, as 'persons of note' were seen standing at some of the fires.[40]

Further news from Darien provoked a renewal of crowd action on the evening of 20 June 1700. Many parliamentarians were still in Edinburgh, awaiting a reconvening of the adjourned May parliament. On hearing that a skirmish had been won by the colonists over the Spanish, Country party leaders meeting at the Cross Keys tavern added plans for unauthorised illuminations to their discussion of the party's second national address. That evening, the circulation of a paper calling on 'all true Caledonians' to put candles in their windows generated significant levels of participation. The town's bells were taken over to play the tune 'Wilful Willy, wilt thou be wilful still'. Some individuals began to throw stones at dark windows, targeting in particular those belonging to Court party figures. In a further escalation, groups attempted to break into the home of Lord Carmichael, the king's secretary, and succeeded in entering the home of Sir James Stewart of Goodtrees, the Lord Advocate. The invaders forced Stewart to sign a warrant for the release of James Watson and Hugh Paterson, publishers of oppositional pamphlets being held in the Tolbooth. Others in the crowd used more direct

---

36 *Carstares papers*, 499–500.
37 *Marchmont papers*, 179.
38 *Wodrow letters*, 17.
39 Insh, *Company of Scotland*, 199.
40 *Edinburgh burgh extracts, 1689–1701*, 311. Nicholas Rogers has pointed out how Jacobitism could be used by crowds as 'an act of defiance or provocation': 'Riot and popular Jacobitism in early Hanoverian England', in Eveline Cruickshanks (ed.), *Ideology and conspiracy: aspects of Jacobitism, 1689–1759*, Edinburgh 1982, 71.

means to achieve these ends by burning down the Tolbooth door and freeing all the prisoners. While gentlemen with drawn swords prevented the city magistrates and town guard from stopping the attack on the Tolbooth, others in the crowd secured the Netherbow port to prevent royal troops from being brought into the city. After the event, the earl of Melville claimed that a 'great many gentlemen' had been involved in 'one of the most numerous and most insolent rabbles that has been here of a long time'.[41]

The violence of the outbreak in Edinburgh indicated the strength of grassroots feelings for the Darien colony. Unusually high levels of public information in Scotland on Darien had blamed the failure of the colony on the king and his ministers. In this environment, the duke of Hamilton and other noble leaders were able to initiate an increasingly aggressive addressing campaign to pressurise the king for a parliament for the consideration of Scotland's grievances. The party organisers used pamphlets and prayer orders to build support for its programme and demonstrated the strength of oppositional opinion with unauthorised illuminations in Edinburgh that boiled over into violent attacks on the king's officers.

After the death of King William and the accession of Queen Anne early in 1702, the continuing strength of disaffection in Scotland led Anne's ministers to avoid calling a parliament or holding elections, even though a 1696 act required that parliament meet within twenty days of the monarch's death. In a move of questionable legality, Anne chose instead to prorogue parliament, proclaiming that it would not meet until June 1702. In response, the Country party organised oppositional protests to pressure the queen into calling new elections. At the opening of parliament on 9 June 1702, the duke of Hamilton read out a statement of dissent and led a group of between fifty-seven and seventy-nine delegates out of the chamber.[42] Extraparliamentary support for this action was communicated by crowds surrounding Parliament House: on emerging from the House, the protesters were 'huzzaed by the acclamations of an infinite number of people of all degrees and ranks'.[43] Though this description by George Lockhart of Carnwath may exaggerate the size of the crowd, it still indicates a significant degree of public support marshalled by the duke's party in Edinburgh. After the walkout, the opposition produced an address to the queen to protest against the illegal meeting of parliament, in a move that echoed their petitioning of William after the abrogation of the May 1700 session. Some seventy-five members signed the address, plus at least 173 and possibly as many as 300 gentlemen gathered in Edinburgh.[44] To press home the allegations of illegitimacy against the queen's parliament, some oppositional gentlemen refused to pay the land tax voted by the remaining estates. Early in 1703 the earl of Rothes assured the duke of

41 *Edinburgh burgh extracts, 1689–1701*, 314–15; NAS, PC 1/52 (109–10, 121, 161).
42 *APS* xi. 5; *Marchmont papers*, 240; 'Scotland's ruine', 14; Patrick, 'People and parliament', 292.
43 'Scotland's ruine', 14.
44 Patrick, 'People and parliament', 292.

Hamilton that 'our friends here in this country [Fife] are firmly Resolved not to pay cesse'.[45]

Though an episode of much shorter duration than the Darien crisis, the events of June 1702 confirmed the continuing political engagement and Country sympathies of many in Edinburgh and the localities, providing a base of support for Country opposition. The impact of this event was limited by a lack of awareness of the legal issues at stake, indicating the degree to which popular engagement rested on grass-roots understanding of national events. In July 1702 Robert Wylie advised the duke of Hamilton to publish 'a clear full vigorous & well digested Information' explaining the party's dissent, for many 'who have honest enough hearts ... do not apprehend the true grounds of that dissent, nor the nullities of this parliament'.[46] Though this episode was not as popular as the Darien protests, the 1702 protests signalled to Anne the Country party's intention to continue to use public opinion as a political weapon.

The accession of Queen Anne led to a shift in the balance of political power in Scotland. Anne's Tory and Episcopalian sympathies led her to favour like-minded ministers, while elections called after the 1702 session produced a new Jacobite element in parliament, the Cavaliers. The crown hoped to retain control of parliament with a Court–Cavalier alliance, but proved unable to reconcile Cavalier desires for Episcopalian toleration with Court party commitments to the Presbyterian establishment. As a result, a coalition between the Country party and the Cavaliers produced an oppositional majority in Anne's parliament. Chapter 4 will discuss how the Country party used this position of strength to advance demands for constitutional reform, employing print discourse to influence public opinion on the question of union. At the same time, however, prominent Episcopalians adopted the Country party's methods of opposition to urge toleration upon the government, claiming this as the desire of the majority of the country. In response, violent crowds in Glasgow demonstrated the willingness of some Presbyterians to act locally in defence of the established Church. Presbyterians in Dumfries sent a similar message to the state in 1704 with anti-Catholic activities, while Edinburgh rioters protested against an Anglocentric crown in 1705. These local activities indicated the continuing engagement of provincial communities in national affairs during the union crisis.

Recognising the potential for toleration under Anne, a devout Anglican who maintained a toleration for Protestant dissenters in England, a few Episcopalian nobles responded to Anne's accession by sending a representative to London to ask her for 'such an universal indulgence to the episcopal people throughout the kingdome of Scotland as the presbyterians have in England'.[47] Before the 1703 parliamentary session, while Court policy was still being

45 NAS, GD 406/1/5181.
46 NAS, GD 406/1/4900.
47 NAS, CH 8/184.

formulated, dissenters took up mass petitioning tactics to urge toleration of Episcopalian worship. Organised by Episcopalian clergy and sympathetic nobles such as Lord Balcarras, the toleration campaign used national and local petitions to put pressure upon the crown. At the national level Archbishop Paterson organised an address signed by about 100 ministers in the name of the dissenting Episcopalian clergy.[48] This address was supported with mass petitions signed by 'a great many hands in Fife, Stirling and Angus shires' and the towns of Glasgow, Dundee, Aberdeen and Elgin.[49]

Along with addresses, a significant number of pamphlets appeared in favour of toleration. Many of these advanced religious arguments for toleration, initiating a theological debate with Presbyterian divines that continued for the next three years. Others, however, asserted a majority interest in toleration, countering the statement of the 1689 Claim of Right that prelacy was 'contrary to the inclinations of the generality of the people'.[50] Sir Alexander Bruce of Broomhill, parliamentary commissioner for Sanquhar, speculated that 'tho' Presbitry had been the Inclinations of the People at the Revolution, it may be very far from it at present'.[51] The queen's new Tory secretary, George Mackenzie (Viscount Tarbat; earl of Cromarty, 1703), declared in print that 'at least the half of Scotland, do desire a Toleration' as proved by addresses with 'above 400 subscriptions of the prime Inhabitants of Glasgow; by two to one in Dundee; By 4 to one in Aberdeen, Especially of the Chief Merchants and Burghers; By 3 to One in Elgin; And by 5000 subscriptions in Fife'.[52]

Anne gave hope to Scottish Episcopalians with a published letter of 24 February 1703 asking her privy council to protect loyal Episcopalian ministers in the peaceful practice of their religion.[53] Though this did not exceed allowances under existing laws for the comprehension of ministers who qualified themselves with oaths of loyalty, it demonstrated Anne's sympathy for these ministers and suggested a possible *de facto* toleration for private dissenting meetings held by non-jurant clergy. Though the bishop of Edinburgh advised against open preaching, some Episcopalian ministers became bolder in their meetings. According to a Presbyterian commentator, these dissenters sought to incite the fury of local Presbyterians 'to get opposi-

---

48 T. N. Clarke, 'The Scottish Episcopalians, 1688–1720', unpubl. PhD diss. Edinburgh 1987, 136; *To the queen's most excellent majestie, the humble address and supplication of the suffering episcopal clergy in the kingdom of Scotland*, [Edinburgh] 1703.
49 *Wodrow letters*, 255; NAS, GD 406/1/5181; [George Mackenzie, earl of Cromarty], *A few brief and modest reflexions perswading a just indulgence to be granted to the episcopal clergy and people in Scotland*, [Edinburgh] 1703, 4.
50 *APS* ix. 40.
51 [Sir Alexander Bruce of Broomhill], *A speech in the parliament of Scotland, in relation to presbyterian government*, [Edinburgh 1702], 3–4. See also Anon., *Draught of an act for toleration with a few short remarks thereupon*, [Edinburgh 1703], 1.
52 [Mackenzie], *A few brief and modest reflexions*, 4. See also [Robert Calder], *Reasons for a toleration to the episcopal clergy*, Edinburgh 1703.
53 NAS, PC 1/52 (510); *Her Majesties most gracious letter to the privy council of Scotland*, Edinburgh 1703.

tion made to them and thus a pretence that without a legall toleration by Parliament they cannot preach without danger of their lives'.[54]

Glasgow, with its strong local Presbyterian culture, provided the desired opposition. By January 1703, even before the queen wrote her letter in favour of loyal Episcopalian clergy, Glasgow buzzed with talk of toleration.[55] Under William, Episcopalian dissenters in Glasgow had 'in a private way held their meetings in a private place of the toun where they were not disturbed', but from January 1703 they began to meet in the home of a prominent Glasgow citizen, Sir John Bell, in the centre of town. A provost of Glasgow before the Revolution, Bell was elderly by 1703 but his son Colin, a former baillie, acted as a leader for Glasgow dissenters.[56] Those actively dissenting in Glasgow numbered about forty, with most being of high social status.[57]

An atmosphere of conflict and fear grew in Glasgow with the preaching of John Hay, an unqualified minister, on 30 January 1703, the anniversary of the execution of Charles I. Addressing a meeting in Bell's house, Hay characterised Charles I as a martyr for episcopacy and attacked presbyterian church government. A small crowd, reportedly made up of boys and Glasgow University students, reacted to the meeting by breaking the windows of Bell's house.[58] Late in February another altercation was threatened when the arrival of a printed copy of the queen's letter to the privy council sparked some Presbyterians to 'goe about inviting people' to come to the dissenting meeting house on the next Sunday. The organisers claimed that the minister preaching there had not qualified himself with the required oaths of loyalty. Glasgow's provost, Hugh Montgomery, took steps to prevent disorder but wrote to the privy council to ask for clarification as to his obligations towards unqualified ministers, indicating that the queen's letter had given rise to some confusion in law enforcement.[59]

During the next week, more news arrived to agitate Glasgow Presbyterians, this time of the queen's new appointments to the privy council, many of them of men recognised as sympathetic to Episcopalian dissent. Talk of a gathering of Presbyterians at the dissenting meeting flowed through Glasgow again the following Saturday (6 March), indicating the likelihood of violence the next day. Townspeople attributed the boldness of the dissenters to the queen's letter, linking local events to the national political scene. A serious altercation began at Bell's house on the Sunday when a private armed guard warned boys in the street that 'if they or any else came near They would make

54 *Wodrow letters*, 256.
55 Ibid. 250.
56 Bell's influence in town is indicated by the town council's acknowledgement in 1704 of his efforts to secure parliamentary authorisation for a local ale tax: *Glasgow burgh extracts*, 386.
57 Mairianna Birkeland, 'Politics and society in Glasgow, c. 1680–c. 1740', unpubl. PhD diss. Glasgow 1999, 102.
58 NAS, PC 1/52 (523–4); *Wodrow letters*, 254; Birkeland, 'Politics and society', 102–3.
59 NAS, PC 1/52 (523–4); NLS, Wodrow quarto xxviii, fo. 151.

their blood Lye upon the ground'. One of the boys provoked a guard to chase him down the street, drawing people out of the Presbyterian churches in response to the noise. A large crowd gathered at the meeting house and broke down the door and windows before the arrival of the town magistrates and a regiment of royal troops quartered in Glasgow quelled any further violence. In the fracas, the provost was wounded in the leg, but the troops prevented serious injury to the dissenters by escorting them home.[60]

After the Glasgow tumult, an organiser admitted that they 'had gott what they were seeking' by provoking a Presbyterian crowd into action.[61] The Glasgow riots also reveal a key dynamic of popular political culture in pre-Union Scotland: the willingness of Presbyterians in some localities to take action to defend their Kirk, particularly when they felt that the government had failed to do so. Anti-Catholic riots in Dumfries in 1704 further demonstrate the readiness of some Presbyterians to protest against laxity in the enforcement of laws protecting the Kirk. These events also highlight the important role played by the church ministry in priming ordinary people to take action and confirm the role of national news as a trigger for local response.

Within a dominant Covenanting Presbyterian culture, Dumfriesshire contained substantial pockets of Catholics, particularly those under the protection of Lord Maxwell in Nithsdale.[62] Dumfriesshire Presbyterians also included radical separatists: members of the United Societies, known as the Cameronians after their former minister Richard Cameron, and Hebronites, followers of John Hepburn, a hardline Presbyterian minister suspended and eventually ejected from the Church in 1705 for preaching beyond the bounds of his parish of Urr. Hepburn criticised Church and State for not renewing the Covenants since the Revolution and was known to preach vigorously against local Catholics.[63] Open conflict between Presbyterians and local Catholics erupted in January and February of 1704 as reports of a Jacobite invasion plot produced high levels of anxiety in the shire. Fears of the Catholic Pretender brought out latent anti-Catholicism, though the actual threat posed by native Catholics was minimal.[64]

Presbyterian concern about Catholicism in the south-west had been rising since 1702. The presbytery of Kirkcudbright had asked the General Assembly to 'deal with the state to put the laws in execution' against papists, while the presbytery of Dumfries asked for advice on how to cope with local Catholics.[65]

---

60 Wodrow quarto xxviii, fo. 151; NAS, PC 1/52 (520, 524–6); Birkeland, 'Politics and society', 103–6.
61 NAS, PC 1/52 (525); Wodrow Letters, 260.
62 The presbyteries of Kirkcudbright and Dumfries both provided long lists of Catholics to the privy council in 1705 and 1707: NAS, CH 1/2/5/3 (197, 205).
63 William McMillan, John Hepburn and the Hebronites, London 1934.
64 Daniel Szechi, 'Defending the true faith: Kirk, State and Catholic missioners in Scotland, 1653–1755', Catholic Historical Review lxxxii (1996), 397–411.
65 NAS, CH 1/2/22/3 (258); CH 1/2/23/3 (195); CH 1/2/23/3 (181).

In turn, the national Church indicated its concerns on the subject of Catholics in 1703 in a petition from the Commission of the General Assembly to Anne asking her to 'give express orders that the laws for preventing the growth of popery... may be duly executed'.[66]

The synod of Dumfries took steps locally against Catholics with an 'Act against papists and trafficking priests' in April 1703. This recommended the distribution among parishioners of 'Little Books' on the errors of papacy and ordered the synod's ministers to 'exhort & excite their people to do what is proper for them in obedience to the Law in opposing the growth of popery... And that with a prudent courage & zeal, they bestir themselves in apprehending these Trafficquing papists That they may be punished according to Law'.[67] At their next meeting, in October 1703, the synod agreed also to be 'careful and diligent in Instructing their flocks in the Nature of the National Covenant & all the heads and Articles thereof in opposition to popery, prelacy & all other Errors'.[68]

The anti-Catholic atmosphere was aggravated in December 1703 and January 1704 as reports of a Jacobite plot (later known as the Scotch or Queensberry plot) raised the fear of the return of a Catholic monarch. Primed by their ministers to take action against papists, in January 1704 an organised crowd searched for priests in the houses of particular Nithsdale nobles and gentry.[69] Soon after, on 2 February, a 'great Convocatione of the Leidges' gathered at Dumfries 'in a war lyke manner' to burn at the town cross 'vestments & popish books & trinkets', probably seized in the January raids. By appearing on the day of the Candlemas fair in Dumfries, the organisers guaranteed a large audience for their demonstration. In choosing to burn the items, the two unidentified gentlemen leading the crowd appropriated the state's usual method of indicating public disapproval of Catholicism, thus condemning the state's failure to act.[70]

Events at Dumfries, like those in Glasgow, indicate the potential for collective political activity in areas of robust Presbyterian adherence. Fuelled by latent fears of resident Catholics, primed by clerical anti-Catholicism and triggered by rumours of immediate danger from Catholic Jacobites, these protests delivered a clear message upwards from the locality to the government. What happened at Dumfries was not part of a deliberate campaign organised by the Country party; instead, this episode showed how popular activity could boil up under the leadership of local ministers and gentlemen in reaction to national affairs and in defence of local interests.

Similarly, tumults in Edinburgh in 1705 demonstrate, as in 1700, the close connection of many in Edinburgh to national affairs and their willingness to

[66] NAS, CH 1/2/4/1 (3).
[67] NAS, CH 2/98/1 (176).
[68] NAS, CH 2/98/1 (186).
[69] NAS, PC 1/53 (126).
[70] NAS, PC 1/53 (144); Dumfries Archives Centre, A 2/8(7).

attack crown ministers seen to have betrayed patriotic interests. Influenced by news, rumour and pamphlets, crowds gathered in April 1705 to pressurise the privy council against remitting the sentences of execution passed by the Scottish Admiralty Court on the crew of the English merchant ship, the *Worcester*. The crew's trial for piracy against an African Company ship had renewed feelings of resentments towards England raised during the Darien crisis at the same time as the English parliament sought to press Scotland into closer union with the Alien Act.

The *Worcester* had been seized at Leith in December 1704 by representatives of the African Company in retaliation for the seizure of the company's last ship, the *Annandale*, by the East India Company in London. Stray comments by *Worcester* crew members and an inspection of the ship's papers and stock provided grounds for charges of piracy against Captain Green and his crew. Town talk linked a missing African Company ship, Captain Drummond's *Speedy Return*, to Green's suspected piracy, creating widespread anger against Green and his crew.[71] The *Edinburgh Gazette* reported in December a suspicion that 'there is on Board some of the Goods and Tackling which belong'd to one of our Indian and African Company's Ships'.[72] According to a contemporary letter, 'It is surmised here that they had secret orders from the East India Company to destroy our ships and men.'[73]

The *Edinburgh Courant* and *Edinburgh Gazette* kept readers apprised of the progress of the case from the initial indictments in February 1705 to the final judgement against the crew in March.[74] The significance of the trial was augmented by concurrent newspaper reporting of the English parliament's debates on the Alien Act.[75] Other tracts, including a flurry of cheap broadsides, emphasised the connection between the *Worcester* case and English interference with Scotland's interests. One, reportedly funded by the secretary of the African Company, accused the pirates of murdering the African Company's crew and warned readers against the English:

> Scots Men may take care
> Of cruel Neighbours bare.
> Who spitefully us treats we see,
> By Murdering Policie.[76]

---

[71] *Correspondence of George Baillie of Jerviswood MDCCII–MDCCVIII*, ed. Gilbert Eliot-Murray-Kynynmound, 2nd earl of Minto, Edinburgh 1842, 64; Richard Carnac Temple, *New light on the mysterious tragedy of the 'Worcester', 1704–5*, London 1930, 29.

[72] *Edinburgh Gazette*, no. 601 (Thurs. 21 Dec.–Mon. 25 Dec. 1704).

[73] *Jerviswood correspondence*, 64.

[74] *Edinburgh Courant*, no. 1 (Wed. 14 Feb–Mon. 19 Feb 1705); *Edinburgh Gazette*, nos 624–6 (Mon. 12 Mar.–Thurs. 22 Mar. 1705).

[75] *Edinburgh Gazette*, no. 626 (Mon. 19 Mar.–Thurs. 22 Mar. 1705).

[76] Anon., *The horrid murther committed by Captain Green and his crue, on Captain Drummond and his whole men*, [Edinburgh 1705]. A contemporary account linked this particular ballad to the angry mood of the crowds attending the executions on 11 April 1705: Temple, *New light*, 291–2.

Though historians have cast doubt on the judgement of the court, the Edinburgh papers emphasised the guilt of the accused by printing a sailor's post-trial confession.[77] As another ballad said of Green:

> He deserves to be hang'd & all his Crue ...
> No Murther and Robbery was ever more clear
> Made evident, as this as doth now appear
> By their own Declaration after Sentence given ...
> Hanging is too little if they get their due.[78]

All the available information in Edinburgh pointed to a conclusion of guilt on the indictments of murder, piracy and robbery. As a correspondent wrote to the minister Robert Wodrow of Eastwood parish near Glasgow, 'Cap. Green has now got this indictment: no body in short doubts but he is guilty, and would fain think he will hang.'[79]

On 28 March 1705 the privy council received a letter from the queen's secretary, the duke of Argyll, ordering a stay of execution until the queen could review the trial papers. Reports of this soon spread through the town and beyond. Although information not available in Scotland convinced the queen of the innocence of the crew, many in Scotland saw her as favouring English interests. Public anger was at such a pitch that five months later, in August 1705, English travellers to Edinburgh were warned 'not to speak anything there, in relation to Captain Green, Darien or the Succession'.[80]

Recognising the overheated state of public opinion in Scotland, the council sent the requested papers to London with a recommendation against reprieve. The treasurer-depute, George Baillie of Jerviswood, wrote privately to London that 'if the Queen shall grant them remissions, it will spoyle the business of Parliament, and I'm affrayd will so exasperate the nation, as may render it difficult to make them joyne with England upon any termes whatsomever'.[81] Another letter from the queen led the council to postpone the executions by one week, until 11 April, as the city began to build a gibbet on the sands of Leith.[82] On 10 April the privy council voted again on the question of a reprieve. Many members absented themselves or abstained, leaving six votes to be cast, three for and three against. As six votes did not constitute a quorum, the executions stood by default. At another meeting early the next morning, the council upheld the executions of Captain Green and two of his crew for later that day, ignoring letters from the queen requesting further delays.[83]

---

77 *Edinburgh Gazette*, no. 627 (Thurs. 23 Mar.–Mon. 26 Mar. 1705).
78 Anon., *The merits of piracie, or a new song on Captain Green and his bloody crue*, [Edinburgh 1705].
79 *Analecta scotica*, i. 239.
80 Taylor, *Journey to Edenborough*, 122.
81 *Jerviswood correspondence*, 64. See also NAS, GD 406/1/5343.
82 *Edinburgh Gazette*, no. 631 (Thurs. 5 Apr.–Tues. 10 Apr. 1705).
83 NAS, PC 1/53 (377–87).

The strength of public feeling against Green had convinced many on the privy council that they should not oppose the scheduled executions. Well aware that the council was meeting to consider reprieves, great crowds gathered outside the Council House during the 11 April meeting. As an eyewitness reported,

> About 11 the word came out of the Council that three were to be hanged, viz. Captain Green, Mather and Simson. This appeased the mob, and made many post away to Leith, where many thousands had been, and were upon the point of coming up in a great rage; when the Chancellor came out, he gott many huzzas at first, but at the Trone Kirk some surmized to the mobb, that all this was but a sham, upon which they assaulted his coach and broke the glasses, and forced him to come out, and goe into Mills Square and stay for a considerable time.[84]

As someone in the crowd had closed the Netherbow port to prevent troops from entering the city, the magistrates and privy council could do little to stop the attack on the queen's chancellor. An eyewitness predicted that had the executions not taken place, 'we would, in all probability have had the confusedest night we saw this seven years'. The crowds at the hangings were described by the same witness as 'the greatest confluence of people there that ever I saw in my life', estimated in another contemporary account at 80,000 armed men from Edinburgh and the surrounding area.[85]

The gathering of informed individuals at the *Worcester* executions reveals the degree of political awareness and engagement that had developed in Scotland since the Darien crisis. Resentment towards the English, cultivated by Country print and addresses in 1699–1701, had been revived with a fresh batch of aggressive pamphlets, broadsides and news reports on the *Worcester* case and the Alien Act. As in the Darien riot of 1700, some in Edinburgh were willing to attack senior governmental figures in the name of Scottish interests. Moreover, by 1705, ministers had become more attuned to oppositional opinion and its influence on parliamentary affairs.

From Darien onwards, politics in Scotland entered a new phase in which political communications increased, awareness of national affairs rose and oppositional groups made deliberate attempts to influence government through expressions of public opinion. Rising numbers of pamphlets advanced oppositional viewpoints, influencing grass-roots concerns along party lines. Mass addressing emerged as a key method for the representation of public opinion, with organisers collecting thousands of signatures in increasingly populist and aggressive campaigns. Primed by national political discourse, and often led by oppositional gentlemen, crowds took action to defend economic, religious and political interests believed to be under threat. These developments paved the way for the significant levels of popular participa-

---

84 *Analecta scotica*, ii. 60. See also NAS, GD 406/1/7091.
85 *Analecta scotica*, ii. 60; Temple, *New light*, 291.

tion seen in the union debates of 1706–7, setting precedents for the Country party and local communities to follow. Nevertheless, these activities did not develop unchecked. As the next chapter will show, the government strove to restrict popular participation and maintain limits on the legitimacy of public opinion. From 1699 to 1705 the Court party learned lessons in the management of public opinion that would be applied in 1706–7.

3

The Government and Public Opinion

A key moment in the development of an early modern public sphere occurs when the government moves from a defensive to an offensive strategy, countering oppositional activities with similarly aggressive methods of opinion formation and expression. Early modern governments preferred to use patronage and civic pageantry to manage the political nation and maintain the goodwill of ordinary subjects. Held back by customary notions of the dangers of popularity, monarchs and their ministers hesitated to participate in propaganda or claims based on public opinion unless pressed by oppositional publicity.[1] In moments of crisis, as censorship broke down and oppositional populism gained strength, individuals in the government began to emulate oppositional practices to maintain the good opinion of the king's subjects. This process was aided by the co-opting of oppositional leaders into the government, bringing expertise, connections and a willingness to employ propaganda.[2] Nevertheless, even as the government began to participate in a more inclusive public sphere, it contested the legitimacy of public opinion and used censorship, management and repression to maintain a degree of control over popular participation.

Initially, as the Country party in Scotland sought to pressurise the government through representations of public opinion from the late 1690s, ministers responded with greater efforts in civic pageantry, management and censorship. The parliamentary disorders of 1700–1, and a change in leadership with Anne's accession, led to a shift in approach. From 1702 Anne's ministers began to allow, and even sponsor, a small quantity of polemical printing in support of government policy. Though dwarfed by larger volumes of Country party publications, these pamphlets indicated the development of a new level of public debate in which the government provided not just proclamations but tract-based defences of its policies. These new essays and speeches sought to influence readers towards a court point of view while claiming to speak for a public opinion sympathetic to the crown.

The government had long encouraged civic demonstrations of loyalty.[3] Such events became more important after the Revolution as indicating the

---

[1] For England see Cust, 'Charles I and popularity', 235–58. See also Sawyer, *Printed poison*.
[2] Downie, *Robert Harley and the press*; Raymond, *Invention of the newspaper*; Harris, '"Venerating the honesty of a tinker"', 195–232.
[3] For England see David Cressy, *Bonfires and bells: national memory and the Protestant calendar in Elizabethan and Stuart England*, London 1989.

adherence of public bodies to William as the *de facto* monarch. Recognising that 'Nothing will more effectually disappoint the bad designes of our... enemies Then that it does appear That our Subjects are firme in their Loyalty and affection to us', William's government encouraged demonstrations of fidelity in civic solemnities and loyal addresses.[4] Edinburgh marked royal occasions, such as the monarch's birthday, with a ceremony at the market cross attended by city magistrates and members of the privy council, accompanied by the ringing of bells and the firing of guns from Edinburgh Castle. At night, residents lit bonfires on the High Street or, from 1692, followed the less disorderly practice of placing candles in their windows.[5] Other towns, such as Aberdeen and Perth, followed Edinburgh's example in recognising birthdays with bells and toasts.[6] Similar ceremonies marked William's funeral in April 1702, while 1,600 men of the Glasgow town militia fired salvos to mark the proclamation of Queen Anne.[7] From 1699 the *Edinburgh Gazette* reported on major civic events, spreading awareness of these demonstrations of loyalty.

The *Gazette* also advertised the submission of loyal addresses to the crown marking moments such as victories in war or accessions.[8] In the post-Revolution environment, loyal addresses also appeared when events challenged the monarch's legitimacy, as in 1701 when Louis XIV recognised the son of James VII and II as the rightful king of Scotland and England on the death of his father. This sparked a string of loyal addresses from shires and burgh councils. The latter included Edinburgh, Dumfries, Sanquhar, Annan, Lochmaben, Linlithgow, Culross and Aberdeen, all declaring their constancy to the Revolution settlement.[9]

Like oppositional addresses, loyal addresses were organised by local nobles and gentlemen. In November 1701, for example, the earls of Mar and Buchan urged the Stirlingshire justiciary court to address the king against Louis XIV's declaration. In response, loyal addresses were produced by the justiciary court and the shire's commissioners of supply (the local heritors responsible for collecting the land tax). At the same time there was 'a great humour of addressing' among Lanarkshire's gentlemen, with Lord Galloway proposing an address from the shire. Though promoted by Court figures, loyal addresses often involved oppositional leaders as they seized a chance to rehabilitate their standing with the monarch. These motivations spurred the Hamilton family and the earl of Tullibardine to participate in the loyal addresses of

4 NAS, PC 1/52 (318).
5 *Edinburgh burgh extracts, 1689–1701*, 63.
6 *Edinburgh Gazette*, no. 407 (Thurs. 11 Feb.–Tues. 16 Feb. 1703).
7 Ibid. nos 315 (Thurs. 19 Mar.–Mon. 23 Mar. 1702), 318 (Mon. 30 Mar.–Thurs. 2 Apr. 1702), 320 (Mon. 6 Apr.–Fri. 10 Apr. 1702).
8 Ibid. nos 328 (Mon. 4 May–Thurs. 7 May 1702), 348 (Thurs. 16 July–Mon. 20 July 1702); *Edinburgh burgh extracts, 1689–1701*, 122.
9 *Edinburgh burgh extracts, 1689–1701*, 290–1; *Edinburgh Gazette*, nos 292 (Thurs. 1 Jan.–Mon. 5 Jan. 1702), 294 (Tues. 6 Jan.–Thurs 8 Jan. 1702), 298 (Mon. 19 Jan.–Thurs. 22 Jan. 1702).

1701. By organising and signing addresses refuting Louis XIV's support for 'James VIII and III', they avoided accusations of Jacobitism and confirmed their loyalty to the monarch despite their adversarial actions in the parliaments of 1700–1.[10]

While encouraging loyal addresses and civic events, William's government in Scotland did little to develop support for its policies through positive propaganda. Printed proclamations, acts of parliament and the privy council, royal letters and ministerial speeches provided only limited rationale for state policy. The licensing of the *Edinburgh Gazette* from 1699 improved the reach of some official communications as well as providing reports on the proceedings of the privy council. Nevertheless, these authorised publications did not engage with oppositional arguments; they provided only assertions of policy and assurances of the crown's good intentions. During the Darien crisis William's government published speeches of the royal commissioner and chancellor and letters from William to his privy council with conciliatory messages, but did not provide a compelling justification for the crown's stance on the African Company.[11]

To control Scottish politics, the government relied on the private persuasion of MPs. Ministers drew on personal links, including friendship, kinship and commercial relationships, to create and sustain followings in parliament. This was augmented by patronage in the form of pensions, commissions and salaries. The weak state of the Scottish treasury reduced the power of patronage but still provided leverage for the crown among parliamentarians pinched by severe recession. Even when the government amassed significant arrears of salary, loyalty could be maintained on credit with promises of future payment. Ministers maintained their networks of adherents through active canvassing prior to and during every parliamentary session. In 1696 Lord Polwarth indicated the importance of canvassing in his comment that 'I am confirming, all I can, friendships older and later that I may employ the interest I had, or gain, in the service of our King.'[12] Ministers also used loyal lieutenants to organise support within the estates, as in the 1698 parliamentary session when the provost of Edinburgh entertained burgh commissioners to urge them to vote for supply.[13] Though requiring significant effort and funding, these methods offered a more direct, immediate and personal effect in parliament than pamphlets.

The crown used management techniques to reduce opposition within the Church as well as parliament. William Carstares, chaplain to William and principal of Edinburgh University under Anne, and the royal commissioners to the General Assembly worked with moderate clergy and lay elders to build

[10] NAS, GD 406/1/10926, 4948, 4944, 5004.
[11] *APS* x. 201, appendix at pp. 34, 43–5.
[12] *Marchmont papers*, 111.
[13] Patrick, 'People and parliament', 210.

support for crown interests.[14] Crown influence in the General Assembly's committee for overtures and the Church's executive committee, the Commission of the General Assembly, could neutralise the efforts of presbyteries like that of Hamilton, which year after year instructed its representative to insist that 'the intrinsick pouer of the Church and the Divine Right of presbyterian Government be ... asserted by ane express act of assembly'.[15] Crown supporters also sought to moderate attempts by the Country opposition to use church fasts to develop public awareness of political issues, as in 1699 when 'Court Divins' in the Commission of the General Assembly resisted initial requests by the company for a national fast on the colony's first abandonment, compromising eventually on a prayer order.[16] Special 'pains' were taken with identified troublemakers, as in 1704 when Chancellor Seafield recommended that Carstares seek to moderate the influence of Robert Wylie and his associates.[17]

The Court party's loss of control of parliament during the Darien crisis revealed limitations in the crown's management methods. Reliant on an accumulation of individual loyalties, crown ministers were vulnerable to the eruption of serious and widespread disaffection. In 1698, as discontent over the African Company appeared among Court followers, Lord Polwarth complained that 'these we had the greatest influence upon could not be prevailed with to support us'.[18] Prior to this session, ministers had all taken 'much pains' in private conversation with MPs, with limited results.[19] By late 1699 Polwarth, now earl of Marchmont, found it even more difficult to maintain his following.[20]

Court leaders responded by increasing their management activities in 1700, going out to the localities in the summer to counter the effects of Country party persuasion. Ministers had hoped that the king would come to Scotland to lend his personal support. Though lacking the extra leverage that a royal visit would have provided, the duke of Argyll and Viscount Seafield travelled widely to lobby individual MPs, offering pensions, jobs and concessions on new laws in exchange for moderating their opposition over Darien. Those helping the government included William Paterson, the originator of the Darien vision, who was paid £100 for his services. As a result of these efforts, enough votes swung back to the Court party to allow it to muster a majority in January 1701 against an act asserting the rights of the African Company

---

[14] A. Ian Dunlop, *William Carstares and the Kirk by law established*, Edinburgh 1964, chs iv–v.
[15] NAS, CH 1/2/5/1 (31).
[16] NAS, GD 406/1/4368.
[17] *Carstares papers*, 725.
[18] Patrick, 'People and parliament', 212.
[19] *Marchmont papers*, 158.
[20] *Carstares papers*, 512.

and its colony, though the party had to concede an address to the king from parliament and an act of *habeas corpus*.[21]

In reacting to the challenge of public opinion on Darien, the government also attempted to reassert its power of censorship over political print. Unlike in England where the crown used the Stationers' Company as a first line of control on print, Scottish book traders and printers were not organised into a gild. Nor did the Scottish parliament take on licensing responsibilities as had the English parliament through licensing acts. Instead, the crown maintained regulatory oversight of print through the issuing of individual book licences by the privy council, with some additional licensing by the Church and burgh councils. On a day-to-day basis, the crown relied on the burgh councils where printing was established (Edinburgh, Glasgow and Aberdeen) to enforce these licences. Since conviction for illicit printing carried the threat of banishment, closure of presses or loss of burgess status, these considerations tended to keep most printers and booksellers in line as long as the regulations were enforced.[22]

The state had maintained a firm grip on political print in the Restoration period with the aggressive application of control measures against Covenanting publications.[23] As book volumes rose, however, the licensing system came under pressure. Publishers began to issue books without a licence unless they wanted monopoly protection for popular works like almanacs. In response, the privy council in the 1690s chose to focus on the threat of sedition and blasphemy, requiring political and religious works to be submitted for licensing to committees of the council. Laws against leasing-making (*lèse-majesty*) gave the council additional grounds to pursue unacceptable works. Under this system, the privy council maintained a tenuous control of political texts after the Revolution.[24] The council also limited the dissemination of news with the imprisonment and banishment of those who spread 'false news'.[25]

Since Scottish censorship relied upon the voluntary submission of manuscripts for pre-publication approval, printers could test the limits of the system in moments of crisis. The capacity of the privy council to maintain control depended on the robustness of its response to unauthorised printing. In July 1699, as political printing increased, the council renewed its 1697 act requiring review of political books and called the printer George Jaffray before it to account for the publication of unacceptable Darien pamphlets.[26]

21 Riley, *King William*, 147; Insh, *Company of Scotland*, 229–2.
22 Mann, *Scottish book trade*.
23 Jackson, *Restoration Scotland*, 40–3.
24 Mann, *Scottish book trade*, 146–7, 174–5.
25 The council pursued William Murray, an Edinburgh burgess, several times in the 1690s for spreading 'false news' from London newsletters, leading to his banishment from Edinburgh: *Edinburgh burgh extracts, 1689–1701*, 184.
26 NAS, PC 1/52 (7).

After the failure of the May 1700 parliamentary session, the council created a new committee 'to consider what prints are lately Emitted Reflecting upon his Majesty or his Government'. One week later, the committee arrested the printer James Watson and the apothecary Hugh Paterson for printing and distributing several pamphlets.[27] Watson protested that by 'the dayly custom' of 'all the printers in Town,' 'printed books or papers publickly sold are not in use to be licensed', but both men were banished from Edinburgh for a year and a day for leasing-making.[28] During the May 1700 parliamentary session, William Seton of Pitmedden was imprisoned for writing his *Memorial to the members of parliament of the Court party* (1700) and forced to apologise at the bar of the House; in addition, his tract was burned at the Edinburgh market cross.[29] By 1701 the government's new severity had made publishers more cautious. In that year James Hodges found that his agent in Edinburgh was unwilling to print one of his pamphlets without showing a copy of the manuscript to the Lord Advocate 'by reason of the hazard in printing without authority'.[30]

The privy council also tried to pursue those oppositional nobles who were sponsoring political prints on Darien. A high-quality copperplate engraving was published early in 1701 featuring a figure of Scotia seated on a thistle-wrapped monument listing 'Caledonia's Supporters or the Eighty four Dissenters'. This inflammatory poster celebrated the members of the Country party, led by the duke of Hamilton, who had dissented formally from the vote against an act on Darien in January 1701.[31] In March 1701 the privy council questioned the duke of Hamilton and the marquis of Tweeddale on the engraving. It was clear that senior individuals in the African Company had been involved in its production, but the council was unable to pin responsibility on the two peers. The council ordered the print to be burned at the market cross in Edinburgh and prosecuted two low-level employees of the African Company for treason.[32]

The council also acted in 1701 against Jacobite prints. In February 1701 it pursued several booksellers and printers who were connected with the publishing of a letter by the Jacobite earl of Melfort that was 'selling throw the streets of Edinburgh reprinted verbatim from the Coppy printed at London'.[33] These included James Wardlaw and John Porteous, both of whom had sold pamphlets on Darien; and the printers George Jaffray and John Reid.[34] The

27 NAS, PC 1/52 (104–8).
28 NAS, PC 1/52 (105, 117).
29 APS x, appendix at pp. 51, 53.
30 NAS, GD 406/1/4910.
31 NAS, JC 26/81/31. I am grateful to Douglas Watt of Edinburgh University for this reference.
32 NAS, PC 1/52 (199, 202–4).
33 NAS, PC 1/52 (189).
34 Wardlaw and Porteous advertised their Darien pamphlets in the *Edinburgh Gazette*, nos 7 (Mon 20 Mar.–Thurs. 23 Mar. 1699) and 185 (Thurs. 28 Nov.–Mon. 2 Dec. 1700).

privy council ordered the Edinburgh magistrates to shut down the presses of Jaffray and Reid. It pursued Reid again in September 1701 for printing news from London of Louis XIV's recognition of James VII's son. Though Reid protested that he had intended no offence, someone had posted his news bulletin like a proclamation at the Edinburgh market cross. Unable to iden-tify the culprit, the privy council instead arrested Reid and his co-publisher James Donaldson, editor of the *Edinburgh Gazette*.[35]

In 1702 the privy council condemned a pamphlet expressing Episcopalian sympathies, Sir Alexander Bruce's *A speech in the parliament of Scotland, in relation to presbyterian government* (1702), but by 1703 its efforts at censor-ship were weakening as its membership changed.[36] The council now included figures like George Mackenzie, who published pamphlets in favour of union and toleration in 1702 and 1703.[37] Though the privy council expressed its disapproval of the proliferation of prints on toleration seen in 1703, it did not pursue authors directly. Instead it delegated the problem by ordering the Edinburgh magistrates to keep the city's printers in line. In response, the city announced that 'no printer is to print anything unless the samen be dewly allowed and authorized' and demanded that all printers put their names on their publications.[38] This had little effect. Presbyterians in the Court party attempted to use parliament to censor pro-toleration tracts with an act proposed by the duke of Argyll against 'a great many Libels' in the 1703 session.[39] The motion failed and print expanded as Presbyterian writers responded to Episcopalian tracts in a pamphlet debate that continued into 1705.

In addition to rejecting Argyll's attempt to tighten up censorship in 1703, the Country party majority in parliament modified the penalties against leasing-making. This new law weakened controls on political tracts and indi-cated a growing appreciation of the usefulness of print for political purposes. Citing the 'dangerous consequence' of former laws that included the possi-bility of capital punishment for seditious printing, the act removed the death penalty for writing or speaking against the crown, allowing only fines, impris-onment, banishment or corporal punishment.[40]

Though by 1703 the privy council had relaxed its control of pamphlets, it maintained the censorship of Scottish newspapers through its licensing

George Jaffray had been in trouble for Darien prints in 1699, while John Reid was the printer of the *Edinburgh Gazette* from 1699.

[35] NAS, PC 1/52 (285, 303).

[36] NAS, PC 1/52 (464–6).

[37] [George Mackenzie, Viscount Tarbat], *Speech in the parliament of Scotland upon the union and upon limitations*, [Edinburgh 1702]; *Parainesis pacifica*, Edinburgh–London 1702; *A few brief and modest reflexions*; and [George Mackenzie, earl of Cromarty], *A continuation of a few brief and modest reflexions*, [Edinburgh 1703].

[38] *Edinburgh burgh extracts, 1701–1718*, 63.

[39] [George Ridpath], *The proceedings of the parliament of Scotland begun at Edinburgh, 6th May 1703*, [Edinburgh?] 1704, 19.

[40] APS xi. 105.

powers. In contrast to England, where the periodical market included papers with extensive political commentary, some funded by crown ministers, the *Edinburgh Gazette* (founded 1699) and *Edinburgh Courant* (founded 1705) only provided news and commercial information.[41] They reported on privy council proceedings but did not cover the proceedings of parliament or the General Assembly. Nor did they offer any obvious party angle on the news, though the *Edinburgh Courant* occasionally revealed a Whig bias in reprinting items from Daniel Defoe's *Review* or John Tutchin's *Observator*.[42]

In its early days, the *Edinburgh Gazette* learned the limits of its privy council licence when overenthusiastic commentary on the Darien colony led to the arrest of its publisher James Donaldson. The privy council ordered pre-publication review of all future issues.[43] The *Edinburgh Courant* also experienced censorship when it was shut down for several months in 1705 after a printer's advertisement questioned the council's book licensing authority.[44] Under privy council control, no domestic periodical offered essay commentary on the news until the brief appearance of the *Observator*, an unlicensed periodical that ran for eight issues from March to July 1705 during the *Worcester* crisis.[45]

The appearance of the unlicensed *Observator* indicated that government control over political print was slipping. Although censorship orders proliferated in parliament during this period, many were instigated by the Country party to make political points. In November 1700 parliament ordered that three anti-Darien pamphlets be burned at the market cross in Edinburgh and authorised a reward of £6,000 Scots for the arrest of Walter Herries or Harris, the author of two of them.[46] It also ordered the burning of James Drake's *Historia anglo-scotica* (1703) for 'many false and injurious reflections upon the Sovereignty and Independency of this Crown and Nation' and of William Atwood's *The superiority and direct dominion of the imperial crown of England, over the crown and kingdom of Scotland* (1704) and *The Scotch patriot unmask'd* (1705). The 1705 parliament went on to encourage polemical printing in

---

41 Downie, *Robert Harley and the press.*

42 *Edinburgh Courant*, nos 22 (Fri. 6 Apr.–Mon. 9 Apr. 1705) and 31 (Mon. 30 Apr.–Wed. 2 May 1705).

43 Mann, *Scottish book trade*, 175; W. J. Couper, *The Edinburgh periodical press*, Stirling 1908, i. 75, 90, 209.

44 *Edinburgh Courant*, nos 53 (Wed. 20 June–Fri. 22 June 1705) and 55 (Mon. 25 June–Mon. 8 Oct. 1705).

45 Anon., *Observator or a dialogue between a country man and a landwart school-master*, nos 1–8, [Edinburgh] 1705. W. R. Owens and P. N. Furbank have suggested that the author of the *Observator* was John Pierce, an Englishman and Whig associate of Daniel Defoe who fled to Scotland in 1704 after publishing a mock address to the House of Lords considered seditious by the English government. As an English Whig writer in Scotland, Pierce may have adapted the dialogue model of John Tutchin's *Observator* to the Scottish situation in 1705: 'New light on John Pierce, Defoe's agent in Scotland', *Transactions of the Edinburgh Bibliographical Society* vi/4 (1998), 134–43.

46 APS x, appendix at p. 51.

Scotland by rewarding James Hodges and James Anderson for publishing tracts in support of Scottish sovereignty.[47]

During the Darien crisis the government increased its censorship efforts and did not publish in response to the Country party, but by 1702 the new members of Anne's Court party were beginning to embrace positive propaganda and to relax controls on pamphlets. In England William's ministers had engaged with the public sphere by publishing tracts in favour of crown policy, particularly during the standing army crisis of 1697–9.[48] In contrast, William had not supported the publication of Court print in Scotland, even though the earl of Marchmont had advocated the publication of a full explanation of the king's position on the Darien colony in June 1700. Marchmont expected that such a publication would win back former Court followers in parliament and would 'probably have an influence upon the body of the nation'.[49] Under Anne, Court figures, such as George Mackenzie, Viscount Tarbat began to publish tracts in support of royal policy. During 1703–4, the Court writing pool expanded to include John Clerk of Penicuik, a follower of the duke of Queensberry and others who remain anonymous. These writers published pamphlets in favour of Court party positions on the Hanoverian succession, the Act of Security, the Act anent Peace and War, limitations and the export of wool.[50] While the Court party still did not use print to the same extent as the Country party, it was taking a greater interest in responding to Country propaganda.

Court engagement with print arose in part out of the need for ministers to manage opinion in London as well as Scotland. Rising English influence over Scottish affairs from 1690 made Scottish ministers more attuned to London opinion and more adept at using print to speak to this audience. Reflecting this, Tarbat printed his 1702 pamphlet on union in London, addressing it to English as well as Scottish readers. In 1704 Lord Clerk Register James Johnston published a tract in London to defend his New Party against Tory criticisms.[51] He also urged the Scottish government to print an account of the

47 APS xi. 66, 221.

48 Lois G. Schwoerer, 'No standing armies!' The anti-army ideology in seventeenth-century England, Baltimore 1974, ch. vii.

49 Marchmont papers, 208.

50 Anon., A seasonable alarm for Scotland ... concerning the present danger of the kingdom, and of the Protestant religion, [Edinburgh] 1703; Anon., The great danger of Scotland as to all its sacred and civil concerns, from these, who are commonly known by the name of Jacobites, [Edinburgh] 1704; Anon., A watch-word to Scotland in perilous times, [Edinburgh] 1704; [John Clerk of Penicuik], A short essay upon the limitations, Edinburgh 1703, in W. R. McLeod and V. B. McLeod, Anglo-Scottish tracts, 1701–1714, Lawrence 1979, no. 404; It is resolved, that the parliament shall consider an act ... and therefore, prop. The Act for Peace and War is altogether useless, [Edinburgh 1703]; [George Mackenzie, earl of Cromarty], A speech in parliament, concerning the exportation of wool, 1704, in McLeod and McLeod, Anglo-Scottish tracts, no. 430.

51 [James Johnston], Reflections on a late speech by the Lord Haversham, in so far as it relates to the affairs of Scotland, London 1704.

1705 *Worcester* trial in London.[52] Writing from London, Secretary-Depute Sir David Nairn concurred: 'not publishing Greens tryall', he wrote, 'is a great disadvantage to all Scotsmen here'.[53] Ministers also maintained links with sympathetic authors in London: connections between George Ridpath and the New Party government are indicated by the authorisation of a payment of £100 to him by the earl of Roxburgh in December 1704.[54] In 1705 a correspondent to the earl of Seafield praised Ridpath's defence of the *Worcester* trial in his *Flying Post* and recommended that the author be rewarded.[55]

In Scotland, the crown's ministers began to acknowledge a need to win over what they called 'country opinion' in order to secure a parliamentary majority. This realisation can be seen in 1705 when the privy council chose to allow the executions of Green and two of his crew to avoid angering country opinion before the next parliament.[56] This recognition of the power of public opinion marked a significant shift in Court party attitudes towards the emerging Scottish public sphere. The crown did not take up Country party methods in mass petitioning or riotous crowds, limiting itself to loyal addressing and authorised civic events. Nevertheless, the developing public sphere in Scotland required the crown to begin to produce positive propaganda for its policies. Its output remained small before 1705, but the stage was set for an explosion of pro-union print in 1706–7.

While responding to oppositional populism with its own propaganda, the government still upheld constitutional limits on the authority of public opinion. With the expansion of the public sphere from the late 1690s, public opinion began to appear as a rhetorical entity in pamphlets, petitions and crowd protests. Oppositional groups demanded policy change on the basis of popular preference, but this was not acknowledged as a legitimate authority. Though the adversarial use of public opinion had evolved from traditional consultative practices, the power of this practice relied not just on the moral authority of a claimed consensus, but on an implied threat of popular disaffection and potential rebellion. The association of oppositional demands with mass petitions or disruptive crowds, especially any that seemed to contain Jacobite or Presbyterian extremists, emphasised this connection. This underlying danger exposed opinion politics to accusations of sedition and democratic anarchy. During the union crisis, crown ministers expressed doubts about the safety and legitimacy of public opinion even as some began to combat Country appeals to opinion with their own propaganda. The lack of constitutional legitimacy for public opinion allowed the government to disregard, undermine and repress representations of 'the sense of the nation' while at the same time publishing their own persuasive efforts.

---

52 *Jerviswood correspondence*, 71.
53 *Seafield correspondence*, 404.
54 *Jerviswood correspondence*, 21.
55 *Seafield correspondence*, 398.
56 *Jerviswood correspondence*, 64–6.

Pamphlet discourse reveals the insecure position of public comment and invocations of public opinion. The law against leasing-making required that 'all his Majesty's Subjects Content themselves in quiet & dutifull obedience … and that none of them presume, To take upon hand to speak or write any purpose of Reproach or Slander of his Majesty's person, Estate or Government'.[57] To build their legitimacy in this legal climate, many pamphlets of this period addressed themselves to members of parliament.[58] Authors invoked the duty of citizens to advise parliament for the common good. As one pamphleteer claimed, 'It is the Duty, of every Good Country-Man at all times, to contribute to the promoting of the publick Weal, particularly at the Meetings of Parliament.'[59] Others saw 'just ground for any Person to complain' when the government had failed to rectify problems.[60] A 1703 pamphleteer argued that 'Tho' the Representatives of a Nation are indeed more immediately concerned [in national politics]…yet Private Men may be allowed to give their thoughts on such matters; and it is the duty of every Member of the Society to exert themselves in their several capacities with the utmost vigor for the common welfare.' For this author, the 'warm Debates in the House, the Thundering Declamations from the Pulpits, and the sweating labours of the Press' were an appropriate response to the political problems of the day.[61] The radical Whig Andrew Fletcher of Saltoun stated an obligation on parliament to attend to the opinions of constituents, asserting a 'right and duty of every man to write or speak his mind freely in all things that may come before any parliament; to the end that they who represent the nation in that assembly, may be truly informed of the sentiments of those they represent'.[62]

These statements pushed against a long tradition of classical teachings and conservative political thought rejecting popular involvement in politics. Moreover, recent Scottish history connected popular practices with faction, rebellion and anarchy driven by Covenanting Presbyterianism.[63] Given this, the crown and many of its followers resisted the widening of public discourse and participation.[64] As the earl of Leven lamented, 'every man thinks he

---

57 NAS, PC 1/52 (114).
58 Anon., *A letter to a member of parliament, occasioned, by the growing poverty of the nation*, [Edinburgh 1703?]; [John Bannatyne], *A letter from a Presbyterian minister in the countrey, to a member of parliament*, [Edinburgh] 1703; [James Donaldson], *A letter to a member of parliament, from a wel-wisher of his country*, [Edinburgh 1705].
59 Anon., *Scotland's interest: or, the great benefit and necessity of a communication of trade with England*, [Edinburgh] 1704, 3.
60 Anon., *The sin and shame of Scotland*, Edinburgh 1704.
61 [Sir Archibald Sinclair], *Some thoughts on the present state of affairs*, [Edinburgh] 1703, 2.
62 Andrew Fletcher of Saltoun, 'Two discourses concerning the affairs of Scotland', in *Political works*, 34.
63 Colin Kidd, *Subverting Scotland's past: Scottish Whig historians and the creation of an Anglo-British identity, 1689- c. 1830*, Cambridge 1993, 53–8; Cust, 'Charles I and popularity', 238–43.
64 NAS, PC 1/52 (206).

knows more than his neighbour; nor is any man respected, it seems, though spending his strength and estate for the public; but they will judge of matters at a distance, which they little understand'.[65] Court pamphleteers bemoaned the need to respond to Country tracts and pointed to the dangers of involving the masses in politics. The author of A *watchword to Scotland in perillous times* (1704) condemned the 'Fatal Spirit of division [that] ferments mightily at this day among our Nobles and Gentrie, and is advancing also to even the commonality', while A *plea against pamphlets* (1703) accused readers of only reading tracts that confirmed their prior opinions.[66]

The practice of adversarial addressing illustrates many of the ambiguities contained in early modern representations of opinion. These addresses operated under conventions of supplication established in medieval requests made by feudal vassals to their superiors. These begged the superior to employ his power to resolve conflicts, grant gifts or dispense justice. The medieval petitioning event was a highly choreographed ritual in which the humble stance of the petitioner signalled his loyal and willing subjection while the superior's acknowledgement of the petition confirmed his gracious authority. In practice, petitions made their way to monarchs through lower officials, often with the sponsorship of a powerful patron. Advance negotiations with interested parties prepared the ground, sometimes leading to the editing or withdrawal of a petition. As a feudal process, petitioning worked as long as the superior was not embarrassed by the presentation of impossible requests and the subordinate was not frustrated by a failure to resolve problems.[67]

In the early modern period, written petitions became the accepted medium in Scotland for administrative applications. A private individual or a corporate body could petition the privy council, parliament or monarch for the grant of a patent, monopoly, licence, fair or other privilege.[68] Lobbying efforts by burgh or shire representatives supported these petitions, indicating the need for advance preparation.[69] The petition was also employed in the routine operation of the judiciary, where appeals to superior courts were usually written as petitions.

The petition was also used to express grievances to higher authorities, framed as humble supplications for relief. According to conventions of consensus politics, such a petition expressed the views of a corporate body in the political nation. In Scotland, recognised bodies like the General Assembly, the Convention of Royal Burghs or the parliamentary estates could bring grievances to parliament, the privy council or the monarch via petitions. Petitioning operated in a hierarchical fashion, with subordinate bodies appealing to the next higher authority. This could create chains of

---

65 *Carstares papers*, 718.
66 Anon., A *watch-word*.
67 Koziol, *Begging pardon and favor*, pt I. See also Zaret, *Origins of democratic culture*, 81–99.
68 See, for example, APS viii, appendix at pp. 14, 18.
69 *Glasgow burgh extracts*, 384.

petitions, as in 1625 when the baron and burgh estates supplicated parliament to ask for a petition to Charles I requesting consultations on his judicial reforms.[70] Individual shires and burghs did not normally petition parliament on political issues, though they might provide private instructions to their commissioner on particular grievances. Similarly, parishes did not normally petition parliament or the General Assembly. Within the Church, presbyteries could instruct their General Assembly members to propose a petition to the civil authorities.

The use of petitions to make a public supplication on grievances indicated a failure of private means of consensus-building. By delivering a formal, public complaint, a petition placed pressure on the recipient to acknowledge a problem and negotiate a solution. A petition could not force the adoption of a particular policy; instead, it pushed the recipient towards a settlement by asserting a consensus of negative opinion. Its leverage was moral, resting on the duty of higher authorities to govern for the common good. Nevertheless, the ultimate judge of the common good was the monarch and negative answers to petitions were to be considered final. Repeated petitioning on the same issue suggested a dangerous lack of respect for authority.

The soft powers of the political petition could be sharpened with more adversarial practices, adding the threat of mass resistance to humble supplications. In the early seventeenth century this can be seen in the increasing aggressiveness and populism of petitioning under Charles I in both Scotland and England.[71] Oppositional groups began to initiate mass petitioning campaigns to generate repeated petitions signed by hundreds of ordinary people. The supplications organised in Scotland against the king's new book of common prayer of 1637 provide an ideal case study of an escalation in populist petitioning, culminating in a drive for universal subscription to the National Covenant of 1638.[72] By breaking the rules of petitioning, these more assertive appeals brought greater force to bear against the king, but at the expense of some of their legitimacy as humble supplications.

Organisers of these new types of petitions sought to shore up their legitimacy in several ways. They retained many conventions of humble presentation, expressing strong demands within the traditional petitionary form. Petitions also followed the traditional practice of blaming unpopular policy on evil councillors rather than the king himself. Most important, adversarial petitions portrayed their complaints as the unified voice of a corporate body.[73] Organisers downplayed the rebellious implications of popular subscription by portraying signatories as members of the petitioning body. Even where local opinion was divided, petitions clung to the practice of corporate presenta-

---

[70] *APS* v. 184.
[71] Zaret, *Origins of democratic culture*; Allan I. Macinnes, *Charles I and the making of the Covenanting movement, 1625–1641*, Edinburgh 1991.
[72] John Leslie, earl of Rothes, *A relation of proceedings concerning the affairs of the Kirk of Scotland, from August 1637 to July 1638*, Edinburgh 1830.
[73] Zaret, *Origins of democratic culture*, 91–7.

tion. In January 1701, for example, a Country party petition presented to parliament from Glasgow did not have the backing of the city's council or parliamentary commissioner, but the 474 signatories still claimed to represent 'the Inhabitants of the City of Glasgow'.[74]

The government recognised the subversive power of these innovations. As successive Stewart administrations in seventeenth-century Scotland attempted to repress adversarial petitioning, the right to petition for relief of grievances emerged as a key political issue. One of the many concerns contributing to the rebellion against Charles I in 1637–9 was the crown's prosecution of John Elphinstone, Lord Balmerino, for treason in 1635 for possession of a petition citing political grievances.[75] Reacting to Stewart controls, the 1689 Revolution Convention secured a liberty to petition in the Claim of Right. This declared that 'it is the right of all subjects to petition the King, and that all imprisonments and prosecutions for such petitioning, are Contrary to law'.[76]

Although the Claim of Right confirmed a right to petition in the time of the union crisis, petitioning remained bound up in conventions of humble presentation and corporate consensus. Moreover, the civil wars and revolutions of the seventeenth century had associated adversarial petitioning with disorder, allowing the crown to continue to resist such addresses. William and Anne found that they could not forbid the practice of addressing, but they could use more subtle means of management to discourage the signing or presentation of unwelcome addresses.

On learning that the Country party was organising a national address in December 1699, some members of the privy council urged strong repression. Sir James Stewart of Goodtrees, the Lord Advocate, argued that meetings for subscription defied standing laws against unauthorised convocations of subjects.[77] Though a committee concluded that 'the council could not in law prescribe the ways and methods of the subjects' petitioning', the council voted by thirteen to ten to issue a royal proclamation from William denouncing the party's petition.[78] Issued on 18 December, this proclamation did not deny the subject's liberty to petition but condemned the Country party for overturning normal practices. The African Company had petitioned the king for a parliament in October and had been told that 'the parliament shall meet when we judge that the Good of the Nation does require it'. This, the king declared, 'ought to have given intire Satisfaction to all our Good Subjects'. The party's 'Design of Addressing Us of New, on the same heads' was unacceptable. The proclamation further accused the organisers of fomenting sedition in their 'unusual Method' of generating subscriptions.[79]

74 APS x, appendix at p. 84.
75 Macinnes, *Charles I*, 137–41.
76 APS ix. 40.
77 Patrick, 'People and parliament', 232.
78 NAS, PC 1/52 (23); *Marchmont papers*, 193–4.
79 African Company, *A full and exact collection*, 87–8, 103–5.

The royal proclamation backfired, creating widespread resentment and encouraging greater support for the party's national address. According to the earl of Marchmont, 'all the matter of discourse here, is quite changed from that of the company and the colony, to that of the subjects' privilege and freedom of addressing to, and petitioning the king'.[80] The manuscript tract 'A few remarks on the proclamation' (1699) asserted the acceptability of repeated petitioning where there were 'just and weighty reasons of Adressing of new' and declared any attempt to limit petitioning to be unlawful.[81] As the Country party continued to circulate its petition, Archibald Pitcairne claimed that 'Twice So many have signed since the proclamation anent Petitioning, as signed it before.'[82]

In response, the crown's ministers turned to their usual management method of 'private pains'.[83] Pressure was exerted on corporations and localities to discourage subscriptions, with demonstrable results: in a January 1700 meeting of the Edinburgh Merchant Company, only thirty of 300 members attended to sign the national address after Court discouragement, while in Glasgow and Ayr, the provosts opposed the petition locally. Later in the summer, counter-canvassing by Seafield in Banffshire and Marchmont in Berwickshire reduced support for the third national address.[84]

William and Anne also discouraged petitioners when they brought unwanted addresses to London. William refused to give an immediate reply to the Country party's June 1700 address, stating that 'you shall know my intentions in Scotland'.[85] An answer was provided several weeks later in a letter to the privy council. The monarchs also at times refused to accept addresses in person, ordering petitioners to submit their papers via a minister. In November 1699 William would not receive an African Company address from Lord Basil Hamilton, younger brother of the duke of Hamilton and a prominent figure in the Country opposition and the African Company. In denying Hamilton an audience, William said that he would only take the address through his Scottish secretaries.[86] Similarly, Anne refused to accept the address presented by the Country party after they walked out of her first parliament in protest in June 1702.[87] In an initial private conference in late June Anne asked the carrier of the petition, Lord Blantyre, to take it back to Scotland to her royal commissioner, the duke of Queensberry. After this rebuff, Lord Blantyre came to see Anne again, accompanied by William Keith. Though Keith warned Anne that the return of the address to Scotland would 'incense the whole body of her people and occasion such disorders as

---

80 *Marchmont papers*, 198.
81 Wodrow quarto lxxiii, fo. 234.
82 NAS, PC 1/52 (67).
83 *Marchmont papers*, 194.
84 Patrick, 'People and parliament', 234, 237–8, 264, 268.
85 African Company, A *full and exact collection*, 130.
86 Insh, *Company of Scotland*, 207.
87 'Scotland's ruine', 14.

perhaps could not so easily be quelled', Anne continued to insist that the petition be presented to Queensberry in Scotland. Blantyre and Keith sought the intercession of Sarah Churchill, wife of the duke of Marlborough and friend to the queen, but Anne's stalling continued and the petition returned to Scotland unpresented.[88]

When addresses could not be refused, the Court made calculated concessions to petitioned grievances to reduce public opposition. Though William had refused to accept Lord Basil Hamilton's address in 1699, he still responded to some of the points in the address, promising in particular to demand the release of a Scottish captain and his crew from Spanish captivity. This was achieved by early 1701 as part of the steps taken to smooth the management of the 1700–1 parliament.[89] William's managers also won voters back to the government's side in 1700–1 by supporting new laws to resolve grievances, such as a *habeas corpus* act, and agreeing to allow an address to the king on the Darien colony.[90]

In contrast to England where counter-addressing had become part of the political culture, the post-Revolution government in Scotland did not generate mass petitions in its own interest.[91] Though the Country party claimed to represent the national interest, the Court party still contained a significant sector of Presbyterian Revolution interests. In the 1703 toleration debates, petitions could have been generated by Court Presbyterians against toleration but were not. Faced with Episcopalian addressing, Presbyterian clergy in Edinburgh consulted the Lord Advocate, Sir James Stewart of Goodtrees, on the advisability of counter-addressing. Stewart discouraged mass addressing by the established Church, suggesting that the clergy collect information to undermine the Episcopalian addresses instead. In 1703 only the Commission of the General Assembly addressed on behalf of the Church with one petition to parliament against toleration. The Church also used the opportunity of a congratulatory address to Anne on military victories to warn her against the disaffection of Scottish Episcopalian dissenters.[92]

The Lord Advocate's conservative position on addressing in this case, and in December 1699, might seem surprising given Stewart's personal history as the author of a radical Covenanting tract on popular resistance, *Jus populi vindicatum* (1669). Stewart's ideological reversal as a member of the post-Revolution government confirms the oppositional nature of adversarial addressing and the state's interest in maintaining controls on it. Loyal addresses had become an accepted means of expressing support for the post-Revolution monarchy, but mass petitioning remained controversial. Bodies

88 NAS, GD 406/1/4813, 4815, 4830.
89 Insh, *Company of Scotland*, 207, 226–7.
90 APS x. 89, appendix at pp. 44–5; Riley, *King William*, 150–1.
91 Zaret, *Origins of democratic culture*, ch. viii; Harris, '"Venerating the honesty of a tinker"'.
92 *Wodrow letters*, 255; *The humble representation of the Commission of the late General Assembly*, [Edinburgh 1703]; APS xi. 46; NAS, CH 1/2/4/1 (3).

like the General Assembly and the Convention of Royal Burghs maintained a traditional right to represent the concerns of their estates to government through petitioning; and, more generally, the liberty of the subject to petition for relief of grievances had been protected in the Claim of Right. Beyond this, however, it remained unclear how far the Claim of Right protected aggressive adversarial petitioning. The government confirmed these limitations by eschewing counter-addressing and focusing instead on the discouragement of adversarial petitioning.

Of all forms of popular participation, crowd activities remained the least legitimate yet potentially the most powerful. Contemporary political culture associated mobs with mindless violence, seeing crowds as an extreme example of the dangers of popular political engagement. Though condemned in principle, in practice crowds could have a strong short-term impact. Like a petition, a riot signalled a public eruption of discontent requiring negotiation and compromise, with a threat of further disorder if grievances were not resolved. This made collective action attractive to party organisers. Since leaders could not afford to be associated with illegal tumults, organisers drew on civic rituals, judicial practices or standing law to construct a form of legitimacy for the expression of public opinion in organised crowds. This can be seen in the encouragement of illuminations before the June 1700 Darien riot or the burning of seized Catholic materials in Dumfries in 1704, both of which echoed typical state practices. Yet despite these attempts to legitimise crowds, laws against unauthorised collective actions gave the government grounds on which to use force to re-establish public order, such as the deployment of town guards or royal forces. In combination with coercive methods, concessions and negotiation were also employed to reduce high levels of discontent and remove the risk of continuing disorder.

Scots law established the basic illegitimacy of crowd actions. Parliamentary statutes made in the reigns of James II and IV banned disorder in royal burghs, while a law of James VI ordered 'That no person within burgh take upon hand under whatsomever pretext to convocat without the knowledge and License of the Magistrats under the pain to be punished in their body and goods with all Rigor.' This law required burgh residents to cooperate with the magistrates in controlling crowds and punishing the disorderly 'under the pain of being repute Fosterers and Mantainers of the said Tumults'. More particularly, a law of James VI banned anyone from invading the privy council or interfering with the king's officers in their pursuit of his business, under penalty of death.[93]

Laws alone could not stop tumults, so burgh leaders tried to talk crowds down before violence could erupt. In early 1703 Glasgow town leaders met with Colin Bell, the coordinator of unauthorised Episcopalian meetings, to try to persuade him not to antagonise local Presbyterians any further. Though they failed to stop him from holding further dissenting meetings in the centre

[93] NAS, PC 1/53 (389).

of town, further talks managed to avert a riot at Bell's house in late February.[94] Similarly, before the anti-Catholic demonstration in Dumfries in February 1704, the town's magistrates met oppositional leaders at the bridge leading into the town, hoping to dissuade them from entering their burgh.[95]

When negotiation failed or was not attempted, magistrates turned to the town guard. A volunteer militia, consisting of officers and men drawn from burgess households, the guard was charged with keeping the peace, suppressing immorality and maintaining a night watch. As burgess members of their own community, however, guardsmen could have conflicting interests. Since 1682 Edinburgh had supplemented its town guard with paid forces, whose numbers rose and fell according to the dangers of invasion and insurrection. After the June 1700 Darien riot, Edinburgh increased its paid guard by ninety men as its volunteer force had proved inadequate during the riot.[96]

When town guards failed to suppress crowds, royal forces could be employed. Such forces might be readily available, having been quartered in the town, or they could be dispatched to tumultuous towns by the privy council. In Edinburgh the burgh's privileges included an exemption from the burden of quartering and magistrates interpreted the admission of royal troops to the city as a high affront to the city's privileges. Nevertheless, the government could call in forces if necessary. During the June 1700 riot, rioters closed the Netherbow port to prevent troops from entering the city from their usual quarters in the suburb of Canongate. On the following day, a privy council act authorised the placing of 145 soldiers in the burgh at the Council-House, the Tron and the Netherbow port.[97] In addition, a privy council proclamation banned unauthorised bonfires in all Scottish burghs and empowered magistrates to call in troops to stop them.[98]

The government again threatened the use of troops in Edinburgh at the time of the *Worcester* hangings in 1705. On the morning of 11 April, royal troops were sent to Leith to keep the peace at the gallows.[99] After a crowd attacked the chancellor in Edinburgh, the privy council warned that if the city authorities could not suppress further rioting, 'we may be obleidged to bring in sufficient Guards into the said citie to abyde and quarter therein'. The council also threatened to remove the king's courts from Edinburgh to another town if the city could not keep them safe.[100] In Glasgow the magistrates relied on quartered royal troops to quell the anti-toleration riot of 7 March 1703; afterwards, the privy council approved this use of the forces and considered sending more dragoons.[101]

---

94 Wodrow quarto xxviii, fos 151–2; NAS, PC 1/52(524).
95 Dumfries Archive Centre, A 2/8(7).
96 *Edinburgh burgh extracts, 1689–1701*, pp. xix–xx, 265.
97 NAS, PC 1/52 (109).
98 NAS, PC 1/52 (111).
99 Insh, *Company of Scotland*, 308–9.
100 NAS, PC 1/53 (390).
101 NAS, PC 1/52 (526).

The council's threats to Edinburgh after the 1705 riots indicate the care taken to reestablish law and order after tumultuous events. Proclamations condemned disorder, reiterated standing laws against rioting and renewed the obligations of burgh residents to maintain order. Following the Darien rioting, the Edinburgh council required its householders to guarantee the good behaviour of servants and apprentices. Since the crowd had blocked the Netherbow port and liberated political prisoners from the Tolbooth, the government chained the port open for eight months and renewed its prosecution of the prisoners, eventually banishing them from Edinburgh.[102] A privy council proclamation after the *Worcester* disturbance again required householders to police their families, adding the masters of Edinburgh University as well. This proclamation stated that in future any person found on the street after being ordered to retire would be considered a participant in the riot and liable to arrest.[103]

Recognising that troops and proclamations alone could not quell popular discontent, authorities also sought to assuage concerns through limited concessions. Following the 1703 anti-toleration riots in Glasgow, the privy council clarified its position on non-jurant Episcopalian preachers. Though stating that 'a mobb and rable can never be Justified; whither the Episcopall Minister that preaches be qualified or not', they acknowledged that 'non should be Imployed to preach but such as are qualified'.[104] After recommending that unqualified preachers be reported to the Lord Advocate, the council proceeded to prosecute several unqualified ministers in 1703.[105]

Central action was also taken against Catholics after the 1704 disorders in Dumfriesshire. In reaction to initial attacks on Catholic households, the council appointed a committee to consider how to deal with Catholic priests in the area, leading to a proclamation 'anent preists and Trafecquing papists'.[106] This proclamation, published in March, acknowledged 'Complaints and Informations from severall pairts of the Kingdome' as well as a General Assembly petition on the Catholic threat. The council ordered local officers to enforce standing laws against Catholics, offered a reward for the arrest and conviction of Catholics and ordered presbyteries to send in lists of known Catholics.[107] In addition, the council scheduled a burning of seized Catholic items at Edinburgh.[108]

During the *Worcester* crisis of 1705, the privy council sought to prevent rioting by acknowledging popular pressure for the carrying-out of scheduled executions. Disregarding the queen's request for a second stay of execution, the council authorised the first three hangings on 11 April. The strategy

102 NAS, PC 1/53 (114, 179).
103 *Edinburgh burgh extracts, 1689–1701*, 267; NAS, PC 1/53 (390).
104 NAS, PC 1/52 (527).
105 NAS, PC 1/53 (70–4).
106 NAS, PC 1/53 (126, 144).
107 NAS, PC 1/53 (194–5).
108 NAS, PC 1/53 (184–5).

was not entirely successful, as a rumour of a reprieve sparked an attack on the chancellor after the council meeting. Nevertheless, assurances that the executions would be carried out quieted the crowd and prevented greater violence.

Rejecting the more aggressive innovations of the emerging public sphere, the governments in Scotland of William and Anne took a pragmatic approach to oppositional populism, using personal persuasion, patronage, counter-propaganda, repression and concessions to maintain royal authority and remove any immediate threat of disorder. The Court party's increasing use of print propaganda from 1702 indicated not a desire to encourage popular participation in the public sphere but the acknowledgement of a short-term need to counter the effects of Country propaganda. The government's intention to limit the influence of public opinion can be seen in its discouragement of aggressive petitions and use of force to restore order after rioting. Limited concessions were made in response to the discontent expressed in petitions and crowds, but these did not credit such representations with any constitutional legitimacy. Despite the efforts of oppositional writers, petitioners and crowds to assert the authority of public opinion, the adversarial nature and uncertain constitutional legitimacy of popular participation allowed the government to maintain limits on its influence. To the state, public opinion mattered only insofar as it indicated high levels of disaffection and therefore a significant risk of disorder and challenge to monarchical authority. In these circumstances, ministers made concessions to opinion as a management tactic alongside their more traditional practices of private persuasion and patronage.

PART II

PUBLIC OPINION AND THE UNION, 1699–1707

4

Public Discourse on the Union, 1699–1705

Entwined with the new public debates on Darien from 1699 was an ongoing discourse on the British union. Though historians of the union have tended to focus on the pamphlet exchanges of 1706–7, these tracts represented the final stage of a question that had been under public discussion since the late 1690s. Problems of sovereignty and Anglo-Scottish relations provided grounds for an ongoing critique of the 1603 union of the crowns of England and Scotland. From 1700 authors were also responding to proposals by William and Anne for a closer union between the two kingdoms.[1] Because crown ministers did not actively publish propaganda before Anne's 1702 union proposals, and even then their output was low, the Country party dominated discourse on union until 1706.

This chapter will trace the course of public discussion of union from the Darien crisis, showing how the Country party's publications, though differing in some points, promulgated a shared diagnosis of the problems of the union of crowns and the reforms needed to recover Scotland's eroding sovereignty. These messages developed alongside a Country party parliamentary programme that sought to force a renegotiation of the British union through acts of reform and a treaty with England. This platform, and its associated print propaganda, operated in opposition to Court efforts to secure an act confirming the Hanoverian successor to the crown of England as the heir to the Scottish throne. Limited amounts of Court party publications in favour of the Hanoverian succession, incorporating union and Protestant unity appealed to a growing cadre of religious moderates but did not build a broad opinion base for incorporation; nor did the largely antagonistic English publications circulating in Scotland contribute to Scottish confidence in the idea of a complete union with England.

Country discourse

From 1699 until 1705 oppositional pamphlets attacked the union of crowns and proposed an alternative vision of union. Historical analyses of the regal union advanced by George Ridpath, Andrew Fletcher of Saltoun, James

---

[1] King William recommended a closer union in messages to the English House of Lords in February 1700 and the House of Commons in February 1702. After her accession in 1702 Queen Anne asked the Scottish and English parliaments to authorise commissioners for union talks.

Hodges, Robert Wylie and others portrayed the Scottish king as trapped under the influence of his English ministers and parliament and forced to act against Scottish interests. Through English encroachment, the original liberties of the Scottish parliament had been lost since 1603, leaving the Scots at the mercy of their stronger neighbours. English control extended to the direction of Scottish ministers and MPs through bribery and other forms of management. Both Scottish sovereignty and the Presbyterian Church were at risk from the designs of the English, especially the High Church Tory party.

To solve these problems, authors pressed for reforms championed by the Scottish parliament as the guardian of the country's interests. In 1700–1 new laws securing Scottish civil liberties and asserting her trading rights were proposed. From 1702 three reform elements were advanced, appearing in different combinations across Country discourse: a shifting of power from the crown to the Scottish parliament through limitations on the prerogatives of Anne's successor; a communication of trade with England to improve Scottish access to English markets and capital; and a re-establishment of the British regal union on a federal basis. Limitations were to be achieved through acts of parliament while treaty negotiations with England would reform the terms of union. Throughout, Country discourse minimised the threat of a Jacobite claim on the open Scottish succession and amplified a sense of immediate danger to the Scottish Church, especially after toleration proposals in 1703. While this Country discourse owed much to a Revolution Whig perspective, particularly in its emphasis on parliament as the guardian of Scottish liberties and its focus on the security of the Presbyterian Church, it also included Tory viewpoints, broadening its appeal.

Country print on union was produced by professional writers, clergy, private gentlemen and MPs. Many of these authors can be linked to noble leaders of the Country party, confirming the relationship between oppositional publications and parliamentary activity. Key authors in this period included Robert Wylie, James Hodges, George Ridpath, Andrew Fletcher of Saltoun, William Seton of Pitmedden and John Hamilton Lord Belhaven. Alongside pamphlets attributed to these known authors, a number of anonymous writers also published in support of Country objectives.

Robert Wylie published on the toleration debates and on union while providing political advice to the Hamilton family and acting as a communication link between the family and church assemblies. Wylie was associated with ongoing Country opposition in the General Assembly, where he worked with ministers like Archibald Foyer of Stonehouse parish, author of tracts on Darien and union, and John Bannatyne of Lanark parish, author of tracts on toleration and union. In 1705 the duke of Hamilton praised Wylie as a key source of advice: 'I find noe bodie has a better & a more just notione of things'.[2]

As a Scottish writer based in London, James Hodges corresponded with

[2]   NAS, GD 406/1/7098, 4944, 8025.

the duke of Hamilton from at least 1701, though he also maintained contact with the earl of Seafield in the Court party and members of the Country Whig faction that formed the New Party of 1704. Personal ties linked Hodges to Hamilton through his brother-in-law, who managed a saltworks for the duke. At least some of Hodges's writings were sponsored by Country party leaders, as in 1704 when Hodges sent a tract to Lord Belhaven to be printed in Edinburgh and asked the duke of Hamilton to support its publication. It seems probable that the duke's support extended to funding, as Hodges was expecting a payment of twelve guineas from Hamilton in 1703. By 1704 Hodges had taken on the role of spin doctor to the duke, writing advice to him from London 'that you may remember to charge your memory with all the Arguments you can ... against an Incorporating Union, and, putt your friends also in mind to doe so against the next meeting of parliament'.[3]

George Ridpath seems to have had contact with Hamilton as well, though less than Hodges.[4] Ridpath's political orientation placed him in closer contact with the more Whiggish elements in the Country opposition led by the marquis of Tweeddale. In 1704 the earl of Roxburgh, a member of Tweeddale's New Party, authorised a payment of £100 to Ridpath.[5] Nevertheless, Ridpath did not always find it easy to work with the New Party when his Whig friends came into office, referring to them as 'our Modern Presbyterians who are for giving up the power of parliaments to the princes they make court to'. Declaring himself to be of 'no party but our old & true Constitution in Church & State', Ridpath's personal commitment to the 'Constitution of 1641 to which the Nation was solemnly sworn' kept him in sympathy with Hamilton's Country faction. In 1705 Ridpath was in contact with James Hodges and Robert Wylie, publishing 'Abstracts' of a paper by Wylie in his *Flying Post*.[6]

After publishing in London on the English standing army debates, the radical Whig Andrew Fletcher of Saltoun helped to define Country Whig discourse in Scotland from 1698 as a private gentleman and from 1703 as an MP. Fletcher was associated with Tweeddale's Country Whig faction, particularly the young earls of Rothes and Roxburgh, though like Ridpath he was unhappy with the ideological compromises made by these Whigs in government. Another laird, William Seton of Pitmedden in Aberdeenshire also published for the opposition during the Darien crisis.

During that time Ridpath, Seton, Foyer and several unidentified writers began to popularise a Country critique of the union of crowns. Royal interest in a closer union, expressed in 1700 and 1702, spurred Ridpath further to develop a Country Whig view of the problems of the union in 1702. Together these publications emphasised the subjection of Scottish interests to English

3 NAS, GD 406/1/4910, 7077, 5195, 5119, 5100, 5116, 5118, 7854.
4 NAS, GD 406/1/4927.
5 *Jerviswood correspondence*, 21.
6 Wodrow quarto xxx, fo. 265.

domination in the union of crowns, called on parliament to reassert its historical powers to defend Scotland against English encroachment and accused
the crown and its ministers of bribery and corruption in creating and maintaining Court control of the Scottish parliament and Church.

Ridpath's *Scotland's grievances relating to Darien* (1700) outlined what would
become the dominant account of the united crowns: 'since the Union of the
Crowns, our Kings prefer their Interest to ours, in all matters relating either
to Church or State'.[7] King William's lack of support for Darien resulted from
the king being advised by 'an English and Dutch Faction mixt with some
Scotchmen who have so little Interest in their Country or Affection for it,
as to betray it for Bread, or the Favour of the Court'.[8] Similarly, a manuscript
tract, 'Heads of things fit to be granted and done in the ensuing session of
parliament' (1700), bemoaned 'the irregular tye of the Union of Crowns' by
which 'This Nation hath been depryved of and Lost the ordinary means of
protecting its Forraigne Trade by Naval Force, Ambassadors, Residents and
such like.'[9] A broadside print, *The people of Scotland's groans and lamentable
complaints* (1700), compared Scotland to a child 'deprived of the Kindness
and Protection of One of their Parents' and charged the English with 'having
the Political Fathers of our Country under their Command'.[10] William Seton
of Pitmedden's *Memorial to the members of parliament of the Court party* (1700)
emphasised the absentee nature of the Scottish monarchy in accusing the
king of being 'of the Episcopal side, when he is in England'; and 'whether he
would be Presbyterian or not, when in Scotland, we must suspend our Judgement, till we have the Honour of seeing him here' – an unlikely circumstance
since no reigning monarch of Scotland and England had visited Scotland
since 1641.[11]

For Country Whigs like Ridpath, a key aspect of the damage done by the
union of crowns was the erosion of the powers of the Scottish parliament. From
1700 Ridpath established an influential line of argument blaming the union
for the rise of the royal prerogative in Scotland and a concurrent decline in
the liberties of the parliament. The Scottish Estates, he claimed in 1700, 'had
originally a greater Power than that of England; for what the States of Scotland offer'd to the touch of the Scepter, their Kings had no power to refuse;
or if they did, the Resolves of the States had the force of a Law notwith-
standing'. According to his researches, the 'native Liberties of the People of
Scotland' included the right to make war and peace, to elect kings, to choose

---

7   [Ridpath], *Scotland's grievances*, 31.
8   Ibid. 8.
9   'Heads of things fit to be granted and done in the ensuing session of parliament' (1700),
NLS, Advocates MS.
10   Anon., *The people of Scotland's groans and lamentable complaints, pour'd out before the high
court of parliament*, [Edinburgh 1700], 1.
11   [Seton of Pitmedden], *Memorial*, 4.

the king's councillors and to approve supply.[12] Ridpath's 1702 *Discourse upon the union of Scotland and England* again stated his view of the lost powers of the parliament, rejecting the need for royal assent to legislation and claiming the power of parliament to make war and peace and the right of the barons to attend parliament in person.[13] These comments were expanded in 1703 in *An historical account of the antient rights and power of the parliament of Scotland*, written for the parliament as it debated limitations on the crown.

Accusations of Court party bribery and intimidation formed another important aspect of the oppositional critique. These associated the Country party with the patriotic defence of Scottish interests while linking the Court party to English influence and corruption. In 1700 *A short speech prepared to be spoken, by a worthy member in parliament, concerning the present state of the nation* decried the 'bad Counsel' and 'foul Dealing' of 'Men altogether depending for Places or Pensions on the Court', accusing these 'evil Councillors' of influencing parliament by 'Force and Bribery'.[14] *The people of Scotland's groans* demanded 'Let not this Nation, that they could never Conquer by their Swords, be ingloriously subdued by their Money.'[15] In *Scotland's grievances*, Ridpath called the king's ministers 'Traytors' and 'pernicious Counsellors' while urging parliamentary commissioners not to be 'frighten'd by Red Coats, and other Court Pensioners' or cries of 'the Castle, the Castle, as in the late Reigns'.[16]

Accusations of Court management extended to the Church as well. Archibald Foyer blamed Court party influence for the rejection by the Commission of the General Assembly of proposals for a fast for the Darien colony in October 1699. Writing to urge support for a national fast in the upcoming 1700 General Assembly, Foyer accused some church leaders of reducing their zeal for the colony once they saw it 'frown'd upon by the Favourers of a Foreign Interest'. Like the Scottish bishops before them, he suggested, Court-influenced clergy were acting for English, not Scottish interests.[17] Ridpath also mentioned Court pressures on the General Assembly in *Scotland's grievances* and developed this line in his 1702 *Discourse*, stating that 'Arbitrary Methods of closeting, bribing, threatening and hectoring' had been used to control the General Assembly as well as parliament under the regal union.[18]

The success of Country discourse in establishing clear messages on the union of crowns, parliamentary liberties and Court party corruption can be

---

12 [George Ridpath], *An enquiry into the causes of the miscarriage of the Scots colony at Darien*, Glasgow 1700, 10–11.
13 [George Ridpath], *A discourse upon the union of Scotland and England*, [Edinburgh?] 1702, 162–3, App.
14 [Seton of Pitmedden], *A short speech*, 1700.
15 Anon., *The people of Scotland's groans*, 2.
16 [Ridpath], *Scotland's grievances*, 3, 5, 25.
17 [Foyer], *Scotland's present duty*, 5, 12, 18–19.
18 [Ridpath], *Scotland's grievances*, 39–40; [Ridpath], *Discourse*, 56.

seen in the repeated appearance of these points in subsequent publications. Andrew Fletcher of Saltoun's attack on the problems of the united crowns in his published speeches to the 1703 parliament joined a well-established discourse.[19] James Hodges's 1703 tract, *The rights and interests of the two British monarchies*, assumed that readers would be familiar with the Country view of the union of crowns. Less well-known authors echoed the Country view, as seen in a 1702 printed speech declaring the 1603 union a disaster for Scotland and a 1703 tract explaining the 'low Ebb' of the nation as 'chiefly due to the long, unequal, and irregular Conjunction of this Nation under one Head with England'.[20] The party's corruption message recurred in a poem urging the patriots of the Country party to 'English-Gold and Influence Oppose'.[21]

To rectify the union of crowns, the Country party advanced proposals for constitutional reform and the negotiation of new terms of union with England. To secure these, from 1703 the Country party demanded that the Scottish succession be kept open until new conditions of government were agreed with England. A communication of trade with England featured as a key reform, along with a transfer of powers from the crown in London to parliament in Scotland. Meanwhile, to counter Anne's attempt in 1702 to secure an incorporating union by treaty, writers advanced a federal union as the preferred outcome of treaty talks. Having established the importance of the Scottish parliament as the guardian of Scottish interests, Country Whig writers insisted on its continuation in a renegotiated union of crowns. To back up their arguments they raised the possibility of popular disorder in the event of incorporation.

In his Darien pamphlets, George Ridpath raised the idea of constitutional reform through a new union. As he expressed it in *Scotland's grievances*, union 'upon good and honourable Terms would be the greatest Happiness this Island could enjoy' by providing both countries with an opportunity to 'rectify what is amiss in their respective Constitutions'. The terms of union, however, had to maintain Scottish independence as a sovereign kingdom. Key problems requiring resolution in union talks included 'no Restrictions in matter of Trade more than the English', support for the Darien colony and security for the Scottish Presbyterian Church.[22] Ridpath also urged a new union in his

---

[19] [Andrew Fletcher], *Speeches, by a member of the parliament, which began at Edinburgh, the 6th of May 1703*, [Edinburgh] 1703.

[20] [John Spottiswoode], *A speech of one of the Barons of the shire of B——* [Berwick] *at a meeting of the barons and freeholders of that shire*, [Edinburgh] 1702, 3; [Andrew Brown], *Some very weighty and seasonable considerations tending to dispose, excite and qualify the nation, for the more effectual treating with England in relation to an union of confederacy*, [Edinburgh] 1703, 6. Brown seems to have been Dr Andrew Brown of Dolphington in Lanarkshire, author of several pamphlets on politics and economics. Brown was also a commissioner of supply and attended the Commission of the General Assembly as a ruling elder in October 1706. See McLeod and McLeod, *Anglo-Scottish tracts*, 161; NAS, CH 1/3/8/249.

[21] Anon., *A panegyrick on a noble peer and worthy patriot*, [Edinburgh 1703/4?], 2–3.

[22] [Ridpath], *Scotland's grievances*, 28, 30, 39–42.

1700 *Enquiry into the causes of the miscarriage of the Scots colony*, 'on such Terms as his Majesty and the Parliament of both Kingdoms shall agree, and so as the Civil and Religious Liberties of both People may be preserved'.[23]

For the 1700–1 parliamentary session, Ridpath proposed new laws to protect Scottish rights in the existing union, particularly a triennial act for frequent parliaments and an act of *habeas corpus*.[24] The 1700 'Heads' manuscript urged the same, as did William Seton of Pitmedden's *Memorial* and the Country party's third national address to William. Alongside these, *The people of Scotland's groans* prayed that the 'Noble Patriots' of parliament would 'deliver us from being Oppress'd at home and Despis'd abroad'.[25]

As Anne's ministers urged union negotiations in 1702, Ridpath's *Discourse* argued against incorporating union by reminding his readers of the proposals for union made by England in the sixteenth century when a marriage between Mary Queen of Scots and Edward VI of England was being negotiated. It was proposed then that the Scots would keep their own parliament and enjoy free trade with England. To dissuade the government from proposing complete union, Ridpath raised the spectre of popular resistance: given the precedent of the Covenanting rebellion of 1637–9, 'How do they think that the People in Scotland in General, would ever part with their Crown, Sceptre, Parliament and other Badges of their Soveraignty, and Independency, and submit to new Laws and new Modes of Religion?'[26]

Queen Anne's attempt to secure a closer union in 1702 failed when her English negotiators proved unwilling to concede reimbursement of the African Company's losses as part of the agreement. The collapse of union talks put pressure upon the Scottish parliament to name an heir to Anne, whose children had all died by 1700. In 1703 the Court party sought an act of parliament to confirm Sophia of Hanover, the named successor in England, as the heir to the Scottish crown. The opposition countered with overtures for an Act of Security in an attempt to force a renegotiation of the terms of the union of crowns before accepting the Hanoverian successor.

The opposition's Act of Security provided for the lack of an agreed successor in Scotland by empowering parliament to meet on the queen's death to name a successor 'of the Royal line of Scotland and of the true protestant Religion'. That person, however, could not be the same as the English successor unless parliament had enacted 'such conditions of Government… as may secure the honour and sovereignity of this Crown and Kingdom, the freedom frequency and power of Parliaments, the religion liberty and trade of the Nation from English or any foreigne influence'.[27] Through this act, approved by a Country

[23] [Ridpath], *An enquiry*, 60.
[24] [Ridpath], *Scotland's grievances*, 44.
[25] African Company, *A full and exact collection*, 135; Anon., *The people of Scotland's groans*, 2.
[26] [Ridpath], *Discourse*, 7–8, 98.
[27] APS xi. 136–7.

party majority in the 1703 and 1704 parliaments and given a reluctant royal assent in 1704, radical limitations proposed by Andrew Fletcher of Saltoun, or more moderate conditions of government raised in other overtures, would transfer named powers from the next Scottish monarch to the parliament.[28]

Numerous tracts supported the Country reform agenda advanced by the Act of Security in 1703 and 1704. *The Act of Security is the only rational method of procuring Scotland a happy constitution, free from the illegal invasions of its liberties and laws, and the base usurpation of its ancient sovereignty* (1704) was typical in arguing that the act would 'Secure our Independency from the undue Intermeddling of the English Court' by 'set[ting] us upon such an Equal Foot with the English, that they will be obliged to Grant us Concessions. ... Thus an happy and lasting Union might be Established without Civil Dissention'.[29]

In addition, as public discourse focused on the renegotiation of the union through an agreement on the succession, writers developed a vision of a federal union with England and attacked the crown's notion of an entire or incorporating union. These federalist schemes were presented as a feasible solution to the problem of the union of crowns, exemplified by other constitutions such as those of the United Provinces or the Swiss cantons. As portrayed by James Hodges and other authors, federal union seemed a less radical change than incorporation, requiring only a treaty on trade and foreign policy to accompany the acceptance of the Hanoverian succession.[30] Hodges's 1703 tract, *The rights and interests of the two British monarchies*, shaped Scottish perceptions of incorporation by presenting an entire union as the swallowing up of Scotland by England. Having 'a great name with not a few in Scotland', this pamphlet's influence was such that by early 1706 federal union was 'most favoured by the people of Scotland'.[31]

As Hodges explained at length in *The rights and interests*, in an entire union Scotland would be ruled by England. In contrast, federal union was 'that, whereby Distinct, Free, and Independent Kingdoms, Dominions or States,

---

[28] [Andrew Fletcher], *Overture for limitations on the successors of Her Majesty ... who shall be likewise kings of England*, [Edinburgh 1703]. These recalled the transfer of powers from crown to parliament seen in the Covenanting legislation of the early 1640s.

[29] Anon., *The Act of Security is the only rational method of procuring Scotland a happy constitution, free from the illegal invasions of its liberties and laws, and the base usurpation of its ancient sovereignty*, [Edinburgh] 1704, 3, 6.

[30] The issue of federal union raises a problem of terminology. Scottish alternatives to incorporating union are usually referred to as 'federal' in the historiography, following James Hodges's use of the term. Allan Macinnes has stressed the difference between federal and confederal constitutions and characterised the Covenanting vision of union in the 1640s as confederal. The literature of the 1707 union used both terms, and both meanings, often without making clear distinctions between them. See Allan I. Macinnes, 'Politically reactionary Brits? The promotion of Anglo-Scottish union, 1603–1707', in S. J. Connolly (ed.), *Great Britain and Ireland since 1500*, Dublin 1999, 47–8.

[31] *The manuscripts of his grace the duke of Portland*, London 1897, iv. 68; Sir John Clerk of Penicuik, quoted in Scott, *Andrew Fletcher*, 150.

do unite their seperate Interests into one common Interest, for the mutual benefit of both, so far as it relates to certain Conditions and Articles agreed upon betwixt them, retaining in the mean time their several Independencies, National Distinctions, and the different Laws, Customs and Government of each', including their parliaments and national Churches. In the British union envisioned by Hodges, Scotland and England would co-operate on foreign alliances, war and trade. Hodges saw the British federal union as resting on the union of crowns, with one monarch for two separate kingdoms: 'I do not mean such an Union, as consisting barely in Articles of Confederacy betwixt the two Kingdoms, otherways altogether disunited: but an Union of a closer nature, whereby both Kingdoms are to be united under one common Monarch of both.'[32]

Hodges outlined a series of objections to incorporating union that became standard points of contention through the 1706-7 debates: that Scottish representation in the British parliament would be inadequate to ensure the enforcement of articles of union; the movement of parliament to London would drain people and money from the kingdom; the nobles and gentry would lose their political rights, privileges and hereditary offices; and the resignation of Scotland's status as an ancient kingdom, defended against conquest for 2,000 years, would be an unacceptable blow to Scottish honour. Economically, the offer of free trade would benefit England rather than Scotland, as Scotland needed protective tariffs to develop its economy; and the tax burden would rise, with malt taxes pulling down rental values and excise taxes increasing three-fold. Like Ridpath, Hodges also pointed to the risks of popular dissatisfaction, asking 'How are the People like to be pleas'd with their Incorporating Union, when they must pay six pence for the Scots Pint of Ale, which they us'd to buy for Two pence?' He also raised the threat of disorder in suggesting that 'perhaps there are few Consequences of an Incorporating Union, about which more Difficulties should be found to satisfie [the people], than about giving up the Crown'.[33]

By Scots law, Hodges argued, it was 'Treason to endeavour the Overturning of the Constitution of the Parliament.' Since governors did not have the power to 'dispose of the fundamental Rights and Liberties of the People', any such act would be invalid.[34] These arguments followed points advanced by Ridpath since 1700 requiring freeholder approval for changes to the fundamental constitution of Scotland. In analysing the decline of the historical powers of the Scottish parliament, Ridpath's 1700 *Enquiry* denied that the 'pack'd Parliaments' of the past had commissions from their constituents to 'give away those Liberties'.[35] In his 1702 *Discourse*, Ridpath cited

---

[32] [James Hodges], *The rights and interests of the two British monarchies, inquir'd into, and clear'd: with a special respect to an united or separate state: treatise I*, London 1703, 3, 6.
[33] Ibid. 28-36, 44.
[34] Ibid. 39-40.
[35] [Ridpath], *An enquiry*, 13.

the legal opinion of Sir John Nisbet of Dirleton, Lord Advocate during the 1670 union discussions, to argue that parliament could not vote to change the kingdom's fundamental constitution without 'positive Instructions' from baron and burgess constituents.[36] Similarly, A discourse of present importance (1704) argued that 'when the Legislative is altered without the consent of the People, it is an Innovation, and encroachment upon their fundamental Constitution'.[37] In 1705 an anonymous Speech concerning a treaty of union with England insisted that 'Our Parliaments ... cannot give up the Liberties of the Nation, or alter the Constitution of the Government' unless its members were 'called Expressly for that Affair' and 'Instructed from their Constituents for that Effect'.[38] Like Ridpath, the author of this tract referenced the views of Sir John Nisbet on constituent instructions.

Together these oppositional tracts set expectations for the nature of an acceptable Anglo-Scottish union and established arguments against incorporation among a significant readership. The multiplying influence of Ridpath and Hodges in particular can be seen in direct references to their pamphlets in other texts, including John Bannatyne's A letter from a Presbyterian minister in the countrey, to a member of parliament and also the Commission of the Church concerning toleration and patronages (1703), Andrew Brown's Some very weighty and seasonable considerations tending to dispose, excite and qualify the nation, for the more effectual treating with England in relation to an union of confederacy (1703) and A letter from one of the Country party to his friend of the Court party ([1704]). The strong impact of Hodges's tract of 1703 was aided by its active promotion by Edinburgh booksellers, who advertised Rights and interests in the Edinburgh Gazette in August–September 1704 during the meeting of parliament, again in April 1705 during the Worcester crisis, and in November–December 1705 as the Gazette reported on moves towards the nomination of union commissioners in England.[39]

In developing a federalist platform, Country party writers were careful to suggest that England, rather than the Jacobites, presented a greater and more immediate peril to the Scottish constitution and Church. As one tract put it in 1704, 'to receive the English Successour before reasonable terms can be Agreed ... is as great an Error as we can be guilty of, Next to the Choosing of K. James the 8th'.[40] The proposal of an act for toleration of Episcopalian

---

36 [Ridpath], Discourse, 46, 88.
37 Anon., A discourse of present importance, [Edinburgh] 1704, 28.
38 Anon., A speech concerning a treaty of union with England, [Edinburgh 1705], 1–4.
39 Edinburgh Gazette, nos 563 (Thurs. 10 Aug.–Mon. 14 Aug. 1704), 567 (Thurs. 24 Aug.–Mon. 28 Aug. 1704), 574 (Tues. 19 Sept.–Thurs. 22 Sept 1704), 629 (Thurs. 29 Mar.–Tues. 3 Apr. 1705), 636 (Mon. 23 Apr.–Thurs. 26 Apr. 1705), 692 (Thurs. 15 Nov.–Tues. 20 Nov. 1705), 695 (Tues. 27 Nov.–Thurs. 29 Nov. 1705), 697 (Mon. 3 Dec.–Thurs. 6 Dec. 1705), 699–700 (Tues. 11 Dec.–Mon. 17 Dec. 1705), 703 (Tues. 25 Dec.–Thurs. 27 Dec. 1705).
40 [James Webster?], A letter from one of the Country party to his friend of the Court party, [Edinburgh 1704].

dissenters in 1703 contributed to a sense of imminent danger to the Church from English Episcopalian interests. Appearing in parallel with Ridpath and Hodges's tracts on union, numerous anti-toleration pamphlets followed Country Whig lines in portraying the Scottish Church as endangered by England and identifying parliament as the protector of Scottish religious liberties. Robert Wylie echoed Ridpath's historical analysis in arguing that 'a State design to conform us to England, upon the Prospect of the Junction of the two Crowns...was the first Occasion under K. James 6 of the first Attempts to Subvert our Reformation, Constitution and to bring back Prelacy'. In his view, prelacy was 'an Ingine for subjecting us to an English Court'.[41] James Hadow, Principal of the New College at St Andrews, warned of 'the grand design of the craved Toleration; That the Prelatick and Jacobite party aim at no less, than the overthrow of the present Establishment, and the Restauration of Prelacy in this Church in spite of the Claim of Right'.[42]

Given this, the duty of MPs as 'worthy Patriots', Wylie asserted, was to uphold the Claim of Right and protect the Church.[43] James Webster, minister of Edinburgh's Tolbooth church, pointed out that riots had already erupted on the possibility of toleration and called on parliament as the 'Guardians of our Laws, Liberty, Property and ... our Religion' to protect the Church.[44] *A three-fold cord for ensuring and securing of Presbytery in Scotland* (1703) also asserted the role of parliament as the guardian of Presbytery, alongside the Claim of Right and 'the people their fixed resolution to stand by it'.

While most Country messages emphasised a Presbyterian Whig perspective on the Scottish constitution, royalist views also appeared, giving Country discourse a wider appeal. A Tory version of the critique of the union of crowns managed to portray limitations as increasing the Scottish monarch's prerogative. A 1703 speech published by John Hamilton, Lord Belhaven, suggested that limitations on the power of the Scottish crown would advance the royal interest by allowing a stronger Scottish parliament to support crown objectives against the English parliament.[45] Similarly, the writer of *A speech in parliament touching the freedom and frequency of parliament* concluded that constitutional reform would give the monarch 'the real power to be exercised by him, according to the Direction and Advice of his Scots Parliament'.[46] This royalist thread in Country discourse can be linked to Episcopalian inter-

[41] [Robert Wylie], *A speech without doors concerning toleration*, [Edinburgh] 1703, 5. See also [James Ramsay], *A letter from a gentleman to a member of parliament concerning toleration*, Edinburgh 1703, 7.

[42] [James Hadow], *A survey of the case of the Episcopal clergy*, Edinburgh 1703, 4. See also [Bannatyne], *A letter from a Presbyterian minister*.

[43] [Wylie], *A speech without doors*, 8.

[44] [James Webster], *An essay upon toleration by a sincere lover of the Church and State*, [Edinburgh] 1703, 22, 24.

[45] See also [John Hamilton, Lord Belhaven], *A speech in parliament, by the Lord Belhaven; upon the Act for Security of the Kingdom*, Edinburgh 1703.

[46] Anon., *A speech in parliament touching the freedom and frequency of parliament*, [Edinburgh 1703], 1–2, 5.

ests, as seen in a 1703 pamphlet recommending parliamentary reforms, such as a triennial act, as well as toleration for dissent.[47]

Alongside constitutional and religious concerns, the Country party also continued to emphasise trading issues. Having highlighted widespread economic grievances during the Darien crisis, the Country party and its writers pressed for reform of Anglo-Scottish commercial relations in 1703–5. Proposals focused on a communication of trade to remove the restraints of the English navigation acts and provide Scottish access to English markets and capital. In addition, the Country party's programme of limitations sought to improve the economy by forcing the monarch to take account of Scottish commercial interests in the conduct of foreign policy. Both approaches had significant support among parliamentarians. This can be seen in the passage of the 1703 Act anent Peace and War, which blocked Anne's successor from involving Scotland in war without parliamentary approval. Many members also backed resolves offered by the duke of Hamilton in 1704 and 1705 which countered Court party proposals for the Hanoverian succession with demands for a prior treaty with England on commercial matters.[48]

While Hodges had some concerns with free trade, most Country writers insisted on the need for a treaty on trade.[49] Ridpath argued that the Scots deserved equal trading privileges in the union of crowns, their tie with England having caused them to lose lucrative commercial liberties with France, their former ally.[50] The 1704 tract *Scotland's interest: or, the great benefit and necessity of a communication of trade with England* emphasised the need to secure free trade alongside limitations on the monarch. Similarly, in the 1705 session of parliament, the duke of Hamilton's resolve for a commercial treaty was supported by a printed speech from Lord Belhaven urging a treaty and limitations.[51] Other tracts like *Some weighty considerations, why Scotland should stipulate terms of an union with England: by a letter from the country to his friend in parliament* also demanded a treaty to prevent English influence in Scottish affairs and secure free trade.

Other pamphlets advised parliament to pass laws to strengthen Scotland's bargaining position in a treaty with rich and powerful England.[52] In 1705 the Glasgow merchant John Spreull proposed steps to increase Scotland's exports

47 [Sir Archibald Sinclair], *Some thoughts on the present state of affairs*, [Edinburgh] 1703, 4, 10.
48 *APS* xi. 107, 127, 216.
49 [Ridpath], *Discourse*, 150.
50 [George Ridpath], *The reducing of Scotland by arms ... considered*, London 1705, 35; [Hodges], *Rights and interests*, 10, 52.
51 John Hamilton, Lord Belhaven, *The Lord Belhaven's speech in parliament, the 17th of July 1705*, [Edinburgh] 1705.
52 Anon., *An essay for promoting of trade, and increasing the coin of the nation, in a letter from a gentleman in the country to his friend at Edinburgh, a member of parliament*, Edinburgh 1705.

to show that 'tho England joyn with us in Union, or Communication of Trade, they will not be Married to a Beggar'.[53] The author of another 1705 tract urged the appointment of a parliamentary committee to consider immediate means of improvement in Scotland's fishing, mining and manufactures while also advocating union negotiations to prevent English influence in Scottish affairs and secure a communication of trade to the English plantations.[54]

Widespread interest in proposals for a commercial treaty can be seen in the experience of an Englishman riding through the countryside south of Edinburgh after the 1705 parliamentary session. Joseph Taylor found women as well as men asking 'what was done in the Parliament, and whether they were to have a free trade with England'.[55] Nevertheless, while trading issues increased interest in negotiations with the English in 1705, at the same time the *Worcester* affair and the English Alien Act raised fresh animosities towards the English and their proposals for an incorporating union. This act, passed by the English House of Commons on 5 February 1705, asked the queen to nominate commissioners to negotiate 'a nearer and more compleat' union with Scotland. The act outlined penalties to be imposed if the Scottish parliament did not nominate commissioners for union or accept the Hano-verian succession by 25 December 1705, including bans on the import of Scottish cattle, linen and coal and the revocation of the naturalisation of Scots in England.[56] The act threatened significant trading sectors in Scotland and Scottish inheritance of English property. News of the act created anger in Scotland, with a correspondent to the duke of Hamilton writing in March 1705 that 'As to the inclination of the people generally speaking, I find every bodye very ill satisfied with the treatment of the Parliament of England.'[57]

Scotland's first periodical paper providing political commentary rather than licensed news, the *Observator*, emerged at this point, targeting 'Vulgar Capacities' with political discussions designed to present 'such a Schem of the Union of the two Kingdoms, as can reasonably be expected Scotland should agree to … together with some other Improvements which may tend towards the Retriving the Honour, Power and Wealth of the Nation'. Speaking in a dialogue with a rural schoolmaster, the 'Country-Man' rejected incorporating union, characterising free trade in an entire union as 'Bait' with a 'Hook in the Heart of it'. Echoing James Hodges, the Country-Man declared that in an incorporating union 'We must become the Tail end of England; We must no more be a distinct Nation, but only a Remot Province of Britain, we must

---

53 J[ohn] S[preull], *An accompt current betwixt Scotland and England balanced*, [Edinburgh?] 1705, preface.
54 Anon., *Some weighty considerations, why Scotland should stipulate terms of an union with England: by a letter from the country to his friend in parliament*, [Edinburgh 1705].
55 Taylor, *A journey to Edenborough*, 145.
56 *The statutes at large*, ed. Owen Ruffhead, London 1769, iv. 78–9, 186–8.
57 *The manuscripts of the duke of Hamilton*, ed. W. Fraser, London 1887, 200.

have not distinct Laws, nor distinct Government in Church or State, but whatever the Parliament of the whole Isle shall Determine.'[58]

A flurry of *Worcester* broadsides reminded readers of the centuries of animosity between Scotland and England and of more recent troubles. One such ballad provided lyrics spoken by Captain Green 'As it were from his own mouth':

> They thought the SCOTS would never dar
> An English to Sentence
> But they're beguiled very far,
> Tho' they pretended Sence.
> They're SCOTS, not Sots, as they did say,
> Yea, Honest Men, and Bold ...
>
> And tho' it's true, WALLACE is dead,
> Yet take no Hope from that,
> For sure there are some in his stead,
> Who some way fill his Hat ...
>
> What e're we think to do 'gainst them
> I know they sure will stand.
> For I can say, and all my Men,
> GOD is at their Right Hand.
> Therefore my Country Men, I pray
> be war [beware] ye wrong the SCOTS.[59]

Similarly, belligerent pamphlets like *A pil for pork-eaters, or, a Scots lancet for an English swelling* (1705) declared incorporation 'morally impossible'. Written by William Forbes of Disblair, this tract urged the Scots to defend their honour and sovereignty:

> Let England Bully, but let Scotland fight.
> And let another Bannockburn redress,
> Too long endur'd Affronts and Grievances ...
> Let us be no more bubbl'd and abus'd
> Nor with their Shamms of Union more amused;
> 'Tis nothing but a treacherous Decoy,
> To bring Us to their Measures, then destroy
> The Rights and Just Pretences of our Crown.[60]

At the start of the 1705 parliamentary session, the queen's letter asked for the settlement of the Scottish succession and 'an Union of Scotland and England'.

---

58 [*Observator, or*] *A dialogue between a country-man and a landwart schoolmaster*, [no. 1], Edinburgh 1705, 2, 5, 8.
59 Anon., *A seasonable advice to all who encline to go in pirrating*, [Edinburgh 1705]. See also Anon., *Horrid murther*, and Anon., *Merits of piracie*.
60 [William Forbes], *A pil for pork eaters, or a Scots lancet for an English swelling*, [Edinburgh] 1705, 9, 11.

The duke of Hamilton responded with demands for a commercial treaty and limitations, leading the queen's new commissioner, John Campbell, duke of Argyll, to seek an act for a treaty of union instead of the succession. Andrew Fletcher of Saltoun tried to block this by proposing an address to the queen asserting parliament's inability to comply with the dishonourable duress of the Alien Act.[61] This tactic was supported by *A speech concerning a treaty of union with England* (1705), arguing in favour of Fletcher's address. Nevertheless, according to Lockhart of Carnwath, 'there was a great inclination in the house to set a treaty on foot'. This interest in a treaty on trade allowed the queen's ministers to draw votes from the Country majority. A clause presented by the duke of Hamilton requiring the treaty not to derogate from Scotland's fundamental laws and ancient liberties failed by a margin of two votes when the Court party argued that limitations on the negotiators would sink the talks. Similarly, the Court party defeated a clause offered by the duke of Atholl requiring the Alien Act to be rescinded before negotiations could commence, promising that this would be handled by a separate parliamentary order. On 1 September an act authorising negotiations for a treaty of union was passed, aided by the absence of a number of Cavaliers who left the house in frustration when the duke of Hamilton unexpectedly proposed that the nomination of commissioners be left to the queen.[62]

Ministers succeeded in generating a Court majority in 1705 and breaking the impasse on the succession by capitalising on wide interest in a commercial treaty with England. They also acknowledged Presbyterian opinion by barring the negotiators from discussing church matters. This victory, however, was not a mandate for incorporating union. Neither the queen's letter to parliament nor the act for a treaty specified an incorporating union, even though the Alien Act had required a closer union.[63] Continuing support for federalist ideas among a majority in parliament can be seen in a 1705 vote to reward James Hodges with a gift of £4,800 Scots.[64] Many in Scotland doubted the intentions of the English, with tracts like *A speech concerning a treaty of union with England* encouraging scepticism towards the union talks. This tract stressed Scotland's interest in a federal union and declared that 'it is plain, [the Alien Act] hath been purely designed, not to procure an Union, but to cudgel us into nominating their Successor'.[65]

Since the late 1690s Country discourse had demanded reform of the union of crowns, including a treaty for a communication of trade with England. While these messages contributed to the passage of an act for a treaty of union

[61] *APS* xi. 213–16, 224.

[62] *APS* xi. 236; '*Scotland's ruine*', 100–6. This move by the duke indicates his desire to maintain a degree of good will with the queen to enhance his employability. Hamilton's personal political capital as a leader of the opposition lay in the possibility that he would bring a large following to the Court party if employed.

[63] *APS* xi. 213–14, 295.

[64] *APS* xi. 221.

[65] Anon., *A speech concerning a treaty of union*, 1, 4.

in 1705, Country publications also shaped a broad, though not universal, opinion base against the idea of an incorporating union. Many tracts, especially those of Ridpath, Hodges and Wylie, emphasised the role of parliament as the guardian of Scottish interests and the Presbyterian Church. In January 1706 George Lockhart of Carnwath reported to a correspondent in London that Presbyterian Whigs in Scotland were 'not very fond of ane Union (I mean ane incorporating one) least ther beloved Kirk should be impaird of its native strength' but they were 'willing to enter into a federall Union (which long ago was called a Covenant)'.[66] In the view of the contemporary historian Gilbert Burnet, many in Scotland 'had got among them the notion of a federal union, like that of the United Provinces, or of the cantons of Switzerland'.[67] Country discourse, including cheap, accessible publications, had contributed to the establishment of arguments against incorporation that were to influence public responses to the treaty of 1706.

Court discourse

A 1702 tract observed that 'there is nothing more the Subject of Common discourse and general resentment; than Englands dealing unequally by Scotland, in most of affairs, since we joyned with them under one Sovereign'.[68] In these public debates on union, only a limited amount of print argued for incorporation before 1706 despite the wishes of William and Anne for a closer union. These few publications show that support for incorporation rested on pragmatic desires to reduce Anglo-Scottish conflict, secure the Protestant succession and grow the Scottish economy through English trade and investment. Relative indifference to questions of church government allowed incorporationists to prioritise the political and religious threat presented by the French Catholic king, Louis XIV, and the Catholic Stewarts over any threat presented by the English to the Scottish Church. By focusing on a common Protestantism, tracts in favour of closer union sought to create a sense of identity between England and Scotland against a joint Catholic foe.[69] Though this position cut across the dual loyalties of Presbyterian supporters of the Revolution, trends towards religious moderation in Scottish society since the Restoration made acceptance of incorporating union possible.

On her accession Queen Anne publicised her interest in a closer union through a printed letter to her 1702 parliament asking for the authorisation of union negotiations. Separately, in a reply to the January 1701 address of

66 NAS, GD 406/1/5321. On Lockhart's reference to a union by covenant see David Stevenson, 'The early Covenanters and the federal union of Britain', in Roger A. Mason (ed.), *Scotland and England, 1286–1815*, Edinburgh 1987.
67 Gilbert Burnet, *History of my own time*, ed. M. J. Routh, Oxford 1833, v. 261.
68 [Mackenzie], *Parainesis pacifica*, 21.
69 This became a key element in post-union British identity: Linda Colley, *Britons: forging the nation, 1707–1837*, New Haven 1992.

parliament to King William, the queen proposed 'an intire Union' between Scotland and England.[70] The rump parliament remaining after the duke of Hamilton's Country party walkout replied positively, stating that 'the Union of the two Kingdoms of Scotland and England hath been long desired by all good men' for peace.[71] All three of these letters were published in the *Edinburgh Gazette*, followed by a notice of an act empowering the queen to nominate commissioners for union.[72]

Alongside these official publications, Anne's secretary, George Mackenzie, published a speech and a pamphlet in support of incorporation in 1702. Advocating an act for union negotiations, his speech claimed to speak for 'many of us, who wish for a full Union' and warned that 'I do not hope that England will grant us any valuable Branch of Trade, when we are a separate nation to them.'[73] With *Parainesis pacifica* (1702), Mackenzie addressed both Scotland and England, urging incorporation for an 'increase of Strength, Honour, Riches, Peace, Security'. In statements directed to the English, he threatened them with separation if Scotland's grievances were not relieved through trading concessions. To the Scots, he acknowledged Scotland's position as 'a Cockboat at England's Stern,' but saw the problem as arising 'Because we are under their Head, but not of their Politick Body.' Mackenzie offered union as a pragmatic solution to Scotland's difficult situation: 'May be the event will bring us to a worse Fate than what we are now chained to' but 'the odds lyes on the other side.'[74]

Mackenzie's writings on incorporation reflect a pragmatic perspective seen also in William Seton of Pitmedden's pamphlets. Though Seton in 1700–1 wrote for the opposition, both he and Mackenzie appear to have been convinced of the merits of incorporation based on a shared indifference to modes of church government. Mackenzie's fervour for incorporation also reflected his allegiance to Queen Anne and her government, for which he was rewarded with the title of earl of Cromarty in 1703. In contrast, Seton's unionism seems to have rested on his own convictions formed during the Darien crisis. Seton's *The interest of Scotland, in three essays* (1700) saw incorporation as the long-term solution to the problems of the union of crowns. Elected as a commissioner for Aberdeenshire in 1702, Seton acted for the opposition in 1704 with a parliamentary resolve in favour of limitations and a federal union, but by 1705 he had moved to the Court party, asking Chancellor Seafield for a £100 pension to fix his allegiance.[75] He was nominated to

---

[70] *APS* xi. 12–14.
[71] *APS* xi. 19.
[72] *Edinburgh Gazette*, nos 338, (Thurs. 11 June–Mon. 15 June 1702), 339 (Mon. 15 June–Thurs. 18 June 1702), 341 (Mon. 22 June–Thurs. 25 June 1702), 343 (Mon. 29 June–Thurs. 2 July 1702).
[73] [Mackenzie], *Speech in the parliament*, 1, 8–9.
[74] [Mackenzie], *Parainesis pacifica*, iii. 8–10, 20.
[75] *Portland manuscripts*, iv. 100; Ferguson, *Scotland's relations*, 221.

act as a commissioner for union in 1706 and, like Mackenzie, published and spoke in favour of incorporation in the 1706–7 parliamentary session.

Both Seton and Mackenzie saw incorporating union as necessary to improve Scotland's prosperity by encouraging English investment, opening new markets and providing a stable environment for commerce. A manuscript tract of 1702 also advocated union to enable Scottish access to English trade: 'the Honey Lys in the Trade', it argued, for 'having once got in a foot we may possibly scrue into the bowels of their hive'.[76] In addition, access to English capital attracted Mackenzie and Seton, who saw Scotland's sea fisheries as an underdeveloped resource that would benefit from English investment.[77] Scotland's fishing had long been an object of plans for exploitation on a British scale, with Charles I and Charles II both attempting to establish British fishing companies to export salted Scottish herring in competition with the Dutch.[78]

These authors shared a neutrality on matters of church government that allowed them to prioritise British Protestantism above Scottish Presbyterianism. Seton's Britain would have one parliament, one crown, one privy council, one set of civil laws, and one Church with toleration for dissenters and a church government 'most consonant to their Civil Government'. Seton preferred 'Presbyterie, or Superintendencie' but did not insist on this, 'for the Laicks of this Island have drawn too much Blood already upon that Subject'. For the author of the 1702 manuscript tract, an incorporating union with religious toleration for 'all men who hold not Pernicious Principles' would be 'ane effectuall Course for Preventing of Tumults and Insurrections about Religion and Worship'.[79] Instead of church government, the threat of popery should be the priority: Seton urged the reformed clergy to 'lay aside all their Triffling Disputes' lest they 'lose their Ground' against a resurgent Catholicism.[80]

Like these authors, Mackenzie also felt that forms of church government were 'neither Essentiall nor unalterable' and that 'no indifferent thing should hinder so uncontroverted a good' as union.[81] At the Revolution in 1689, Mackenzie had proposed the establishment of a moderate, erastian Church in Scotland in which Episcopalian and Presbyterian ministers would be accommodated under parallel church governments with toleration for other dissenting Protestants. Such a structure, he hoped, would relieve the

76 NAS, GD 406/1/4976.
77 [Mackenzie], *Parainesis pacifica*, 5, 17; [William Seton of Pitmedden], *The interest of Scotland, in three essays*, Edinburgh 1700, 57–8, and *Some thoughts, on ways and means for making this nation a gainer in foreign commerce*, Edinburgh 1705, 26.
78 Bob Harris, 'Scotland's herring fisheries and the prosperity of the nation, c. 1600–1760', *SHR* lxxix (Apr. 2000), 36–60.
79 NAS, GD 406/1/4976.
80 [Seton of Pitmedden], *The interest of Scotland*, 41, 48, 85. See also [Seton of Pitmedden], *A short speech*, 15–16.
81 [Mackenzie], *Parainesis pacifica*, 7, 19.

'divisions and animosities of the nation' and prevent 'the matter of Church Government' being made 'a pretence for the troubles of Scotland' as it had 'for 100 yeare'.[82] A Presbyterian Church having been established instead, Mackenzie recognised in 1702 that Presbyterian opinion would pose a significant barrier to incorporation. *Parainesis pacifica* promised the Scots that the queen and 'the Wise and Good Men of England' would allow Scotland 'to continue in that Ecclesiastick Government, which will be most acceptable to the People'.[83]

Court party writers urged British Protestant unity against Franco-Jacobite peril as the government's legislative objective changed from incorporating union to the Hanoverian succession in 1703–4. The author of *A seasonable alarm for Scotland … concerning the present danger of the kingdom, and of the Protestant religion* (1703) urged 'a perfect understanding betwixt the two Nations' to secure Protestantism, while *A watch-word to Scotland in perillous times* (1704) warned that 'French Tyranny' would be worse than 'English indiscretion'.[84] At the opening of the 1704 parliament, the queen's published letter and her commissioner's speech urged the settlement of the succession, its open status being a 'Matter of Encouragement to Our Enemies beyond Sea'.[85] In *The great danger to Scotland as to all its sacred and civil concerns, from those who are commonly known by the name of Jacobites* (1704), a member of the 'honest revolution party' conceded that the Act of Security was necessary to repair the grievances of the union of crowns by demanding better terms in the joint succession, but warned against holding out for further concessions: 'in the mean time…the Jacobites find here a fair Opportunity to play their Game to advantage by making the Breach still wider'.[86]

The Court party's focus on a Catholic Jacobite threat to British Protestantism had the potential to appeal to religious moderates in Scotland. Since the Restoration 'a spirit of latitude' had been emerging in response to the religious conflicts that had fuelled Scottish Covenanting rebellion and the British civil wars.[87] Moderation suited many who had conformed to the Episcopalian Church during the long Restoration period. As Sir Alexander Bruce of Broomhill, burgh commissioner for Sanquhar, stated in 1702, he and other gentlemen tended to be 'pretty indifferent' on points of church government and resented what they perceived as the righteous extremism

---

[82] *Leven and Melville papers: letters and state papers chiefly addressed to George earl of Melville secretary of state for Scotland, 1689–91*, ed. William H. L. Melville, Edinburgh 1843, 125–7.

[83] [Mackenzie], *Parainesis pacifica*, 18.

[84] Anon., *A seasonable alarm*, 2; Anon., *A watch-word*, 1. In response, the Country point of view was reasserted in Anon., *An essay, shewing, that there is no probability of there being so much French interest, as it's certain there's English influence in our present parliament of Scotland*, [Edinburgh] 1704.

[85] *Her Majesties most gracious letter to the parliament of Scotland: together with His Grace the Lord Commissioner, and the Lord High Chancellor their speeches*, Edinburgh 1704, 1, 4.

[86] Anon., *The great danger of Scotland*, 2–4.

[87] Kidd, 'Religious realignment', 147.

of some Presbyterians. Scots Episcopalians, he suggested, 'preferr'd Order and Decency in the House of God to the Pride and Infallibility of a Pope in every Parish'.[88] Sermons on 30 January, the anniversary of the beheading of Charles I, provided an ideal opportunity for Episcopalians to claim that 'our Holie Religion is not chargeable with justifying anie degree of Rebellion'.[89] From 1703 publications in favour of toleration further supported religious moderation.[90]

More relaxed attitudes towards church government can also be seen among Presbyterians such as Francis Grant, an Edinburgh advocate. Although Grant published in 1703 against toleration for Episcopalian dissent, he echoed Seton in suggesting that while he preferred presbytery, episcopacy was 'warrantable' in some constitutional circumstances.[91] This stance allowed Grant to accept the establishment of episcopacy in England while supporting presbytery in Scotland.

Among Presbyterian clergy, the dependence of the Church on an erastian settlement had discouraged Presbyterian extremism since the Revolution. Leading ministers such as William Wisheart, minister at Leith and moderator of the Commission of the General Assembly in 1706–7, advocated the moderating of Presbyterian intransigence. In a printed sermon to his synod in 1702, Wisheart reminded his fellow clergy of the importance of discretion: 'Let us keep the Things entrusted to us prudently, that we betray not our Trust by our imprudent Management of it. ... It is necessary to time our Contentions and Appearances for the Truth, and to Regulate the Manner of them. ... Else our Zeal will produce very hurtful Effects.' Setting a tone echoed by other Court-affiliated ministers, Wisheart advocated a balance of 'Holy Zeal and Prudence'.[92] This message resonated with local ministers like Robert Wodrow of Eastwood. In 1702, as Robert Wylie agitated in synod for an assertion of the intrinsic right of the Church to call meetings of the General Assembly, Wodrow feared that 'the ill timed zeal of some may bring us into difficultyes'.[93]

Though erastian moderation had the potential to translate into support for incorporating union, most clergy still worried about the possible dangers of a closer union with prelatical England. After the 1702 union negotiations, for example, David Williamson expressed his willingness to eschew the Covenants and tolerate prelacy in England but still prayed that England 'neither

88 [Bruce of Broomhill], A speech in the parliament, 3–4.
89 [Andrew Cant], A sermon preached on the XXX day of January 1702/3, Edinburgh 1703, 21.
90 [George Garden], A letter to the episcopal clergy in Scotland, Edinburgh 1703; [Mackenzie], A few brief and modest reflexions. See also John Wilson, An essay on enthusiasm, Edinburgh 1706.
91 [Francis Grant], An essay for peace, Edinburgh 1703, 3.
92 William Wisheart, A sermon preached before the synod of Lothian and Tweeddale, Edinburgh 1703. See also David Williamson, A sermon preached in Edinburgh at the opening of the General Assembly, Edinburgh 1703, 30.
93 Wodrow letters, 201.

designed nor urged as Terms of Union, conformity of our Church Government to theirs, which I hope shall never be yielded to'.[94] Otherwise moderate clerical leaders fought to defeat toleration for Episcopalian dissent in 1703, publishing pamphlets and organising an address from the Commission of the General Assembly against this threatened invasion of the national Church.[95] To back an entire union, church leaders would have to be convinced that incorporation would remove both the Anglican threat to the Presbyterian Church in Scotland and the Franco-Jacobite threat to Protestantism in Britain.

From 1699 to 1705 there were few public advocates for incorporating union in Scotland besides the queen, her secretary George Mackenzie and William Seton of Pitmedden. Their limited output argued that incorporation would solve the problem of the union of crowns by creating a peaceful and prosperous Britain under a Protestant monarch. After the failure of Anne's 1702 union attempt, promotion of the Hanoverian succession in 1703–4 encouraged British unity against the threat of Catholic Jacobites. Within Scotland, increasing religious latitude and erastian pragmatism may have made some receptive to these arguments. In the short term, Country discourse on an English-Anglican threat spoke more loudly than Court party tracts on the Jacobite-Catholic peril and by 1705 the Court had not succeeded in building a significant opinion base for an incorporating union. This failure meant that while the queen's ministers secured an act for a treaty in 1705, they faced a major battle in 1706–7 to pass an incorporating union. Nevertheless, the opportunity remained open for the Court party to build support for their promised peaceful, prosperous, Protestant Britain.

News from London

The formation of Scottish opinion on incorporation was complicated by the availability in Scotland of news and tracts from London. These publications tended to reinforce Country arguments against incorporation by confirming fears of English designs to destroy Scotland's trade, religion and sovereignty. London news came from several sources: newspapers, such as the Tory *Post Boy* or Ridpath's Whig *Flying Post*, were posted to Edinburgh for sale in Scotland; Scottish newspapers printed London news and English parliamentary proceedings; Scottish booksellers imported English pamphlets and books; and the post, common carriers and travellers brought books, letters and manuscripts from the south. From 1699 to 1705 English tracts on Darien and the succession fuelled resentment in Scotland, while tracts on toleration and incorporation confirmed Country warnings on the dangers presented by the English to the Scottish Church and Scottish sovereignty.

94 Williamson, A sermon, 51.
95 *The humble representation of the late General Assembly.*

English pamphlets on Darien challenged the Country view on the colony's failure by placing the blame on the Scots. The colonists were portrayed as pirates who had illegally settled on Spanish territory. Moreover, as Darien pamphleteers exchanged blows under the pseudonyms of Philo-Britan and Philo-Caledon, Philo-Britan questioned the independence of the Scottish kingdom.[96] Parliament increased public awareness of the more obnoxious English pamphlets by condemning three to be burned by the Edinburgh hangman in November 1700.[97]

Following the Darien crisis, Mackenzie's publications in favour of the 1702 union talks were joined by several London pamphlets that seemed to confirm English plans to use the union to undermine the Scottish Church. One author proposed a complete union, with one British Church and 'a perpetual toleration to all, whose Principles and Practices were consistent with the civil security'.[98] Similarly, a 1702 reprint of Sir Francis Bacon's *Brief discourse of the happy union betwixt the two kingdoms of Scotland and England*, originally written for James VI and I at the union of crowns, urged unity in forms of church government.[99] More ominously, *A discourse upon the uniting Scotland with England* (1702), written as if from a Scots point of view but by an English writer, declared Presbytery 'wholly inconsistent with the monarchy we all pretend to uphold ... wholly adapted to ... tumultuary Government ... [and] not at all agreeable to our ancient, or our present Constitution'. Was not union, he asked, 'of greater Importance than the humouring the Hot-headed, Improvident Kirk?' The author even proposed barring Presbyterians from membership of the new British parliament.[100] A similar proposal was made in *A letter to Sir J.P. Bart.*, first published in 1702 and addressed to the Tory MP Sir John Pakington. This tract had an ongoing impact on union perceptions in Scotland through its reprints in 1705 and 1706.[101] The Country party amplified these messages in a 1703 pamphlet by Robert Wylie warning that 'it is plainly and above-board insisted upon, and argued by the English in Print,

96   Philo-Caledon, *A defence of the Scots settlement at Darien*, [Edinburgh] 1699; Philo-Britan [Walter Harris], *The defence of the Scots settlement at Darien, answered*, London 1699.
97   APS x, appendix at p. 51.
98   Anon., *A memorial briefly pointing at some advantages of the union of the two kingdoms*, London 1702, 7. See also [John Humfrey], *A draught for a national church accommodation: whereby the subjects of England and Scotland, however different in their judgements concerning episcopacy and presbytery, may yet be united ... in one church and kingdom of Great Britain*, London 1705.
99   Sir Francis Bacon, *A brief discourse of the happy union betwixt the two kingdoms of Scotland and England*, [Edinburgh?] 1702.
100   [Blackerby Fairfax], *A discourse upon the uniting Scotland with England*, London 1702, 30, 32, 37.
101   Anon., *A letter to Sir J. P. Bart.* [Sir John Pakington] *a member for the ensuing parliament, relating to the union of England and Scotland*, London? 1706? On the reprints see McLeod and McLeod, *Anglo-Scottish tracts*, no. 233A.

that there can never be an Union, unless Scotland be intirely brought over into a full Conformity with the Church of England'.[102]

With the Scottish succession remaining open in 1703–4, English authors sought to prove that the Scots possessed no sovereignty independent of England and therefore had to follow the English parliament in accepting the Hanoverian heir. These included James Drake's 1703 *Historia anglo-scotica* and William Atwood's *The superiority and direct dominion of the imperial crown of England, over the crown and kingdom of Scotland* (1704). Atwood republished his arguments in a 1705 edition in order to assert 'the true foundation of a compleat union'.[103]

These tracts sparked a well-publicised print debate with Scottish authors. Robert Sibbald's 1702 *The liberty and independency of the kingdom and Church of Scotland, asserted*, was reprinted with additions in 1703 and 1704 and strongly promoted by Edinburgh booksellers.[104] In 1705 James Anderson produced a counter-history to Atwood with *An historical essay, shewing that the crown and kingdom of Scotland, is imperial and independent*. Like Sibbald's work, Anderson's book was advertised to potential readers in the *Edinburgh Gazette*.[105] Parliamentary orders in 1703 and 1705 for the burning of Drake and Atwood's books reveal the negative impact made by these books in Scotland; in addition, parliament voted to reward James Anderson with £4,800 Scots and the thanks of the House for his reply to Atwood.[106]

Other English reactions to the Scottish Act of Security supported the picture of a bullying nation trying to force acceptance of the Hanoverian succession on Scotland. Tracts like *A manifesto, asserting and clearing the legal right of the Princess Sophia, and her issue, the serene House of Hanover, to the succession of Scotland* (1704) insisted that the Scots had no alternative but to accept Sophia, having, like England, no other Protestant heir. *Hereditary succession in the Protestant line, unalterable: in answer to the Scots Bill of Security* (1704), condemned the Act of Security as a Jacobite ploy to break up the British union. The author did not intend to smooth relations with Scotland when he blamed the failure of Darien on Scottish 'saints turned Freebooters', though he did concede that Scotland had trading grievances

---

[102] [Robert Wylie], *A letter from a gentleman in the city, to a minister in the countrey*, [Edinburgh 1703], 21.

[103] William Atwood, *The superiority and direct dominion of the imperial crown of England over the crown and kingdom of Scotland, the true foundation of a compleat union, reasserted*, London 1705, in McLeod and McLeod, *Anglo-Scottish tracts*, no. 451.

[104] [Robert Sibbald], *The liberty and independency of the kingdom and Church of Scotland asserted to which is added, a speech at the proclamation of K. James VI concerning the succession to the crown of England*, Edinburgh 1703; [Robert Sibbald], *The liberty and independency of the kingdom and Church of Scotland...wherein all the objections of Mr. Atwood, and others against the same, are fully answered*, Edinburgh 1704, in McLeod and McLeod, *Anglo-Scottish tracts*, no. 236; *Edinburgh Gazette*, nos 384–6 (Thurs. 19 Nov.–Mon. 30 Nov. 1702), 398–400 (Mon. 11 Jan.–Thurs. 21 Jan. 1703), 559 (Thurs. 27 July–Mon. 31 July 1704).

[105] *Edinburgh Gazette*, no. 665 (Thurs. 9 Aug.–Mon. 13 Aug. 1705).

[106] APS xi. 66, 221.

that could be resolved in a closer union. The tract concluded by calling on the English parliament to force the Scots to accept the Hanoverian succession.[107] A manuscript of 1703, 'A short conference ... anent the union of the two kingdoms', proposed that the succession could be secured in Scotland with the application of £20–£30,000 sterling in bribes, supplied by the house of Hanover and distributed to MPs by the earl of Seafield.[108]

News of the English Alien Act raised fresh concerns in Scotland. Just as the *Worcester* crisis was unfolding in Edinburgh, reports of the English parliament's reaction to the Act of Security began to reach Scotland. In December 1704 readers of the *Edinburgh Gazette* learned that the queen had attended the House of Lords to hear their discussion of a 'Bill for promoting an intire Union with Scotland' and that the Lords had addressed the queen to request the fortification of border towns and the readying of the northern militia in response to the Act of Security.[109] Soon after, the Scottish papers reported the English parliament's intention to make the Scots aliens if the Hanoverian succession was not settled, followed by prints of the full Alien Act stating as its goal that 'a perfect and Entire Union may be Treated and Agreed upon'.[110] By March 1705 Robert Wylie could write to a correspondent that 'their hectoring us, committing acts of hostility against us and running us down in their pamphlets hath so far opened the eyes of some who were for union & Hanoverian succession that now they begin to declare themselves against Both'.[111] By the end of 1705 Scots with access to the *Edinburgh Gazette* knew that the House of Lords intended a 'nearer and more Compleat Union between the two Kingdoms' as the outcome of the forthcoming treaty negotiations.[112]

Not all print from London supported an incorporationist position. *An essay upon the union of the kingdoms of England and Scotland* (1705) and *A scheme of union between England and Scotland, with advantages to both kingdoms* (1705) both proposed a union of trade only, while *Great Britain's union, and the security of the Hanover succession, consider'd* (1705) advocated the conceding of free trade to Scotland in order to secure the Hanoverian succession in union. These tracts reinforced expectations that England would make significant concessions to Scotland in return for confirmation of the Hanoverian succession in the northern kingdom. Most London prints, however, suggested the

---

107 Anon., *Hereditary succession in the Protestant line, unalterable: in answer to the Scots Bill of Security*, London 1704, 5, 20, 25.
108 A. M., 'A short conference ... anent the union of the two kingdoms', London 1703, 7: Glasgow University Special Collections.
109 *Edinburgh Gazette*, nos 601 (Thurs. 21 Dec.–Mon. 25 Dec. 1704) and 602 (Mon. 25 Dec.–Thurs. 28 Dec. 1704).
110 Ibid. nos 608 (Mon. 15 Jan.–Thurs. 18 Jan. 1705) and 612 (Mon. 29 Jan.–Thurs. 1 Feb. 1705).
111 NAS, GD 406/1/5297.
112 *Edinburgh Gazette*, nos 688 (Thurs. 1 Nov.–Tues. 6 Nov. 1705) and 692 Postscript (20 Nov. 1705).

reality of English, or at least Tory and Anglican, plans to subdue Scotland and the Presbyterian Church in an incorporating union.

From the Darien crisis onwards, oppositional voices in Scotland condemned the terms of the 1603 Anglo-Scottish union of crowns, advocating constitutional reforms to relieve Scottish grievances. Through limitations on the agreed successor and a treaty with England, power was to shift from the Scottish crown to parliament and free trade was to be conceded by England in a federal union with security for the Presbyterian Church. Rather than being 'a complete delusion created by propaganda', the vision of federal union, or a renegotiated union of crowns, was a real aspiration developed in print discourse to support the Country party's parliamentary reform objectives.[113] A few Court authors advanced incorporationist views before 1706, promising peaceful economic development under a Protestant monarch, but as Francis Grant admitted in 1707, 'these Prints which we had a while ago, were more industriously composed and spread, against an incorporating Union, than for it'.[114] These included tracts from London reinforcing Country warnings on the dangers of incorporation. The act for a treaty secured by the government in 1705 did not commit Scotland to an incorporating union, indicating the strength of opinion in parliament for a treaty but not for an entire union. Opinion, however, was not static. The next chapter will show how views on union responded to changing events and new propaganda initiatives as the government brought a treaty of incorporating union to the Scottish parliament in 1706.

113 Riley, *Union of England and Scotland*, 35.
114 [Francis Grant], *The patriot resolved in a letter to an addresser, from his friend*, [Edinburgh] 1707, 5.

5

Public Discourse on the Union Treaty

Histories of the union of 1707 have tended either to downplay popular anti-unionism as the product of manipulation by oppositional elites or to celebrate it as the spontaneous manifestation of a deep-seated patriotism. The development of a more inclusive public sphere in Scotland, outlined in part I, and the proliferation of public discourse against an incorporating union, described in chapter 4, suggest a more nuanced picture. Public opinion on the union was not simply manipulated or instinctive but shaped and informed by discourse and events. During the parliamentary debates of 1706–7 a lack of effective censorship meant that the volume of print appearing in Scotland exceeded anything seen before in the kingdom.[1] Though in July 1706 Robert Wylie complained of a 'stupid unconcernedness' about the treaty among many, by the autumn there was 'no talk more common than of a Union'.[2] The reading of the treaty in parliament during most of October provided a crucial window of time for the dissemination of communications, so that by November it was claimed that 'none of any Intelligence or Conversation are ignorant of the great and weighty Affair of the Union now before the Parliament'.[3]

Numerous pamphlets from a widening pool of authors represented Court and Country views on the treaty to audiences. Writers associated with Country party leaders asserted the sovereignty of parliamentary constituents, suggesting that the consent of the people would be needed to ratify the treaty. Country tracts also sought to undermine earlier Country interest in free trade and reinforce Presbyterian concerns over incorporating union. Within this, Covenanting and radical Whig views re-emerged into the political mainstream accompanied by a growing threat of crowd violence and possible rebellion. Meanwhile, pro-incorporation discourse expanded rapidly as professional writers like Daniel Defoe joined Scottish Court party writers to advocate the benefits of union and highlight the dangers of oppositional radicalism. As events progressed, the previously strong opinion base formed by the Country party against incorporation loosened and new voices began to advocate acceptance of an amended treaty.

1   Parliament ordered the burning of a few extreme tracts, including a Covenanting pamphlet and an English tract that denied the sovereignty of the Scottish crown, but there was no real attempt by the privy council to control the production of pamphlets: *APS* xi. 355, 357.
2   NAS, GD 406/1/9747; [Andrew Brown], *A scheme proposing a true touch-stone for the due trial of a proper union betwixt Scotland & England*, Edinburgh 1706, preface.
3   [Daniel Defoe], *A seasonable warning or the pope and king of France unmasked*, [Edinburgh] 1706, 3.

Anti-incorporation discourse

Between the negotiation of the union treaty in early 1706 and the opening of the Scottish parliament in October 1706, leading Country party writers published against incorporating union. A few pamphlets proposed new federalist compromises with British, English and Scottish parliaments, but most tracts amplified prior arguments that incorporation would threaten Scotland's interests and that some degree of popular approval would be needed for any treaty of union. The beginnings of a radicalisation in Country opposition can be seen in mentions of the National Covenant, greater emphasis on the security of the Presbyterian Church and the escalation of the idea of constituent consent to demands for a wider plebiscite. As parliament began to debate the treaty, oppositional discourse radicalised further with the publication of Covenanting and extremist Whig pamphlets and petitions.

Reacting to the treaty negotiations, *Essay upon the union* (1706) was printed in London in April and in Edinburgh in May.[4] This proposed a union in which the English and Scots would become one people under one king with one British parliament and free trade, but would retain Scottish and English parliaments with the power to veto harmful acts passed by the British parliament. A committee of English and Scots would meet before each gathering of the British assembly to review overtures on shared matters. On 30 May Robert Wodrow in Scotland reported to George Ridpath in London that this view 'relishes very much here'.[5]

George Ridpath echoed these arguments in his *Considerations upon the union of the two kingdoms* (1706), printed in September. Expressing his hope for 'such Measures as may Secure our Liberties... and Cement a Lasting Union with our Neighbours', Ridpath argued that the 'Gordian knot' of 'federal, incorporating, compleat, and intire Unions' should be cut with 'a General Act of Naturalisation' to create one people.[6] Like the *Essay upon the union*, Ridpath proposed a common British parliament to consider shared issues of peace, war, trade and property, with a Scottish parliament to handle local matters and judicial appeals. He recommended that separate Churches be maintained, as any attempt to force the Scots to a religious conformity with

---

[4] This tract has been attributed to James Hodges, but this can be questioned. Though Wodrow says that this pamphlet was 'said to be by Mr. Hodges', the tract differs from Hodges's 1703 and 1706 *Rights and interests* treatises in its support for free trade. Moreover, George Ridpath, who knew James Hodges in London, described this tract as written by a 'cavalier': *Wodrow letters*, 291; 'Correspondence between George Ridpath and the Reverend Robert Wodrow', ed. James Maidment, *Miscellany of the Abbotsford Club*, Edinburgh 1837, i. 390.

[5] *Wodrow letters*, 291.

[6] [George Ridpath], *Considerations upon the union of the two kingdoms*, [Edinburgh] 1706, pp. vii, 12.

England would result in 'constant Uneasiness' due to the 'resolute Adherence of so great a part of the Nation' to Presbytery.[7]

Ridpath also reinforced prior Country arguments for constituent approval of incorporation. Declaring that 'proprietors of the Country, had from the beginning, a Sovereign Right of Legislature and Judicature invested in them for the Security and Government of that Property', Ridpath stated that such freeholders reserved the right to attend parliament in person and demand satisfaction from their representatives.[8] His argument had clear implications for potential freeholder action against parliament, though he did not advocate direct resistance.

Robert Wylie also emphasised popular consent in a July pamphlet, *Letter concerning the union*. This tract reflected recommendations on party strategy made by him to the duke of Hamilton based on consultation with Country party opinion in Scotland: 'that which seems to take as most plausible with all is That no Treaty be ratified in parliament till by printing it the nation be acquainted with it and be able to send their commissioners to a subsequent session (or rather to a new parliament) with the fresh and deliberat sentiments of the nation about it'. Crucially for an ideologically divided country, and Country party, this plan to demand a parliamentary recess or new elections would be 'what both Jacobites & Revolutionists ought to agree in'.[9]

In keeping with this strategy, Wylie's pamphlet argued that Scotland's sovereignty could 'never be alienated by Delegates' without 'Consulting the whole Nation'. Incorporation would be unacceptable to the nation because there would be no security for Scottish interests or its Church without the Scottish parliament. Given that it was unheard of to have 'two legally Authorised and Established Religions or Form of Church Government' in one state, Presbytery was likely to be 'reduced to a Toleration' by a British parliament.[10] In addition, Wylie argued that 'this Nation is sworn to maintain' laws protecting parliament 'by their National Covenant (the Covenant of their Protestancy and Reformation)'.[11] Contemporaries were quick to note even this brief mention of the Covenant: in writing to his brother the earl of Mar, James Erskine characterised Wylie's pamphlet as having two main arguments against the union, one of which was the betrayal of the Covenants.[12]

---

7 Ibid. 33.
8 Ibid. 58.
9 NAS, GD 406/1/9747.
10 Anon., *State of the controversy betwixt united and separate parliaments* ([Edinburgh] 1706) made similar arguments on the threat posed by the British parliament to the Scottish Church, as well as to Scottish trade. The attribution of this tract to Andrew Fletcher has been challenged by John Robertson in 'Andrew Fletcher's vision of union', in Mason, *Scotland and England*, 203.
11 [Robert Wylie], *A letter concerning the union, with Sir George Mackenzie's observations and Sir John Nisbet's opinion upon the same subject*, [Edinburgh] 1706, 4, 6, 7.
12 *Report on the manuscripts of the earl of Mar and Kellie*, ed. Henry Paton, London 1904, 273.

In a new tract completed by September, James Hodges also raised popular consent and the National Covenant within a wide range of arguments against the treaty. With his *The rights and interests of the two British monarchies* (1706), Hodges hoped to define the Country party's position against the treaty. In September he sent his pamphlet to Robert Wylie, the duke of Hamilton and the duke of Atholl with the recommendation that Wylie discuss 'prudent measures' against the treaty with the dukes. Hodges also hoped to travel to Edinburgh to attend the parliamentary debates, but his request through Wylie for travel expenses seems to have been unsuccessful.[13]

With a more strident tone than his 1703 *Rights and interests*, Hodges's new treatise provided more than a hundred pages of argument on how Scottish interests would be betrayed by incorporation, from the clashing of English and Scottish trade priorities to the burden of English taxes and the undermining of the Presbyterian Church. Deriding constituent consultation as a 'gross Mistake', Hodges declared that the only constitutional means to create incorporation would be the unanimous consent of 'the Whole Freeborn Subjects of Scotland, Conven'd in ONE Great Assembly'.[14]

Hodges's new tract had a significant impact on opinion: being 'right calculated to catch the ministers and commonalty', the earl of Mar reported to London, early in November, that 'really it has done harm'.[15] One aspect of its appeal lay in its strong Presbyterian line, developed to a much greater extent than in Hodges's earlier work. Hodges warned that incorporation would sully the purity of the Scottish Church by association with English 'Arminianism, Socinianism, Popish Ceremonies, and a Cold, Lazie, and Lifeless Form of Worship'. Incorporation would lead to public discontent, for 'a great multitude of the Scots Nation, account themselves Engag'd to the support of the Presbyterian Ecclesiastick Government... by the Obligation of a most solemn National Oath to God, and Compact or Covenant with Him'. Hodges insisted that 'an incorporating Union with England is Absolutely Inconsistent with Adhering to the Obligation of that National Oath'.[16] He closed with a call for a national fast, asking Robert Wylie to print his comments on the fast separately so that they could be sent to every parish.[17] The extract was reprinted as *That part of a late book which relates to a general fast and humiliation*.

After the publication of the articles of union in October, other pamphlet writers attacked the provisions of the treaty as parliament began to debate the articles. The printing of petitions against the treaty supported the Country party's emphasis on popular consent and reinforced economic and religious arguments against the treaty. In addition, party leaders like Lord Belhaven used patriotic rhetoric already associated with the Country party to make

13 Wodrow quarto xxx, fo. 269.
14 [Hodges], *Rights and interests*, 71.
15 *Manuscripts of the earl of Mar*, 310.
16 [Hodges], *Rights and interest*, 49, 56, 58.
17 Wodrow quarto xxx, fo. 269.

emotional pleas for the preservation of the Scottish kingdom. At the same time, printed Covenanting and Whig petitions and pamphlets offered increasingly radical opposition to incorporation.

William Black, an advocate and Aberdeen-based cloth manufacturer, began to publish condemnations of the economic provisions of the treaty. After his first essay, *Some considerations in relation to trade* (1706), Black engaged in an ongoing print debate with Daniel Defoe which provided significant publicity for his critique.[18] Like other oppositional writers, Black indicated an interest in union with England but expected it to be on terms that would advance 'the Honour as well as the Interest of this Nation'.[19] Black demanded changes to the treaty in the form of drawbacks, duty reductions and regulatory exemptions for Scotland and dismissed the Equivalent as nothing more than a loan to be repaid by the Scots with interest.[20] Similar complaints on taxes appeared in printed addresses such as *Remarks for the salt-masters, fishers of salmond, herrings and white-fish, and others who make use of Scots salt, humbly offered upon the eighth article of the Treaty of Union* (1706) and a fictional address in vernacular Scots from 'te Fishers on te Highland Coasts, an all ather Inhapiting te Highlands'.[21]

These economic attacks were reinforced in anti-treaty criticisms from the Convention of Royal Burghs. After narrowly voting to oppose the treaty, the Convention's printed address of 6 November provided a strong attack on free trade from the institution representing the merchants and tradesmen of Scotland's burghs. These oppositional burgesses saw the proposed trade with England and its colonies as 'uncertain, involved, and wholly precarious'. Focusing on existing rather than potential trade, they observed that 'the most considerable branches of our trade are different from those of England', making it vulnerable to an English majority in the British parliament. In addition, English customs and excise rates would be 'a certain unsupportable burden'. Like Hodges and others, the burgesses argued that in the British parliament, 'our religione, Church government, claim of right, lawes, liberties, trade, and all that is dear to us' would be 'dayly in danger of being encroached upon'.[22]

---

18 For the Black–Defoe exchange see McLeod and McLeod, *Anglo-Scottish tracts*, 412.

19 [William Black], *Some considerations in relation to trade*, [Edinburgh] 1706, 3.

20 As part of the communication of trade agreed in the treaty, English customs duties were to be extended to Scotland. The Equivalent was a lump sum payment of £398,085 10s. sterling designed to compensate Scotland for the payment after 1707 of customs duties created by England to repay English national debt incurred before the union. Further payments were to be made over time. Rather than reimbursing those paying the new customs duties, the Equivalent was to be used for other purposes designated in the treaty, primarily the buyout of African Company shareholders and the payment of public debts in Scotland.

21 *Ta hir grace her majesties high commissioner, an te honourable estates of parliament; te address far te fishers on te Highland coasts, an all uthers inhapiting te Highlands*, [Edinburgh 1706].

22 NAS, PA 7/20/18, printed as *To his grace, her majesty's high commissioner, and the right honourable, the estates of parliament, the address of the commissioners to the General Convention of the Royal Burrows*, [Edinburgh 1706].

Like the Convention, the African Company voted narrowly to oppose the treaty and on 26 December printed an address to parliament which protested against the proposed dissolution of the company and the terms upon which the Equivalent would be used to buy out shareholders. The company's petition criticised the interest rate and the total sum proposed as well as a lack of security for the promised pay-out.[23]

These tracts and petitions on trade issues sought to weaken opinion in favour of a communication of trade by highlighting the risks of free trade combined with incorporation. Since the Darien crisis, much Country discourse had pressed for a treaty with England for a communication of trade, contributing to the passage of an act for a treaty in 1705. In May of 1706 Robert Wodrow observed that 'not a feu that are taken for men of sense and piety are like to goe in to ane incorporating union, and ... it may very easily take in Parliament' thanks to interest in 'a liberty of trade'.[24] After a proliferation of criticism on the treaty's economic provisions, however, the opinion of some shifted. In late October the duke of Hamilton felt that 'the treading people who war amussed with the talk of itt since they have seen it & considered it ar totally avers to itt'.[25]

While undermining the treaty's promise of free trade, Country publications also sought to awaken a spirit of Scottish patriotism. In his new *Rights and interests* tract, Hodges reminded his readers that the Scottish kingdom had been independent for 'above a Third Part of the World's Age since the Creation'.[26] Patriotism had always been an important part of Country rhetoric since Darien; now writers began to draw more heavily on patriotic imagery as they called on parliament to protect their country from incorporation. This approach tapped the feelings of those who, like Robert Wodrow, had 'a great many melancholy thoughts of living to see this antient kingdome made a province'.[27]

Lord Belhaven's speech of 2 November, delivered during impassioned debates on the first article of union for one united kingdom, has become the most famous manifestation of this strategy. Accusing the union negotiators of betraying the nation's desire for a federal union, Belhaven called on parliament to reject the treaty and maintain Scotland's 2,000 years of independence. Continuing the Country party practice of associating Court followers with corruption, he castigated those members who sat in silence from 'a Fear of Frowns of Great Men and Parties'.[28] Similarly, *Scotland's speech to her sons*

---

[23] *The humble representation of the council-general of the Company of Scotland trading to Africa and the Indies*, [Edinburgh] 1706. This address was signed by the earl of Cromarty on behalf of the company with the *caveat* that it was 'contrary to my own Vote and Opinion'.
[24] *Wodrow letters*, 291.
[25] NAS, GD 406/1/5294.
[26] [Hodges], *Rights and interests*, 75.
[27] *Wodrow letters*, 291.
[28] John Hamilton, Lord Belhaven, *The Lord Belhaven's speech in parliament the second day of November 1706*, [Edinburgh 1706], 7.

(1706), attributed to James Clark of Glasgow's Tron church, condemned the negative effect of 'Pensions, Places and Preferments' and called on members of parliament to 'lay by your little private selfish Designs, generously sink them all in the Grand Project of my Honour, and your Posterity's Happiness'.[29]

While Clark spoke in his tract as the voice of Scotland, vernacular Scots was used to represent the voice of the people in *A copy of a letter from a country farmer to his laird, a member of parliament* (1706). The country farmer bemoaned the lack of patriotism in parliament and begged his laird to join 'True-hearted Scotsmen' in rejecting the treaty.[30] Patriotic appeals also appeared in sermons and printed ephemera. In October a cleric spoke in the high kirk of Edinburgh on the text 'Hold fast to that which thou hast; let no man take thy Crown', while prints of a king list and the Declaration of Arbroath emphasised the historic independence of the ancient Scottish crown and kingdom.[31]

Alongside these economic complaints and patriotic appeals, tracts urged support for the Presbyterian Church as petitions from the Commission of the General Assembly raised concerns about the security of the Church in union. In an address on 17 October the commission asked parliament to guarantee the establishment of the Presbyterian Church in union. A more aggressive second address of 8 November listed a series of objections to closer union. These were seconded by pamphlets by several clergy who had published before on Darien or toleration, plus the printed petitions of three presbyteries.

As one of the most political of the established clergy, Robert Wylie remained focused on the constitutional dangers of incorporation. His *The insecurity of a printed overture for an act for the Church's security* (1706) demanded 'Let any Thinking Person say what possible Security can be contriv'd or made secure, for the very Being or Subsisting of this Church, in the Event of a Treaty taking place, whereby a surrender is made of the Parliament, and Civil Constitution of this Kingdom ... there being no co-ordinat Authority provided or retain'd, as Guarantee of the Separate Interests of the Church of Scotland.' In his view, the likely outcome of incorporation was toleration for episcopacy in Scotland, 'to the Destruction and Ruine of the present Legal Establishment'.[32]

Wylie called for a meeting of the General Assembly to discuss the treaty, a demand repeated in a printed address organised by Wylie from Hamilton

---

29 [James Clark], *Scotland's speech to her sons*, [Edinburgh 1706].

30 Anon., *A copy of a letter from a country farmer to his laird, a member of parliament*, [Edinburgh 1706], 2–4.

31 *The letters of Daniel Defoe*, ed. George Harris Healey, Oxford 1955, 137; Anon., *A true and exact list of the whole kings of Scotland since Fergus the First*, Edinburgh 1707; *Letter in 1320 to Pope John declaring for Robert the Bruce*, [Edinburgh] 1706. Edward J. Cowan, 'For freedom alone': the Declaration of Arbroath, 1320, East Linton 2003, 101–3.

32 [Robert Wylie], *The insecurity of a printed overture for an act for the Church's security*, [Edinburgh] 1706, 4.

presbytery in November. The Hamilton address insisted that there was a 'full unanimity therein amongst the Ministers of this National Church' on the concerns raised by the addressers of the Commission of the General Assembly. The presbytery clergy did not mention the Covenants directly but stated that their parishioners were convinced that the union would incur 'the Guilt of National perjury'. As an alternative to incorporation, they proposed an address to the queen asking her to allow the Hanoverian succession to be voted instead of the treaty.[33] Concern with the perjury of a covenanted nation also appeared in *Some queries proposed to consideration, relative to the union now intended* by John Bannatyne, minister of Lanark parish and author of an anti-toleration tract. Bannatyne echoed Wylie and Hamilton presbytery in asking whether the union would 'involve the Nation in perjury; Seeing the National Covenant obliges this Nation to maintain the Authority of Parliaments?'[34]

The prominent Edinburgh minister James Webster, also an anti-toleration author, founded a series of objections to incorporation on the requirements of the Covenants. In *Lawful prejudices against an incorporating union with England* (1707), Webster saw the presence of bishops in the British parliament as 'a Breach of our National Engagements' barring clergy from civil posts. Moreover, the protection of the Church of England in union was 'a manifold Breach of the Solemn League' of 1643 obliging Scotland to improve the Reformation in England. In an incorporating union, he argued, the Presbyterian Church would have no allies, not even the English dissenters as they had accepted toleration.[35]

Going even further, Archibald Foyer issued a tract reasserting the Covenants and rejecting the Hanoverian succession. A minister at Stonehouse parish in Lanarkshire who published during the Darien crisis, Foyer offered what was effectively a radical revival of Covenanting politics, starting with the assertion that the union 'for ever buries our Covenanted work of Reformation'. He condemned the neglect of the Covenants since 1690, proposing 'Should we not begin with England, where we left in 1643; and if they will not joyn with us upon such Terms, ought we not to protest against the Breach of Covenant, and look to God for help in choising a King of our own.'[36] As a Lutheran, Sophia of Hanover was not an acceptable solution to Scotland's succession crisis; moreover, she and her heirs would be required by the English Act of Succession to maintain prelacy in England. For the short term Foyer

---

33 NAS, PA 7/20/50 Hamilton, printed as *Unto his grace, her majesties high commissioner and the right honourable the estates of parliament, the humble address of the presbytry of Hamilton*, [Edinburgh 1706].

34 [John Bannatyne], *Some queries proposed to consideration, relative to the union now intended*, [Edinburgh 1706], 1.

35 [James Webster], *Lawful prejudices against an incorporating union with England*, Edinburgh 1707, 4, 5, 7.

36 [Archibald Foyer], *Queries to the Presbyterian noblemen and gentlemen, barons, burgesses, ministers and commoners in Scotland, who are for the scheme of an incorporating union with England*, [Edinburgh 1706], 1–2.

proposed that parliament pass acts against Jacobitism, renew the National Covenant, approve a national fast and name a committee to discuss ways to build Scotland's trade. Foyer's radical rejection of the Hanoverian succession and his adherence to the Covenants exceeded the limits of acceptable public discourse, making his one of the few pamphlets ordered to be burned by the hangman during the union debates.[37]

This revival of extremist Presbyterian politics by a minister of the established Church coincided with the appearance of even more strident tracts from separatist Covenanters. A printed address from the Hebronites in south-western Scotland stated that they were 'not against an Union in the Lord with England', but such a union had to be consistent with 'our sacred Covenants', as well as 'the liberty of our Nation' and 'security of our Church'.[38] Since the Covenants required the Scots to maintain their parliament, the Hebronites felt obliged to resist the treaty. Moreover, by the treaty 'Wee incorporat with a Nation deeply guilty of Many National Abominations, who have openly broke and burnt their Covenant with God and league with us ... have their publick and established Worship horridly Corrupted, with Superstition and their Doctrine dreadfully leavened with Socianism and Arminianism, besides the most gross and deeply lamentable profaneness that abounds amongst them.' As Webster also pointed out, the treaty prevented the Scots from advancing any further reformation of England. The address closed with the declaration that the Hebronites did not consider themselves bound by the treaty, 'tho a prevailing party in parliament should Conclude the same'. Instead, they declared their readiness to 'stand by such noble patriots with life and fortune, as are for the Maintinance and defence of the Nations independencie and freedome, and of this Churches just power and propper privileges conform to our Attained reformation from 1638 to 1649'.[39]

Alongside this statement from the Hebronites, the militarised Cameronian separatists of south-west Scotland also declared an anti-incorporation stance in An account of the burning of the articles of the union at Dumfries (1706).[40] Like the Hebronite address, this tract rejected any approval of the treaty by parliament as not 'binding upon the nation now, nor at any time to come'. This protest was based on a claim of popular sovereignty, that only 'the consent of the generality of the same [the nation]' can 'divest them of their sacred and civil liberties'. The Cameronian demonstrators stated their willingness to support the parliamentary opposition in further action against the treaty and

---

[37] APS xi. 355.

[38] McMillan, John Hepburn.

[39] NAS, PA 7/28/22, printed as To his grace, her majesties high commissioner, and honourable estates of parliament, the humble address of a considerable body of people in the south and western shires, [Edinburgh 1706].

[40] See chapter 7 below for more on this event.

suggested that the Scottish army would not be willing to defend parliament against the anti-incorporationists.

Similarly, *A speech in season against the union* (1706) called on 'all true Presbyterians in heart, how far so ever they have slacked their Watch' to be ready to 'sacrafice all your Lives and die in a good cause'. Incorporation, combined with the persecutions of the 'Witnesses' during the Restoration, would bring down God's fury on Scotland: 'Therefore prepare to meet your God O Scotland, for your old Perjurie and Blood shed, and Treacherie against your Land.' Like the Hebronites and the Cameronians, the *Speech* rejected the treaty votes: 'since you have unmagistrate your selvs ... what you are doing will make way for the Lords raising up a partie to renounce, annull, and cast all down, and Call a representative to succeed in your room ... and in the mean time we renounce, annull and cast all down that you do'. Like Foyer's tract, the *Speech* rejected the Hanoverian succession, declaring that 'we will have no Protestant of Englands choising ... we are no more beholden to Hannover then to any other, if he be not Presbyterian'. The new Scottish king must be 'One of our Brethren both in Nation or Religion, or else we will have no King at all.' Instead, Scotland would have 'the Lord that made the Heaven and the Earth to be head Majestie and absolute power'.[41]

Covenanting extremism and activism appeared in yet more pamphlets, including *The smoaking flax unquenchable* (1706), *To the loyal and religious hearts in parliament, some few effects of the union, proposed between Scotland and England* (1706) and *We heard that the parliament is sitting at Edinburgh ... A word to the Unioners and their confederats thee parliamenters* (1706). These urged collective action against the treaty, often in violent terms. *A word to the Unioners*, for example, expressed the fervent wish that the Edinburgh mob would stone the traitorous treaty commissioners and warned that the Lord's sword would be drawn to stop the treaty. *The smoaking flax* proposed not just the stopping of the treaty but the overturning of monarchical rule in Scotland, for 'the true and faithful subjects of Scotland inclines not to Monarchy Government'.[42] Such pamphlets revived the once-familiar ideology of extremist Covenanting Presbyterianism and associated resistance to the treaty with fanatical rebellion.

In a more secular vein, other writers advanced radical Whig theory to defend the idea that Scottish freeholders could call parliament to account for betraying the national interest. *The Scotch echo to the English legion* (1707) provided a digest of Whig writings featuring extracts from two writers now on the government's side: a defence of the 1701 Kentish petitioners by Daniel Defoe and *Jus populi vindicatum* (1669) by Lord Advocate James Stewart of Goodtrees. Originally written to justify resistance to the Episcopalian establishment in the Restoration period, the extract from Stewart's *Jus populi vindicatum* argued that 'the Power of the People is greater than the Power of

41 Anon., *A speech in season against the union*, [Edinburgh 1706], 5, 6, 8, 9.
42 Anon., *The smoaking flax unquenchable*, [Edinburgh] 1706, 5.

any delegated or constituted by them' and that if representatives 'seek the Destruction of the Community, the Community is allowed to see to the preservation of their own Rights and Privileges the best way they can'.[43]

One Whig publication can be linked with a Jacobite author, indicating a disingenuous employment of resistance theory by Jacobite interests in the Country opposition. A tract by Patrick Abercromby, former royal physician to James VII and II, suggested that 'now we are upon the Revolution-Foot, no good Revolutioner will be offended, if I attempt to prove by Revolution-Principles, That the Parliament cannot finally conclude and determine the Whole of the Union, so long as the People shall continue to express their Dissent'. Quoting Defoe's *Original power of the collective body of the people of England* (1701), a tract that 'may be had in any of our Booksellers Shops in Town', Abercromby argued that the people could 're-assume the Right of Government in their own hands, and to reduce their Governors to Reason'.[44]

This Whig emphasis on popular resistance represented an extreme form of the Country party leadership's strategy to demand constituent approval of the treaty. Early on, George Ridpath claimed that 'if all the Freeholders in Scotland were poll'd upon this account, it would be found that the Majority will never agree to it'.[45] In November Lord Belhaven invoked 'the general Aversation that appears by the Addresses from the severall shires of the Kingdom', while Abercromby claimed that addresses from 'all Corners of the Kingdom' had demonstrated that the treaty was rejected by 'most, if not all Scotsmen, Women and Children'.[46] The vernacular voice of *Copy of a letter* observed that 'the maist part of Fock here awal very fair against it' and the presbytery of Hamilton warned of the 'ferment' in their parishes against the proposed union.[47]

These claims reinforced party efforts in parliament to call for consultation with constituents and new elections for a more representative assembly. However, when linked with Covenanting politics and radical theories of popular sovereignty, opinion politics became a double-edged sword. Useful for mobilising action in Covenanting areas, radical tracts also had the potential to alienate moderates with fears for the revival of Covenanting extremism. As the earl of Mar wrote after the burning of the articles of union in Dumfries,

---

[43] Anon., *The Scotch echo to the English legion*, [Edinburgh] 1707, 19–20.
[44] [Patrick Abercromby], *The advantages of the Act of Security, compar'd with these of the intended union: founded on the revolution-principles publish'd by Mr. Daniel De Foe*, [Edinburgh] 1707, 6–7.
[45] [Ridpath], *Considerations upon the union*, 62.
[46] John Hamilton, Lord Belhaven, *The Lord Belhaven's speech in parliament the 15th day of November 1706*, [Edinburgh] 1706. See also [Webster], *Lawful prejudices*, 3; 'Scotland's ruine', 178; [Abercromby], *The advantages of the Act of Security*, 5.
[47] Anon., *Copy of a letter*, 1; NAS, PA 7/20/50. See also [Wylie], *Insecurity of a printed overture*, 6; [Foyer], *Queries*, 3.

'They are mad men, and allways were so, and are thought so by every body.'[48] Despite the persuasions of Country tracts on the economic, religious and political dangers of incorporation, the extremism of some opponents of the treaty pointed to other dangers in active resistance and rebellion.

Pro-incorporation discourse

From the late summer of 1706 an increasing number of Court publications advanced the government's view of union as the pragmatic path to peace, prosperity and Protestant security. Former Court party authors published again, joined by Daniel Defoe, a professional writer hired by the English secretary Robert Harley to work in Edinburgh as a Court party publicist. These writers produced a range of materials appropriate to varying social levels, from nobles to ordinary subjects. Their tracts advanced positive arguments for union, countered Country discourse and condemned adversarial addressing and crowds as irrational, disaffected and dangerous. By late 1706 a vigorous Court campaign in favour of incorporation and the emergence of radical resistance to the treaty combined to persuade some moderates to publish in favour of an amended treaty of incorporation.

Accounts of the print campaign for union tend to focus on Daniel Defoe and his prolific output, obscuring the role played by Scottish politicians in encouraging the print campaign. Before Harley engaged him to go north, Defoe had already agreed to write the first two of his *Essays at removing national prejudices* at the request of Scottish treaty negotiators in London.[49] Against an estimated forty tracts attributed to Defoe, there are at least thirty-eight printed titles by other authors, in addition to an unknown number of manuscript tracts.[50] Defoe's output remains impressive and significant, but should be viewed in the context of the whole pro-treaty campaign, produced by Scottish as well as English hands.

Publications attributed to George Mackenzie, now earl of Cromarty, illustrate in one author the Court party's new efforts to speak to a wider audience, supply more tracts, respond to anti-treaty arguments and weaken oppositional representations of public opinion. Having published one pamphlet and a few speeches on incorporation before 1706, Cromarty is believed to have printed at least eleven tracts in 1706–7 for a variety of readers. Like leading Country party writers, he sought to predispose opinion on the treaty during the negotiations by printing two tracts in early 1706, followed by a reply to Wylie's July assertions of freeholder sovereignty. During the parliamentary session, Cromarty published a seven-issue periodical dialogue for a mass audience, finishing with a pamphlet on the nineteenth article of union.

---

48 *Manuscripts of the earl of Mar*, 332.
49 Paula R. Backscheider, *Daniel Defoe: his life*, Baltimore 1989, 205–9.
50 Idem, *Defoe: ambition & innovation*, Lexington 1986, 56.

Written as two letters to the earl of Wemyss, Cromarty's first two pamphlets addressed a propertied audience familiar with the dynamics of national politics. While responding to commonly held concerns about the dishonourable loss of the ancient name of Scotland and the small Scottish contingent in the British parliament, Cromarty also addressed gentlemen's fears that property laws would be changed and that law cases would become more expensive with appeals going to a British House of Lords. In addition, Cromarty condemned the impracticality of federal union, arguing that the monarch would remain as trapped between Scottish and English interests in a federal arrangement as in the present union. He repeated his argument from 1702 that the English would not concede free trade without a complete union and insisted that the Church would be more secure with incorporation than without.[51]

Indicating the Court party's intention to woo public opinion, Cromarty asked his readers to consider the treaty anew: 'I do earnestly beg and wish, that the Treaters, Parliaments and all Inhabitants of both the Nations, should weigh the Arguments of both sides in an impartial Balance.' Establishing a refrain echoed by other writers, he argued that 'Reason and Prudence are the Motives of this Union.' Rather ominously, Cromarty asserted in a postscript to his second letter that for those who did not recognise that the advantages outweighed the potential disadvantages of union, 'it is in the Interest of the Whole, either by Force or Perswasion, to draw the Divided, or Dividing Part or Party, into a total Union'.[52] These comments signalled the government's commitment to the securing of union by a combination of persuasion and force.

Cromarty's reply to Robert Wylie's Letter concerning the union countered Country attempts to put pressure on parliament with freeholder opinion. The people did not delegate the power of government to their monarch and parliamentary commissioners, but devolved it, making parliament sovereign in conjunction with the crown. Rather than telling parliament what to do, constituents had to recognise that their 'Duty' lay in 'Obedience'. These arguments against freeholder sovereignty may have raised fears of a return to the royalist absolutism of the Restoration, but in this new version Cromarty placed sovereignty in parliament as well as the monarch. He also redefined the obligation of the Covenants as a requirement to uphold the authority of queen and parliament in the making of new laws, including legislation for a treaty of union.[53]

Cromarty spoke to a wider audience with an unusual periodical publication, *Trialogus*, in which Mr Pro, Mr Con and Mr Indifferent argued over incor-

---

51 [George Mackenzie, earl of Cromarty], *Two letters concerning the present union, from a peer in Scotland to a peer in England*, [Edinburgh] 1706. These letters were also published as two separate tracts.
52 Ibid. 8, 11–12, 14, 17.
53 [George Mackenzie, earl of Cromarty], *A friendly return to a letter concerning Sir George Mackenzie's and Sir John Nisbet's observation*, [Edinburgh] 1706, 15–16, 26.

poration in seven weekly conversations from October to November 1706. With these exchanges, Cromarty provided positive arguments for union and characterised the opposition as irrational, over-zealous and dangerous. The second conversation of 7 October, for example, sought to overcome popular concerns at the loss of the kingdom of Scotland. Citing history to show that Scotland was comprised of unions, such as that of the Picts and the Scots, Mr Pro stated that one more change of name would be of no great moment in historical terms, deriding any such fears as 'petty'. When the ensuing debate became heated, Mr Indifferent accused Mr Con of becoming too fiery and called for calm consideration of the issues.[54]

Together Cromarty's tracts provided a Tory perspective aimed at religious moderates and the propertied. A similar pro-union perspective can be seen in the works of William Seton of Pitmedden, commissioner for Aberdeenshire and a 1706 treaty negotiator. Taking the form of a letter from the country, Seton's first tract represented what he wished 'country opinion' would believe about union. Consistent with his own 1700 arguments and Court party pamphlets of 1703–4 on the Jacobite threat, Seton argued that union would form 'the Bulwark of the Protestant Religion and Interest' to secure the 'Safety, Prosperity and Peace of Britain'. Like Cromarty in 1702, he asserted that Scotland 'by all probability, will be in a better, but can be in no worse Condition' with the proposed union. Appealing to those tired of 'Fatal Divisions about the less Essential Parts of Religion', Seton argued that the security of the Church was 'no sufficient reason to oppose the common Good and Advantage of the Island'. He framed parliament's task as a choice between 'Union with Peace and Plenty, or Dis-Union with Slavery and Poverty'. Opponents of union would see this if they would 'Reason calmly, and without Prejudice' instead of trying 'to startle such, who, not understanding the Reasons and Causes of Things, are easily imposed on'.[55]

In a speech of 2 November, Seton argued in favour of the first article of the treaty on the uniting of the kingdoms and attacked counter-proposals for a federal union. He insisted that Scotland as the weaker nation would be at a permanent disadvantage *vis à vis* England in a federal union and that only through incorporation could Scotland become an equal partner with England and receive the full benefits of union. He derided the idea of federal union as 'very Fashionable' and 'handsomely fitted to delude unthinking People'.[56]

Like Seton, William Paterson also attacked Country arguments in favour of federal union. Writing from London before the treaty negotiations were concluded, Paterson referred to federalist tracts like Hodges's 1703 *Rights*

[54] [George Mackenzie, earl of Cromarty], *Trialogus: a conference betwixt Mr. Con, Mr. Pro and Mr. Indifferent, concerning the union: second conversation*, [Edinburgh] 1706, 11, 13.

[55] [William Seton of Pitmedden], *Scotland's great advantages by an union with England: showen in a letter from the country, to a member of parliament*, [Edinburgh] 1706, 4, 5, 7–10, 10.

[56] William Seton of Pitmedden, *A speech in the parliament of Scotland, the second day of November, 1706 on the first article of the treaty of union*, London 1706, 6.

and interests as 'long, tedious and perplext heaps of words'. His tract, he said, offered a readable dialogue, though Robert Wodrow found it 'very dull'.[57] Starting from the premise that all Scots wanted union with England but disagreed on its form, Paterson warned his readers that England would not concede a communication of trade without a 'Communication of Government'. He emphasised the advantage of the Equivalent and its buyout of the African Company and promised substantial economic growth to offset higher English customs and excise rates. Furthermore, the Church would be safer in a British union, 'the two Churches and the Tolleration' forming 'a natural poise and Balance to one another'.[58]

John Clerk of Penicuik, a treaty negotiator in 1706, also emphasised the security of the Scottish Church in union. Clerk published a lengthy essay during the parliamentary debates responding to the leading anti-incorporation arguments found in the works of Hodges and Ridpath. Like Paterson, Clerk rested most of his counter-arguments on the expectation of increased trade and wealth after the union and promised security for Scottish interests, including the Church. Throughout, Clerk emphasised the benefits of the Protestant succession, free trade and the use of the Equivalent as a loan to rebuild the economy.[59]

Published after the first appearance of riots and addresses against the treaty, Clerk's tract sought to reduce active resistance to the treaty by emphasising the need to 'wait with Patience and Submission' for parliament to decide on the union. In his view the addresses against the treaty showed not that parliament should reject the union but that 'there has been too little Time taken to resolve upon a matter of such extraordinary Consequence'. Clerk reassured his readers that parliament would enact whatever 'Rectification or Additional Articles' might be necessary to relieve complaints on tax and trade regulations. He claimed that much of the printed material on duties was erroneous and accused the opposition of exaggerating the risk of higher taxes to inflame the people. Hoping to convince Presbyterians that anti-unionism only aided their enemies, he portrayed a 'Presbyterian Minister, a Popish Priest, and an Episcopal Prelate' as agreeing in their opposition to the union for 'contradictory' reasons.[60]

The Episcopalian John Arbuthnot, physician to the queen, used a mock sermon to deliver a Tory view of union to a popular audience in *A sermon preach'd to the people* (1706). Arbuthnot framed the union problem in simple terms as a choice between riches or poverty, emphasising economic advantages and dismissing religious issues as trifling. Consistent with other Court writers, Arbuthnot portrayed his arguments as the voice of reason, describing

---

57 *Wodrow letters*, 291.
58 [William Paterson], An *inquiry into the reasonableness and consequences of an union*, London 1706, 2, 13, 21.
59 [John Clerk of Penicuik], A *letter to a friend, giving an account how the treaty of union has been received here*, [Edinburgh] 1706.
60 Ibid. 1, 7, 37, 39.

Country notions as 'Precarious, Imaginary and Fantastical'. He called on the lower orders to accept the judgement of their superiors on the union, declaring the treaty 'a matter of such weight as made it a very unfit subject for the Judgement (much more for the Scorn and Contempt) of Boys, Apprentices and Tradesmen'. Suggesting that anti-treaty riots in Edinburgh had been encouraged with French gold, he urged the people to seek instead English guineas through incorporation.[61]

Together, these works by Cromarty, Seton, Paterson, Clerk and Arbuthnot established a consistent Scottish Court party platform emphasising the benefits of union in peace, prosperity and the Protestant succession. Working alongside these Scottish writers, Daniel Defoe developed similar arguments in response to developments in Country discourse and the parliamentary debates. Having published two essays in London to improve English attitudes to union, Defoe wrote two further essays soon after his arrival in Edinburgh.[62] Like Clark's *Letter*, these addressed the range of anti-union arguments that Defoe found current in Scotland, especially those established by Hodges's most recent *Rights and interests* treatise.[63] Defoe used his third essay to counter concerns for the vulnerability of Scottish interests in the British parliament by promising that the Presbyterian Church would be safe with the protection of an act securing the Church in union.[64] His fourth essay responded to a range of economic concerns raised by oppositional writers like William Black. In this, Defoe used his connections with the parliamentary committees on trade and tax amendments to supply a wealth of detail countering the assertions of anti-treaty publications.[65] Additional tracts by Defoe responded to parliamentary debates on the economic articles in November and December, followed in January 1707 by a fifth essay on trade issues.[66] Initially, Defoe sought to minimise economic amendments to the treaty as per his instructions from London. He supported limited changes once it became clear that amendments would be necessary for the treaty to pass. His *Observations on*

---

[61] [John Arbuthnot], *A sermon preach'd to the people, at the mercat cross of Edinburgh: on the subject of the union*, [Edinburgh?] 1706, 4, 10.

[62] The third essay appears to have been printed in late October and the fourth in early November: *Letters of Daniel Defoe*, 138.

[63] Backscheider, *Daniel Defoe*, 218, 223; [Daniel Defoe] *An essay at removing national prejudices, against a union with England, part III*, Edinburgh 1706, and *A fourth essay at removing national prejudices; with some reply to Mr. H[o]dges and some other authors, who have printed their objections against an union with England* (1706), in McLeod and McLeod, *Anglo-Scottish tracts*, no. 138.

[64] [Defoe], *An essay ... part III*, 16, 26.

[65] Backscheider, *Daniel Defoe*, 222.

[66] [Daniel Defoe], *A letter concerning trade, from several Scots gentlemen that are merchants in England, to their country-men that are merchants in Scotland*, [Edinburgh] 1706; *Observations on the fifth article of the treaty of union, humbly offered to the consideration of the parliament, relating to foreign ships*, [Edinburgh] 1706; *The state of the excise after the union, compared with what it is now*, [Edinburgh] 1706; and *A fifth essay, at removing national prejudices*, [Edinburgh] 1707.

the fifth article of the treaty of union (1706), for example, proposed a compromise solution to concerns on the exclusion of part-owned Scottish ships from qualification as British bottoms.

Alongside these contributions to pro-treaty arguments, Defoe also developed the Court party's attacks on representations of anti-treaty opinion. In *A seasonable warning or the pope and king of France unmasked* (1706), Defoe pitched his message to the middling and lower sorts, denouncing popular opposition to the union and reiterating pro-incorporation arguments in simple terms. He stressed the mistaken nature of public aversion to the treaty, accusing Country party leaders of persuading 'poor ignorant People, that they are Asserting the Honour and Liberty of the Nation' while actually encouraging 'Poverty and Slavery'. He claimed that 'the most violent Opposers of a Union' were 'declared Papists' and that most of the addressers were 'Dissenters ... and no Friends to the Civil Government'. Like other Court authors, he recommended that his readers reject 'popular mistakes and prejudices' and rely instead on the 'Wisdom and Decree of the Parliament'.[67]

The stir created by anti-treaty addresses to parliament led Defoe to devote his sixth essay to the question, *What is the obligation of parliaments to the addresses or petitions of the people, and what the duty of the addressers?*[68] In this, his arguments bore more resemblance to Cromarty's Tory views than his own radical Whig *Legion's address* (1701) or 'The original power of the collective body of the people' (1701), but as Paul H. Scott has observed, 'Defoe was too good a propagandist to allow consistency to spoil a good argument.'[69] Defoe claimed that parliament was under no obligation to do more than accept petitions. While Clerk had portrayed the addressers as misguided, Defoe went further in describing them as dangerous, especially in their talk of travelling to Edinburgh to demand answers to their petitions or reclaim the barons' right to sit in parliament. Defoe characterised any popular attempt to call parliament to account as 'absolutely Destructive of the very Being and Substance of Government'.[70]

Publishing in response to riots in Edinburgh, Defoe denounced anti-union crowds as menacing and irrational. *A letter from Mr. Reason, to the high and mighty prince the mob* (1706) emphasised the crowds' anarchic overturning of authority. Similarly, the narrator of *The rabbler convicted* (1706) saw riots

---

67 [Defoe], *A seasonable warning*, 8, 14, 16.
68 [Daniel Defoe], *Two great questions considered, I: What is the obligation of parliaments to the addresses or petitions of the people, and what the duty of the addressers?; II: Whether the obligation of the Covenant or the other national engagements, is concern'd in the treaty of union? Being a sixth essay at removing national prejudices against the union*, [Edinburgh] 1707.
69 Paul H. Scott, 'Defoe in Edinburgh', in *Defoe in Edinburgh and other papers*, East Linton 1995, 10. For a more charitable view of Defoe see Katherine R. Penovich, 'From "revolution principles" to union: Daniel Defoe's intervention in the Scottish debate', in John Robertson (ed.), *A union for empire: political thought and the British union of 1707*, Cambridge 1995, 228–42.
70 [Defoe], *Two great questions*, 3, 5, 6, 11.

as 'destructive to all Society' and 'disagreeable to the Laws of God'. Public clamour against the union 'proceeded from Ignorance and Malice', 'a Popish Party amongst us' and 'giddiness of the brain, which they vainly call zeal for Religion'. Defoe's narrator called on the people to trust parliament to decide the matter of union.[71]

Defoe hit even harder at crowds in *A short letter to the Glasgow-men* (1706). Faced with rioting sparked by Glasgow's deacons of trade, Defoe scolded the burgesses of Glasgow for their tumultuous behaviour and accused them of advancing the Jacobite cause, harming the Church, overturning the Scottish constitution and inviting mass disorder. Referring to a letter from the Commission of the General Assembly asking presbyteries to calm local unrest, he accused the Glaswegians of betraying the Church with their opposition. Whether they realised it or not, 'all the Jacobites are in League with you, the Papists are on your right Hand, the Prelatists on your left, and the French at your Back'. For those rioters who were not freemen of Glasgow, Defoe dismissed any right on their part to communicate with parliament, 'For none but he, that has a Right to be Represented, can have a Right to Limit their Representatives; All you then, that have not a Voice in an Election, are meer Rebels, Rioters, Thieves, [and] Sowers of Sedition.' Rioting, Defoe stressed, was madness, 'against Duty, against Reason, against Laws and Authority'.[72] Defoe reported in a December letter to Harley that he had printed 2,500 copies of his *Letter to the Glasgow-men* for distribution in areas of resistance in and around Glasgow, Lanark, Hamilton, Dumfries and Stirling.[73]

Alongside the publications of these known Court writers, further pamphlets by unidentified writers advanced similar arguments. Though this group included long, sophisticated essays, such as *A discourse concerning the union*, many focused on the exposition of particular issues from a pro-incorporation point of view.[74] These refuted the more popular anti-union arguments while hammering home the Court's association of the opposition with Jacobitism and disaffection. In one example, a dialogue between a coffee-master and a country farmer responded to John Bannatyne's *Queries* with brief, uncomplicated arguments. The coffee-master rejected the Covenants as not binding on posterity, reminded Presbyterians that the Jacobites opposed the treaty because it barred the Pretender from the throne and suggested that they ought to follow their church leaders in supporting the union. On the positive side, a 'Tenant of 100 Merks' would become a 'rich Farmer of a 100l' and the country farmer's wool would sell more quickly. The coffee-master acknowledged that many were 'blinded still, not to see the Interest of the Nation by

---

71 [Daniel Defoe], *The rabbler convicted*, [Edinburgh] 1706, 2, 4.
72 [Daniel Defoe], *A short letter to the Glasgow-men*, [Edinburgh 1706], 2, 5, 7.
73 *Letters of Daniel Defoe*, 170.
74 Anon., *The equivalent explain'd*, [Edinburgh 1706]; 'Resolution of some doubts, with relation to the publick debts of Scotland, as stated in the 15 article of the Treaty of Union' (3 Feb 1707), NLS, Advocates MS; R. S., *Some neutral considerations, with relation to two printed papers, which are cry'd about the streets*, [Edinburgh 1707].

an Union', but explained this as 'owing mostly... to the mists which disaffected people raise before their Eyes'. The farmer, however, knew his duty: to 'submit to what the Parliament shall determine'.[75] Pro-union authors also used the vernacular to represent popular interests, as in a mock petition from the female 'shank workers and fingren spinners of Aberdeen'. These wool workers anticipated an increase in cloth exports with 'Eenion' and denied that the Scottish cloth market would be flooded with cheaper, better-quality English cloth.[76]

The strengthening of the campaign for incorporation in 1706–7 affected opinion in Scotland by providing a rationale for union support and highlighting the association of radical Covenanters, Jacobites and popular disorder with the opposition. In addition, the sheer volume of publications in favour of the treaty indicated the Court's commitment to the union project. By late 1706, alongside the aggressively positive tracts published by Court party writers, new pamphlets began to emerge indicating the presence of a moderate, pragmatic opinion base for the treaty. While insisting on amendments to secure key Scottish interests from the encroachments of a British parliament, these tracts reflected the views of those who were 'so sure that the welfare of church and state depended entirely on Article 2 [establishing the Hanoverian succession] that for the sake of it they were willing to embrace all the others, even if they did not like many of them'.[77]

Two advocates, the Tory John Spottiswoode and the Presbyterian Whig Francis Grant, both published tracts revealing their reluctant conversion to incorporation as the only feasible path forwards for Scotland. Rejecting more enthusiastic Court propaganda for union, both emphasised the need for unity in Britain against a Jacobite threat. Writing at an earlier stage in the debates, Spottiswoode demanded amendments to the treaty, while Grant, publishing in January, indicated his acceptance of the treaty based on the concessions secured by the end of 1706. A third writer, Thomas Spence, also indicated his acceptance of the treaty by early 1707 but urged further changes to protect the Scottish legal system. It is important to note that these authors placed their trust in parliament, not public opinion, as the authority by which the treaty should be accepted.

Having expressed Country views of union in a 1702 pamphlet, by 1706 John Spottiswoode had come to accept incorporation as a political necessity though he sought amendments to protect Scottish interests in an entire

---

[75] Anon., *An answer to some queries, &c. relative to the union: in a conference betwixt a coffee-master, and a countrey-farmer*, [Edinburgh] 1706, 2, 9, 12. See also Anon., *Counter quiries to the quiries burnt at the cross of Edinburgh*, [Edinburgh] 1706.

[76] *To his grace her majesties high commissioner and the honourable estates of parliament: the heemble petition of the peer shank workers and fingren spinners of Aberdeen, and places, thereabout*, [Edinburgh 1706].

[77] Sir John Clerk of Penicuik, *History of the union of Scotland & England*, ed. Douglas Duncan, Edinburgh 1993, 122.

union.[78] In calling his 1706 tract *The trimmer*, Spottiswoode indicated that he was steering a pragmatic course between the Court's vision of a prosperous, united Britain and Country demands for a sovereign Scotland allied with England. While Country tracts urged amendments that would be unacceptable to the English parliament, Spottiswoode sought more realistic changes; conversely, while Court tracts trumpeted the positive benefits of union, Spottiswoode focused on the need to avoid English trade sanctions, outright conquest or a Franco-Jacobite war.[79] Spottiswoode's concern for English coercion can also be seen in the pro-treaty opinion of the burgh council of Montrose, as expressed in a private letter of October 1706 to their commissioner.[80]

Spottiswoode rejected proposals for a federal union with separate parliaments as 'inconsistent with a lasting Union of the Two Kingdoms'. He suggested instead 'a few Articles, Cautions, Restrictions and Declarations' to secure 'the peculiar concerns of this Church and Nation' in the existing treaty.[81] These included an article in the treaty to maintain the Church; further securities for the civil law system, including the supremacy of the Court of Session; a new coronation oath requiring the monarch to uphold the separate interests of Scotland and England; a ban on any sacramental test for offices in Scotland; and the retention of the right of the Estates to meet on an *ad hoc* basis to discuss future amendments to the treaty or Scottish property laws. Spottiswoode's demands were less aggressive than those of most Country writers. Rather than seeking the rejection of the treaty, he seemed to desire a compromise solution to improve Scottish securities in the existing treaty.

Coming from a similarly pragmatic position, Francis Grant's tract showed how a moderate Presbyterian's concern for civil and religious liberties could lead to an acceptance of the treaty. Against the greater threat of a Jacobite succession, incorporation presented the best option for Scotland. Seeing the treaty as a means to secure the Presbyterian Church and the Protestant succession in a united Britain, Grant rejected the emphasis on free trade and economic gain found in most Court propaganda as a 'Vulgar Error'. He stated that he had, at first, supported the notion of separate parliaments as demanded by oppositional pamphlets, but he had been brought round to incorporation after 'several Concessions and Securities' had been passed in parliament. Believing that it would be 'morally impossible' for the British parliament to betray the treaty, Grant chose to trust incorporation as the means to secure the Protestant succession and the Scottish Church in funda-

---

78 [Spottiswoode], *A speech of one of the barons.*
79 [John Spottiswoode], *The trimmer: or, some necessary cautions, concerning the union of the kingdoms of Scotland and England; with an answer to some of the chief objections against an incorporating union,* [Edinburgh] 1706, 15, 4.
80 T. C. Smout, 'The burgh of Montrose and the union of 1707: a document', *SHR* lxvi (Oct. 1987), 182–4.
81 [Spottiswoode], *The trimmer*, 6, 10.

mental law. Instead of dismissing opponents of the treaty, he spoke respect-fully to the 'Men of Knowledge and Honour' who had submitted addresses against it. Grant urged addressers to recognise how their actions, along with crowds, interfered with parliamentary liberties and served to compel some towards union through their fear of disorder.[82]

While Grant did not demand any further amendments to the treaty, in early 1707 Thomas Spence asked the parliament to remedy some remaining issues. Accepting the passage of the treaty as a foregone conclusion, he hoped that parliament would ensure the continuation of the privy council, pass new laws to advance Scottish trade before devolving this responsibility to the more distant British parliament, reform Scottish laws, block appeals to the House of Lords and secure the Church with a Presbyterian sacramental test for Scottish offices.[83] Like Spottiswoode, Spence focused on a few pragmatic areas where treaty amendments could improve Scottish leverage in the new union. Both men showed an unwillingness to trust to the British parliament to adjust the terms of union later, a stance that the earl of Mar encountered in his management of the Court majority. In writing to London, Mar warned that 'trusting to the Parliament of Britain for rectifications … does not sound well here at present; and except those of us who were treaters I'm affraid few will be willing to do it'.[84]

A grudging acceptance of incorporation among some moderates also can be seen in the public support of leading clergy for the treaty. Like Grant, many church leaders were willing to accept incorporation in order to ensure the Protestant Hanoverian succession and the establishment of the Presby-terian Church. As William Carstares wrote to the English secretary Harley, 'The desire I have to see our Church secured makes me in love with the Union as the most probable means to preserve it.'[85] While asking parliament to take steps to protect the Church in union, Court-affiliated ministers like Carstares, John Logan and William Wisheart exerted themselves to minimise popular resistance to the treaty.

The Court party in the Church published their views on union on 17 October with a petition from the Commission of the General Assembly, supported by public sermons. The address cited the queen's letter to parlia-ment authorising 'what may be necessary for security of your present Church Government' and asked parliament to pursue further securities for the Church in union.[86] The Commission hoped that parliament would ratify past acts establishing the Presbyterian Church and confirm presbytery as 'the only Government of the Church within this Kingdom' through 'a funda-mentall article and Essential Condition of any Treaty'. For 'peace and amity

---

82 [Grant], *The patriot resolved*, 5–7, 9, 15, 17.
83 [Thomas Spence], *The testamentary duty of the parliament of Scotland*, [Edinburgh] 1707.
84 *Manuscripts of the earl of Mar*, 312.
85 Dunlop, *William Carstares*, 115.
86 *APS* xi. 306.

in this whole Island, and preserving… the Protestant Interest at home and abroad', erastian church leaders were willing to accept the treaty as long as it secured Presbyterian government against toleration or disestablishment.[87] Acknowledging the Church's moderate approach, Court managers in parliament allowed a formal response to the commission's address. This stated that parliament 'would do every thing necessary for securing the true Protestant Religion and Church Government presently established by law'.[88]

John Logan, minister of Alloa parish and a correspondent of William Carstares and the earl of Mar, reinforced the commission's petition with a sermon delivered to members of parliament on 27 October.[89] Avoiding any reference to the Covenants, Logan asked only that the Church's existing privileges be protected in the treaty. Though he lamented 'the indifferency and neutrality of many in this Church of Scotland', he still recommended that prudence temper zeal in the service of the Church.[90] For a fast day in Edinburgh presbytery secured by Country party efforts, William Carstares chose biblical texts emphasising the role of God, not the people, in protecting the nation.[91]

In parliament, the Court party introduced measures ensuring the promised protection for the Church, with an Act for Security of the Protestant Religion voted on 12 November. The passage of this act restored control of the Commission of the General Assembly to the Court party after managers had lost a vote on a more aggressive petition in early November. The commission issued two more addresses to parliament requesting further protections for the Church, but did not protest against the union or block its passage. To quiet 'the trumpets of sedition' in the parishes, the commission sent a letter to the presbyteries on 6 December, also published in the *Edinburgh Gazette*, instructing ministers to calm popular opposition at the local level. In the same way that Court writers urged Scottish subjects to trust parliament, so the commission asked presbyteries to trust their representatives in the commission. It also denounced rioting as an affront to the queen's authority on which the safety of the Church rested and warned that tumults could be used by Jacobites to disadvantage the Church.[92]

Ministers like William Wisheart of Leith parish, moderator of the Commission of the General Assembly in 1706–7, responded to this call by remonstrating from his pulpit against public disorder.[93] In printed sermons

---

87 NAS, PA 7/20/6.
88 *APS* xi. 307.
89 *Manuscripts of the earl of Mar*, 274.
90 John Logan, *A sermon preached before…the honourable estates of parliament in the New-Church of Edinburgh upon the 27 of October 1706*, Edinburgh 1706, 9, 11–12.
91 Dunlop, *William Carstares*, 116.
92 Clerk of Penicuik, *History of the union*, 121; NAS, CH 1/3/9/61; *Edinburgh Gazette*, no. 59 (Tues. 10 Dec–Mon. 16 Dec. 1706).
93 Like Logan, Wisheart corresponded with Court figures like Carstares and Mar: *Manuscripts of the earl of Mar*, 257.

from December 1706 Wisheart asked that 'all sober and well-meaning People' would help to prevent 'great Confusions in this Nation' by avoiding all crowd activities and doing everything possible in their stations to discourage resistance to parliament. He particularly called upon the better sort to reduce the dangers of popular opposition and recommended trust in the parliament.[94]

As indicated by the publications of Grant, Spottiswoode, Spence and leading clergy, some moderates had, by late 1706 and early 1707, accepted the treaty as a necessary step or an unavoidable fact. Rejecting overenthusiastic economic arguments for union, Presbyterians like Grant focused on the Protestant Hanoverian succession as the key outcome of incorporation. Though Clerk of Penicuik later claimed that it 'was now clear to all that the Franco-Spanish policy of keeping England and Scotland perpetually under separate jurisdictions had become the strongest of all arguments for bringing them together', it would be more accurate to say that some moderates had come to believe that the Jacobite threat made union unavoidable, if unpalatable. With the reassurance of an act confirming the Presbyterian Church in union, mainstream Presbyterians could accept the treaty, even while retaining misgivings about sacramental tests, bishops in parliament and the risk of toleration for Episcopalians.

Though some historians have dismissed print debates on union as ineffective propaganda, public discourse on the treaty constituted a real debate that affected opinions and outcomes. Country discourse established strong arguments against incorporation by 1705 and continued to develop them with fresh attacks on the treaty in 1706, countering the concession of free trade with new representations on the economic and religious risks of an entire union. Though the Country party invoked patriotic rhetoric and sought to convince parliament of the Scottish people's unanimous rejection of the treaty, the radicalisation of anti-treaty discourse and the appearance of public disorder weakened the solidity of oppositional opinion. The Court encouraged this with a flood of printed discourse. Pro-incorporation pamphlets provided glowing predictions of economic growth in union and promised security for the Presbyterian Church while dismissing popular resistance as unconstitutional, dangerous and disaffected. By late 1706 a reluctant acceptance of the treaty as a pragmatic means to secure the Protestant succession and the Presbyterian Church can be seen in some pamphlets, addresses and sermons. This acceptance, however, rested on key concessions and amendments made by the government in response to anti-treaty activity – not just pamphlets but also petitions and crowds, as will be discussed in the next two chapters.

94 William Wisheart, *Two sermons on Jeremiah 30.7*, Edinburgh 1707, 9, 11–12.

6

Addresses against the Treaty

Since the making of the union, historians have disagreed over the meaning of the dozens of anti-treaty addresses submitted to parliament between October 1706 and January 1707. Echoing the view of George Lockhart of Carnwath that they showed 'the nation's aversion to enter into this union', William Ferguson stated that 'Popular opinion asserted itself in numerous addresses against the treaty.'[1] In contrast, Daniel Defoe's *History of the union* (1709) suggested that the addresses were the product of elite Jacobite agitation, while more recently P. W. J. Riley has interpreted them as manifestations of deference to oppositional nobles.[2] In echoing Lockhart and Defoe, historians have accepted Country and Court rhetorical strategies at face value. As the first part of this book has shown, adversarial addresses were generated by partisan interests to influence the political process with claims of corporate grievances. Involving both elite instigation and willing participation by ordinary inhabitants, addresses represented neither straightforward popular opinion nor deference to elite organisers; and they did not necessarily portray an undifferentiated consensus. To understand the anti-treaty addresses, it is necessary to consider how they were generated and deployed by the Country party and how the government responded to this strategy.

The scale of addressing against the union treaty suggests a major organisational effort by the Country party, drawing on precedents from the Darien crisis. Addresses came from national bodies, including the Convention of Royal Burghs, the Commission of the General Assembly and the African Company; and from more than a hundred local political units: fifteen shires, twenty-two royal burghs, nine towns, three presbyteries and sixty-seven parishes. A total of seventy-nine addresses from these localities contained over 20,000 signatures, including many from those of middling to lower social ranks.[3] These addresses strove to convince parliament and the government of an overwhelming public consensus against incorporation. Together they hinted at the danger of popular resistance to union, with some texts making this threat explicit. In response the queen's managers marshalled their own resources and tactics. Wherever possible ministers and their supporters

---

1 '*Scotland's ruine*', 57; Ferguson, 'Making of the treaty of union', 109. See also Scott, *Andrew Fletcher*, 190.
2 Daniel Defoe, *The history of the union of Great Britain*, Edinburgh 1709, 18, 21, 24, 58; Riley, *Union of England and Scotland*, 282.
3 Karin Bowie, 'Scottish public opinion and the making of the union of 1707', unpubl. PhD diss. Glasgow 2004, appendices E, F.

discouraged petitioning, attacked the legitimacy of addresses, restricted collective action in support of addresses and made targeted concessions to win back parliamentary votes and reduce popular opposition in the short term.

Anti-incorporation addresses

From the summer of 1706, oppositional pamphlets signalled the Country party's intention to block the treaty by asserting the sovereignty of parliamentary constituents. As the session began, the opposition 'set on Foot a Notion that the Members of Parliament had no Right to alter the Constitution, without the particular consent of their Constituents'.[4] Lacking any accepted constitutional process for the giving of constituent consent, the Country party generated addresses and instructions to communicate freeholder opposition to the treaty and back calls for delays and new elections.

As early as April 1706 George Ridpath was writing to Scotland to recommend that instructions against the treaty be organised from constituencies.[5] Private instructions to commissioners were not unusual, as commissioners for the shires and burghs in the Scottish parliament were expected to act in the interests of their localities as well as the nation.[6] In addition, burgh councils and presbyteries often provided written instructions to their commissioners to the Convention of Royal Burghs and the General Assembly.[7] Such instructions usually remained private, though the English practice of publishing instructions to MPs would have been familiar to newspaper readers in Scotland.[8] In 1706 Country leaders saw an opportunity to strengthen their hand by using instructions as public representations against the treaty and as assertions of freeholder opinion.

In October the anti-treaty instructions of the royal burgh of Lauder appeared in pamphlet form and in Ridpath's *Flying Post*. Warning that the proposed union would tend to 'the destruction of their ancient Constitution, and all their Rights and Privileges, as a free People in general, and to every individual Person and Society ... especially that of the Boroughs', Lauder

---

4 Defoe, *History of the union*, 22.
5 'Correspondence between Ridpath and the Wodrow', i. 390.
6 *Stirling burgh extracts*, ii. 99; *Lanark burgh extracts*, iv. 253–4, 260–1; William Ferguson, 'Electoral law and procedure in eighteenth- and early nineteenth-century Scotland', unpubl. PhD diss. Glasgow 1957, 31.
7 *Lanark burgh extracts*, iv. 273; NAS, CH 1/2/23/3 (186).
8 Not long before the union debates, the *Edinburgh Courant* reprinted 'Instructions by the Free-Holders of the County of Middlesex, given to their Representatives after their Election, May 28, 1705': no. 53 (Wed. 20 June–Fri. 22 June 1705). For more on the adversarial use of instructions in eighteenth-century English politics see Paul Kelly, 'Constituents' instructions to members of parliament in the eighteenth century', in Clyve Jones (ed.), *Party and management in parliament, 1660–1784*, Leicester 1984, and Nicholas Rogers, *Whigs and cities: popular politics in the age of Walpole and Pitt*, Oxford 1989, 240–51.

required its commissioner to reject the treaty unless parliament amended it to maintain the Scottish parliament. If its member did not obey, the burgh protested that 'his Vote in the contrary thereof is null'. Drawing on the traditionally strong corporate identity of the royal burghs, Lauder said it had published its instructions in order that 'our Opinion and Proceedings may be made known to our Brethren the other Royal Burrows'. In practice, the instructions were used to lobby not just the burghs but all in parliament, as a copy of Lauder's instructions was handed 'to every Member as they entered the House' on 28 October.[9]

Printed instructions from the royal burghs of Dunfermline and Dumbarton also appeared. Dumbarton's burgh council resolve of 4 October directed its commissioner to 'declare their dislike of, and dissent from, the said union, as in their judgement inconsistent with, and subversive of, the fundamental laws and liberties of their nation, and plainly evacuating all the publick oaths this nation lyes under'. It further required that its member have 'due regaird to the judgment of his constituents'. Dumbarton's instructions created some difficulty with its commissioner, who voted for the union. In December 1706 he claimed that the burgh's published instructions differed from guidance provided to him privately.[10]

Instructions also appeared from Dumfriesshire as *Instructions for the commissioners of the sheriffdom of Dumfries* (1706). This asserted that

> nothing can be done by our Representatives in that Matter, conform to their Commissions, unless they have a special Authority for that Purpose. And we have not, by vertue of your said Commissions, delegated any Power to you our Trustees, to evert, alter, or innovate our Fundamental Laws, our Ancient Constitution, and Privileges of Parliament, the Offices, Rights, Liberties, and Dignities of this Kingdom, either belonging to Church or State.

Signed by thirty-one 'Barons, Freeholders, Heritors, and others', the instructions declared the treaty subversive of 'Three great and valuable Interests ... Our Church Government by Law Established, Our Liberty, and Our Trade' and required the shire's commissioners not to vote for any treaty article inconsistent with these interests.[11]

At the start of the parliamentary session, the Country party made great efforts to delay consideration of the treaty to allow time 'for people to consider of it [the treaty] more fully' and to prepare instructions and addresses.[12] As the government attempted to begin debate on the treaty on 15 October, the

---

9 *Flying Post*, no. 1796 (Tues. 5 Nov.–Thurs. 7 Nov. 1706); *Instructions by the magistrates and town council of the burgh of Lauder, to their commissioner in parliament*, [Edinburgh 1706].
10 *Manuscripts of the earl of Mar*, 318; *Dumbarton burgh records, 1627–1746*, Dumbarton 1860, 102.
11 Dumfries Archive Centre, G2/6/17.
12 NAS, GD 406/1/7138.

opposition submitted a motion for a further pause of eight days 'to consider more deliberately the Articles and Minuts' ordered printed on 3 October.[13] On the same day a 'hot debate' erupted over 'whether or not the Parliament without particular instructions from their constituents, could alter the constitution of the government'.[14] Anti-union speakers argued that 'In a matter of such weight ... it will be fruitless for parliament to institute debate without first consulting the people.'[15] Following this, the opposition provided extensive arguments against the articles as they were read one by one from 15 to 30 October, allowing time for addresses to be prepared among 'people of all ranks'.[16]

Having exerted significant 'pains ... to procure addresses', the Country party presented them to parliament between November and January.[17] The arrival of the first locality addresses on 1 November was used to support another motion for a delay so that 'the Members of Parliament may consult these whom they represent'.[18] Addresses were secured from the Commission of the General Assembly and the Convention of Royal Burghs as well as shires, burghs, presbyteries and parishes. Reflecting local and corporate concerns and interests, together these also indicate the many coordinating influences of Country party nobles, gentlemen and clergy.

Though church issues had been excluded from the union negotiations, the queen's letter to parliament of 3 October indicated 'an opportunity for doing what may be necessary for security of your present Church government after the Union within the Limits of Scotland'.[19] This provided a safe opening for the Church to address parliament for a ratification of the Presbyterian establishment as part of the union agreement. The Commission of the General Assembly nominated a committee to draft an address to parliament in early October. The committee included moderate clergymen (William Carstares, William Wisheart, George Meldrum and David Blair) and Court party elders (David Boyle, earl of Glasgow, and Lord Justice Clerk Adam Cockburn of Ormiston). The commission chose to accept the committee's recommendation of what Daniel Defoe called a 'Moderate and well Temper'd' address requesting greater security for the established Church in the proposed union.[20]

At the same time, presbyterial representatives John Bannatyne and Thomas Linning asked the commission also to petition parliament for a national fast on the union. Earlier in the session, the Country party had lost a motion for a fast in parliament, leading the duke of Hamilton to write on 12 October to

13 APS xi. 306–7.
14 'Scotland's ruine', 142.
15 Clerk of Penicuik, History of the union, 95.
16 APS xi. 307–11; NAS, GD 406/1/5294.
17 Jerviswood correspondence, 166.
18 APS xi. 307; 'Scotland's ruine', 158.
19 APS xi. 306.
20 NAS, CH 1/3/8 (226–32); Defoe, History of the union, 26; NAS, PA 7/20/6.

Robert Wylie in Hamilton parish to urge him and his 'bretherene' to come to Edinburgh to fight in the Commission for a fast.[21] The tactic of applying for a national fast on contentious political issues followed Country party practice from the Darien crisis and echoed James Hodges's recent published call for a fast.[22] This request was referred to a committee for public affairs.[23]

After the commission's first petition to parliament of 17 October, oppositional ministers continued to advocate a national fast and a further supplication on religious issues, supported in the commission by Country party elders like John Hamilton, Lord Belhaven. As increasing numbers of activist clergy arrived in Edinburgh to join the commission, the question of a fast was resolved with the authorisation of a local day of prayer on union administered by the presbyteries. This outcome disappointed the duke of Hamilton who felt that the clergy had 'fallen into the Courts trap: for the delay was the main point of importance to us & now what ever they may doe I apprehend it will come too Lait'.[24]

Nevertheless, oppositional ministers and elders succeeded in securing a more assertive second petition from the commission raising specific concerns on the treaty. Though not as aggressive as draft petitions prepared by Robert Wylie, the address asked parliament to ensure that Scottish Presbyterians would not be disadvantaged by the English sacramental test and not asked to take any new oaths or tests inconsistent with their principles.[25] It also asked that the Scottish Church be protected in the British coronation oath and that arrangements be made for a civil authority in union for planting kirks, valuing teinds, judging church cases and approving fasts. Lastly, aspects of the abjuration oath and the presence of Anglican bishops in the British parliament were declared incompatible with Presbyterian principles.[26] Heavily attended commission meetings in late October and early November debated the contents of this address, particularly the presence of bishops.[27]

Before the commission submitted its second address on 8 November, the Convention of Royal Burghs delivered a petition against the treaty on 6 November. As in the Commission of the General Assembly, Court and Country interests battled on the question of union in a special late October meeting of the convention. The securing of a petition from the convention represented a major victory for the opposition, won after a fierce debate and by a narrow margin.[28] The convention's address stressed its 'duty' to commu-

---

21 NAS, GD 406/1/7127.
22 [James Hodges], *That part of a late book which relates to a general fast and humiliation*, [Edinburgh] 1706.
23 NAS, CH 1/3/8 (226–32).
24 NAS, GD 406/1/5294.
25 Wodrow quarto xl, items 16–17.
26 NAS, PA 7/20/19, repr. in 'Scotland's ruine', 153–4.
27 NAS, CH 1/3/8 (259–72).
28 *Extracts from the records of the convention of the royal burghs of Scotland*, Edinburgh 1880, iv. 399–400; Daniel Defoe, *Review*, no. 191 (Tues. 26 Nov. 1706).

nicate 'the sentiments of the people we represent', 'being mostly impouered by our constituents'. The convention acknowledged that it was 'not against a Honourable and safe union with England', but asked that such a union be consistent with 'the being of this kingdome and parliaments'. The burghs focused on the loss of the Scottish parliament, 'without which we concive neither our religious nor our civil interests and trade, as we now by law enjoy them, can be secured to us.' In the British parliament, 'the mean representation aloued for Scotland can never signifie in securing to us the interests reserved by us' for 'all the concerns of trade and other interests, are after the union subject to such alterations, as the parliament of Brittain shall think fitt'. Moreover, the specific economic terms of the treaty could not advantage Scotland. Not only were 'our poor people ... made lyable to the English taxes which is a certain unsupportable burden', but the proposed free trade with England and its colonies was 'uncertain, involved, and wholly precarious'. To protect Scottish interests the Convention asked parliament to reject an incorporating union and to maintain Scotland's sovereign parliament, Presbyterian Church and Protestant succession.[29]

At the same time as the Country party strove to secure addresses from the Church and the convention, party leaders also generated a recommended text for locality petitions. This text, 'framed so as to comprehend everybody's wish', reflected the party's need to develop a platform that could contain Jacobites and Revolutioners alike while adhering to conventions of humble petitioning. The address sought common ground in patriotic rhetoric with its emphasis on the commonly held idea of Scotland as an ancient, undefeated kingdom.[30] The widespread use and adaptation of this standard text demonstrates the links between the Country party and local addressing. In total more than half of the locality addresses used the standard text or a version of it:[31]

To His Grace, Her Majesty's High Commissioner and [the] Right Honourable the Estates of Parliament, the Humble Address of _____

Humbly Sheweth,

That we, undersubscribing, have seen the articles of the Union agreed upon by the commissioners nominated in behalf of Scotland, and the commissioners nominated in behalf of England, in which they have agreed that Scotland and England shall be united in one kingdom, and that the united kingdom shall be represented in one and the same Parliament. And seeing it does evidently appear to us that such an incorporating union as contained in these articles is contrary to the honour, fundamental laws and constitutions of this kingdom, Claim of Right and rights and privileges of the barons and freeholders and burrows of this kingdom and church, as by

---

[29] NAS, PA 7/20/18, repr. in 'Scotland's ruine', 151–3.
[30] Kidd, Subverting Scotland's past, 24–5.
[31] Bowie, 'Scottish public opinion', appendix H.

laws established, and that the same is destructive to the true interest of the nation.

Therefore, we humbly beseech your grace and Honourable Estates, and do confidently expect, that you will not allow of any such incorporating union, but that you will support and preserve entire the soveraignty and independency of this crown and kingdom, and the rights and privileges of Parliament, which have been so valiantly maintained by our heroick ancestors for the space of two thousand years, that the same may be transmitted to succeeding generations as they have been conveyed to us. And we will heartily concur with you for supporting and maintaining our soveraignty and independency and church government with our lives and fortunes, conform to the established laws of the nation.[32]

Aided by the supply of a standard text, addresses tended to appear from territories associated with Country party nobles. The particular influence of the duke of Hamilton and his family and followers can be seen in the concentration in Lanarkshire of over one-third of the seventy-nine locality addresses. In a letter to Robert Harley, Daniel Defoe complained that the 'worst people are about Hamilton and that Side of the Country, and principally because they ... are Dayly Deluded by the party of that family'.[33] The family could not simply command the shire heritors, as indicated by the apparent failure of Hamilton Sheriff-Depute Andrew Hay of Craignethan to secure instructions against the treaty from the shire's Michaelmas head court.[34] Nevertheless, the family's influence, combined with the activism of Robert Wylie and his clerical associates, ensured a strong presence for Lanarkshire localities among the addresses. A number of them used the party text, including the burgh and parish of Rutherglen and a group of fourteen parishes led by Wylie's Hamilton parish.[35] Another group of ten parishes shared a common text found in the papers of the Hamilton of Dalzell family.[36] The gentlemen addressing in the name of the shire of Lanark used their own text, though their petitioning process was instigated by Anne, duchess of Hamilton, at her son's request.[37]

Hamilton influence also reached into nearby Renfrewshire, where the teenaged John Cochrane, 4th earl of Dundonald and nephew of the duke of Hamilton, headed the subscriptions to an address from the shire using the

32 'Scotland's ruine', 149.
33 Letters of Daniel Defoe, 183.
34 NAS, GD 406/1/9731.
35 The Hamilton group of parishes included Biggar, Blantyre, Carmichael and Pettinain, Carnwath, Carstairs, Covington, Crawford, Crawfordjohn, Dunsyre, Glasgow Barony, Liberton, Quothquan and Symington: Bowie, 'Scottish public opinion', appendix F.
36 North Lanarkshire Council Archives, Motherwell, USC 052. This group included Avendale, Bothwell, Cambusnethan, Dalserf, East Monkland, Kilbride, Lesmahago, Old Monkland Shotts and Stonehouse (Archibald Foyer's parish): Bowie, 'Scottish public opinion', appendix F.
37 NAS, GD 406/1/9744.

Country party text.[38] Dundonald held lands in Renfrewshire, Ayrshire and Lanarkshire, including the lordship of the town of Paisley and the barony of Douglas.[39] Local clergy supported the generation of petitions from Dundonald's areas of influence as indicated by the signature of the minister Thomas Browne on an address from Paisley and the signing of a petition from the parish of Douglas at the church.[40] In addition, Dundonald was in communication with his father's cousin, John Cochrane of Waterside in Ayrshire, a former Bothwell Bridge rebel, who collected signatures on an address from Ayrshire. Cochrane's address had the support of John Brisbane the younger, of Bishoptoun, an anti-union commissioner for Ayrshire, though it was not presented to parliament for reasons discussed below.[41]

In addition to the Hamiltons, other prominent oppositional nobles also encouraged addresses against the treaty from their areas of territorial influence. The duke of Atholl appears to have coordinated a set of addresses from Perthshire and western Fife. The Atholl family's lands, including their estate in Falkland, were based in these shires of which the duke was hereditary sheriff.[42] A note on the back of the burgh of Falkland's address states that it was presented to parliament by the duke of Atholl. The Atholl petitions were joined by a pair from several Perthshire parishes associated with the Jacobite earl of Errol.[43] The Atholl and Errol addresses all used the Country party text with the addition of a legal argument citing particular parliamentary acts as bars to incorporation. The duke of Atholl made the same legal points in parliament in a formal protest on 4 November 1706.[44]

The marquis of Annandale also seems to have organised a group of three addresses from the Annandale area, including the stewartry of Annandale and the royal burghs of Annan and Lochmaben.[45] These all used a text that echoed parts of the party address while expressing a willingness for union with England on 'all Warrs, Treaties and Allyances. ... And for securing the Protestane Succession of both kingdoms against all Popish pretenders'.[46] This argument can also be found in a resolve presented to parliament by the marquis on 4 November 1706. This proposed that, in place of the treaty, either a new union be negotiated to cover matters of 'Succession, Warrs, Alliances and

---

38 NAS, PA 7/28/19 Renfrewshire.
39 Sir James Balfour Paul, *The Scots peerage*, Edinburgh 1904, iii. 352–4.
40 NAS, PA 7/28/79 Paisley, 67 Douglas.
41 NAS, GD 406/1/5439, 5370.
42 Leah Leneman, *Living in Atholl: a social history of the estates, 1685–1785*, Edinburgh 1986, 13.
43 The Atholl group is NAS, PA 7/28/16–18 Perthshire, 32 Dysart, 33 Falkland. The Errol group is PA 7/28/69 Errol, Kilspindie, Kinnaird, Inchture, Longforgan, St Madoes & Kinfauns, 58 Caputh, Lethandy, Alyth & Kinloch.
44 NAS, PA 7/20/16.
45 NAS, PA 7/28/3 Annandale, 23 Annan, 42 Lochmaben.
46 NAS, PA 7/28/3 Annandale.

Trade' or the Hanoverian succession be settled with limitations.[47] A connection between these addresses and the marquis is further indicated by his role as provost of Lochmaben.[48] The physical nature of the stewartry's document also suggests that blank copies of the address were provided to locations in Annandale from a central source, as the paper appears to be a manuscript form with the name of the stewartry written onto the document in a different hand and ink.

An assessment of the locality addresses by estate reveals the influence of Country party coordination most clearly at the shire level. Of fifteen shires addressing, thirteen used the party text, though some amended it to emphasise trading or religious concerns.[49] This adherence coincides with a strong presence of oppositional commissioners in addressing shires. In fourteen of the fifteen addressing shires at least half of the shire members voted against the treaty, with only one petitioning shire having a Court majority (Roxburghshire).[50] Party influence in the shires is confirmed by the use of the party text in five of eight addressing towns. As burghs of barony and regality, these towns had stronger connections with local nobles and barons than the royal burghs. All the addressing towns were situated in shires with significant Country party affiliations among their baron commissioners and local nobles.

Only about half of the twenty-three addressing royal burghs had Country party commissioners, but the opposition was able to use the Convention of Royal Burghs as a forum for the organisation of resistance to the treaty. This is best seen in Stirling where the burgh's commissioner to parliament and the convention, Lt Col. John Erskine, followed Court obligations to vote for union but was active in the convention against the treaty. Erskine provided the address text used by the convention and organised another address from his burgh against the treaty.[51] Three royal burghs used the national text of the Convention for their local address, including the burgh of Glasgow where the deacons of trade organised an independent address without the support of the town council. In addition, twelve burghs used the Country party text.[52]

The burghs were more likely than the shires to advance economic and religious objections to the treaty. Many burghs echoed the Convention's concerns about higher taxes and the risks of free trade. Some forecast the ruin of local industries, as in Dunbar where higher salt duties were expected to destroy the

---

47 NAS, PA 7/20/15. See also 'Scotland's ruine', 162–3.
48 The Lochmaben court and council book, 1612–1721, ed. John B. Wilson, Edinburgh 2001, 241.
49 Bowie, 'Scottish public opinion', appendix H.
50 Roxburghshire's address may have been the work of the shire's sole anti-incorporation commissioner, Sir Gilbert Elliot of Minto. Though usually a court follower, Elliot chose to oppose the treaty on religious grounds: Manuscripts of the earl of Mar, 315.
51 Convention records, iv. 399–400; Letters of Daniel Defoe, 153. As an army officer, Erskine had professional obligations to the earl of Mar, the governor of Stirling Castle.
52 Bowie, 'Scottish public opinion', appendices G, H.

herring trade, while others condemned the economics of incorporation in more general terms, as in Perth's emphasis on 'Intollerable Taxes and Impositions'.[53] Alongside economic complaints, burghs also stressed the threat presented by incorporation to the Presbyterian Church and asked parliament to take steps to secure the Protestant succession. The Country party text had taken a soft line on the Church and the succession to maintain the party's coalition of Jacobite and Hanoverian interests, but many burghs emphasised their concern for Presbyterian government and a Protestant crown.

The inclusion of religious concerns in many burgh petitions reflects the influence of activist clergy and parishioners at the local level. The sentiments of many clergy are reflected in a letter to a baillie of Glasgow from Robert Wodrow. In early November 1706 Wodrow wrote to urge the town council to address against the treaty, stating that he and others 'wonder very much that there is noo application from such a place as Glasgow to the parliament ... I am satisfyed that our all is at the stake nou, and if some appearance be not made ... when there is room for addressing, the presbiterian party may Repent it'.[54] In Glasgow, the minister James Clark of the Tron church (author of a pamphlet against the treaty, *Scotland's speech to her sons*) used a sermon to remind his listeners 'how forward Glasgow used to be in the Honest Cause'. He urged them not just to pray, but to be 'valiant for the City of our GOD'. The next day a crowd of Glaswegians supported the city's deacons of trade as they initiated an independent address against the treaty.[55]

Clerical activism became even more important in the parish and presbytery addresses. Key agitators included Robert Wylie, close associate of the duke of Hamilton and author of pamphlets against toleration and union; Archibald Foyer of Stonehouse parish in Hamilton presbytery, the author of pamphlets on Darien and union, including one burned by the hangman in December 1706; John Ballantyne of Lanark parish in Lanark presbytery, also an author of pamphlets against toleration and union; and Thomas Linning of Lesmahagow parish in Lanark presbytery, a former leader of the Cameronians who came into the established Church at the 1690 settlement. These clergymen can be connected with the pressure for addressing seen in the Commission of the General Assembly. According to George Baillie of Jerviswood, Wylie led a 'squadron' of oppositional ministers on the commission.[56] Both Ballantyne and Linning were known as firebrands on the commission, while Wylie and Foyer had been connected with Country agitations on the commission since the 1690s.[57]

With addresses from the presbyteries of Hamilton, Lanarkshire and Dunblane, oppositional clergymen sought to reinforce the objections raised in the commission's second address of 8 November. Dunblane expressed

53 NAS, PA 7/28/30 Dunbar, 44 Perth.
54 Wodrow quarto xl, item 12.
55 Defoe, *History of the union*, 59–63; NAS, PA 7/28/34 Glasgow.
56 *Jerviswood correspondence*, 167.
57 '*Scotland's ruine*', 155; *Letters of Daniel Defoe*, 152.

its wish to 'concurr' with the 'severall faithfull and seasonable Addresses and Representations of our brethren in the Commission of the General Assembly'. Lanark presbytery's address pointed to several concerns in the Church's second address 'of which there is no Notice taken in the Act of Security for the Church', while Hamilton insisted that the second address expressed 'a full unanimity therein amongst the Ministers of this National Church'. Moreover, Hamilton demanded that 'no Incorporating Union with England may be concluded until Her Majestie shall be pleased to call the General Assembly of this Church; Which ... hath an undoubted Right to be consulted'.[58]

The presbyteries stressed the danger represented by popular discontent with the treaty. Hamilton stated that 'tho hither to we have endeavoured to keep them [our parishioners] from breaking out, yet the Ferment and Dissatisfaction doth so increase amongst all that we are Justly afraid of what these things may turn into'. If parliament were to approve the proposed union, Lanark feared 'the fatal consequences thereof', the treaty having created 'such a ferment'. Hamilton explained that this ferment had been caused by popular fears that incorporation would incur 'the Guilt of National perjury' against the Covenants. Similarly, the clergy of Lanark saw the treaty as 'Contrarie To our known principles and Covenants' and Dunblane described it as that which 'we cannot goe in without guilt before God in a manifest breach of our Solemn Covenants'.[59]

Activist ministers tried to recruit more presbyteries to address, but were more successful in generating petitions from their parishes.[60] Twenty-two parish petitions came from Hamilton, Lanark and Dunblane presbyteries, accounting for nearly three-quarters of the thirty parish addresses (excluding parishes petitioning with their burgh). Of the fourteen parishes in Hamilton presbytery, thirteen addressed, as did ten of the eleven parishes in Lanark presbytery.[61] In Dunblane, where there were fewer identifiable Country clergy, nine of the presbytery's twelve ministers subscribed the presbytery address but only the eastern parishes of Logie and Tulliallan addressed in their own right.[62]

As a group, the parish addresses reveal a complex combination of influences. Parishes were not just units of the national Church but local administrative centres in which clergy worked with heritors and elders to manage public services like schooling and poor relief according to parliamentary regulations. In addition, though local elites no longer controlled the patronage of clerical posts, noble families still had strong ties to some parishes. As a result,

58 NAS, PA 7/20/28 Lanark presbytery, 49 Dunblane presbytery, 50 Hamilton presbytery.
59 Ibid.
60 Wodrow quarto lxxiii, fos 271, 277–8.
61 Bowie, 'Scottish public opinion', appendix F.
62 NAS, PA 7/28/75 Logie, 83 Tulliallan.

local power relations influenced the balance of religious and secular concerns in parish addresses. While sharing a common demand for a Protestant Britain in which the Scottish Church and parliament would be preserved, parish addresses ran the gamut from standard Country party statements to florid Covenanting outbursts. Half of the parish addresses used a form of the Country party text, while a group of four parishes from Glen Ken in Galloway used the Convention of Royal Burghs' text.[63] Two sets of Perthshire parishes, where Presbytery was less well established, used a variant of a Country party text associated with the duke of Atholl and earl of Errol that did not emphasise the Church. In contrast, parishes from Lanarkshire and Stirlingshire highlighted religious concerns. These included a group of Lanarkshire parishes led by Avendale that shared a text asserting their interest in 'ane honourable and safe unione, with England, consisting with the being, and Civill Libertyes of this Ancient Kingdom. ... And Consisting with our Covenanted work of Reformatione'.[64] Another group of parishes, led by Hamilton, advanced the constitutional arguments of the Country party text with added complaints about bishops in the British parliament. This group also demanded that any union 'consist with our Glorious work of Reformation According to our Nationall Covenant'.[65] In its own unique text, the parish of Cambuslang went further in declaring that the treaty would 'subvert the present established government of our church ... strip her of her intrinsick pouer and liberties ... bury our most glorious covenanted work of reformation [in] ... an intire inslaving of our church and Nation. ... yea no more to be a church and Nation, but a poor contemptible antiquated colonie'.[66]

The emphasis on the Covenants in many of the parish addresses indicates the degree of grass-roots Covenanting spirit remaining within many parishes of south-west Scotland. A petition from the Hebronites, a separatist coalition of praying societies concentrated in Dumfriesshire, Galloway, Ayrshire and Lanarkshire, gave full voice to this spirit. From 'a Considerable body of People in the South & Western Shyres', it matched the second address of the Commission of the General Assembly in its complaints on the presence of bishops in the parliament, English oaths and sacramental tests. In addition, the Hebronites emphasised their dedication to the vision of British union established by the Solemn League and Covenant, rejecting incorporation with 'a Nation deeply guilty of Many National Abominations, who have openly broke and burnt their Covenant with God and league with us, entred into, in the Year 1643'.[67]

Moreover, the Hebronites denied the legitimacy of a union treaty forced through parliament and indicated their willingness to take action to stop

63 Bowie, 'Scottish public opinion', appendix H; NAS, PA 7/28/70 Glen Ken.
64 NAS, PA 7/28/50 Avendale.
65 NAS, PA 7/28/71 Hamilton.
66 NAS, PA 7/28/56 Cambuslang.
67 NAS, PA 7/28/22 Southern and Western Shires.

the union. While the Country party text promised that subscribers would 'concur' with parliament in 'supporting and maintaining our soveraignty and independency and church government with our lives and fortunes, conform to the established laws of the nation', the Hebronites failed to mention the restraints of law in their promise to 'stand by such noble patriots with life and fortune, as are for the Maintinance and defence of the Nations independencie and freedome, and of this Churches just power and proper privileges conform to our Attained reformation from 1638 to 1649'.[68] A shared desire to dissent from a unionist parliament can be seen in the petition of the parishes of Glen Ken, which added a formal protest against the passage of an incorporating union to the Convention of Royal Burghs' text.[69] A few other parishes also suggested that they were ready to take independent action. According to Bothwell, both natural and statutory law required resistance to the treaty of union.[70]

The assertiveness of these addresses, including that of Hamilton presbytery which 'narrowly escap'd in parliament being censur'd as seditious and being burnt by the Hangman', strained the conventions of humble petitioning.[71] To be effective, addresses had to convince parliament of a strong consensus against the treaty without resorting to overt intimidation. This required a fine balance in wording and presentation not always achieved by the petitioners. While the inclusion of many signatures supported the portrayal of unanimity, large numbers of participants also suggested a dangerously activist public. Many addressers tried to contain this contradiction by arranging signatures in a social hierarchy. The seniority of the first signatures lent stature to the petition, backed by a long tail of ordinary people. In Ayrshire, for example, the organisers of a petition declined to sign it first, believing 'our names to[o] mean to begin sutch a work'.[72]

Many of the locality petitions provided significant numbers of signatories to reinforce their addresses. The fifteen petitions from the shires included four with signatures numbering between 900 and 2,000 and three between 300 and 700, with the remaining eight having less than 200. While many names on the shire addresses indicated a landed status, the larger petitions included numerous rural artisans, cottars and servants. Among the thirty-one burghs and towns, most petitions contained between 100 and 400 signatures. Three collected more than 500 signatures while eight offered less than 100. Burgh signatures indicated the participation of a wide range of social levels, from merchants and professionals to unskilled workers. Parishes delivered similar numbers of signatures with most gathering between 100 and 300 adherents. A few collected more than 500, but these tended to include several parishes

68 Ibid.
69 NAS, PA 7/28/70 Glen Ken.
70 NAS, PA 7/28/53 Bothwell.
71 *Letters of Daniel Defoe*, 187.
72 NAS, GD 406/1/5439.

addressing together.[73] Rough hands and X or initial marks for illiterates appeared more often in parish and burgh addresses. In some localities parish elders and notaries public signed for those who could not.[74]

Alongside these attempts to communicate corporate unanimity, addresses also reinforced their legitimacy by declaring their liberty to petition. Though the Convention of Royal Burghs could claim a traditional privilege to petition parliament on behalf of its estate, its address reinforced this by reminding parliament of the 'priviledge of all subjects to petition' secured by the Claim of Right.[75] This argument was repeated by a number of other localities besides those using the Convention's text. The address of the 'merchants, Deacons trads and other Inhabitants of the Burgh of Air' began with the words 'That as by the claim of right all subjects are allowed the priviledge of petitioning So at this junctur… Wee cannot be silent'.[76] The Hamilton parish group amended the Country party text to justify their supplication on the authority of the Claim of Right, while the texts used by the shire of Lanark and the Avendale group of parishes also made reference to the protections of the Claim of Right. Airth, Larbert, Dunipace and Denny parishes went beyond the 'particular allowance' of the Claim of Right to posit a 'naturall right of all subjects to represent their grievances'.[77]

The arrival of dozens of locality addresses in parliament from 1 November 1706 onwards provided ammunition for Country party speakers in their attempts to block the passage of the treaty. The addresses reinforced grievances raised by the Commission of the General Assembly and the Convention of Royal Burghs, and provided grounds for assertions of widespread anti-unionism. In mid-November the party began to use the addresses to justify calls for direct communication with the queen. On 15 November the duke of Hamilton craved a recess so that the queen's commissioner could inform her of 'the general aversion of the nation, appearing by the multitude of Addresses presented'.[78] Lord Belhaven supported this with a speech referring to the 'the general Aversation that appears by the Addresses from the severall shires of the Kingdom'.[79] The address of the presbytery of Hamilton, delivered on 11 December, also asked for an address to the queen to request a settlement of the Protestant succession instead of incorporating union.[80]

The opposition reinforced the shift towards a national address to the queen by inviting addressers to come to Edinburgh in December to demand answers to their petitions and to sign such an address.[81] Party organisers hoped that

73 Bowie, 'Scottish public opinion', appendix I.
74 NAS, PA 7/28/65 Culross, 31 Dunfermline.
75 NAS, PA 7/20/18.
76 NAS, PA 7/28/25 Ayr (2).
77 NAS, PA 7/28/49 Airth.
78 Hume of Crossrigg, *Diary*, 183; APS xi. 325.
79 Belhaven, *Speech, 15th November 1706*, 1706, 6.
80 NAS, PA 7/20/50 Hamilton.
81 'Scotland's ruine', 184.

'This sudden filling of the toun ... tho in a peaceful manner [would] perswade the court to consider the addresses better than they have done.'[82] A text for a national address was drafted citing the 'almost universal aversion to this treaty' and entreating the queen to call a new parliament.[83] On 7 January 1707 the duke of Atholl used the locality addresses to reinforce a fresh protest demanding an address to the queen for a new parliament, summarising the oppositional stance on constituent powers and the authority of public opinion:

> the present Representatives of the Barons & Burrows in Parliament to offer by any vote or deed of theirs to incapacit their Constituents or deprive them of any part of their inherent right is that which their Constituents may and do justly disallow. ... And since it evidently appears from the multitudes of Addresses and Petitions from the several parts of this Kingdome of the Barons Freeholders Heritors Burrows and Commons and from the Commission of the General Assemblie that there is a generall dislike and aversion to the incorporating Union as contained in these Articles. ... I do therfor further Protest against concluding this and the following articles of this Treaty untill her Majestie shall be fully informed of the Inclinations of her People That if her Majestie think fit she may call a new Parliament to have the immediat Sentiments of the Nation.[84]

Also in January, the duke of Hamilton made plans for his followers to propose the Hanoverian succession as an alternative to incorporation and, if this were refused, to make a formal protest, abandon the house and submit a national address to the queen.[85] Hamilton's draft act of settlement referred to the 'many pregnant evidences' showing that the proposed union was 'disagreeable to the generality of this Nation'.[86] Similarly, his draft protest, possibly written by Lord Advocate James Stewart of Goodtrees, argued that parliamentary representatives could not vote for the constitutional changes contained in the treaty without 'express power and warrant for that effect from the constituent'. It also pointed to the 'utter aversion' to incorporation shown by parliamentary protests, addresses from the Commission of the General Assembly, the Convention of Royal Burghs, presbyteries and 'an unprecedented number of addresses subscribed by the generality of the freeholders, magistrates and burgesses'.[87]

By gathering petitioners in Edinburgh and planning a national address, the Country party played on the threat of mass disaffection implied by the locality addresses. As the addresses arrived in parliament, Country speakers had reminded the government of this danger. In a resolution of 4 November,

---

82 Wodrow quarto lxxiii, fo. 276.
83 'Scotland's ruine', 185–6.
84 APS xi. 387.
85 'Scotland's ruine', 188–9.
86 NAS, GD 406/1/7855.
87 'Scotland's ruine', 189–93.

the marquis of Annandale pointed out that since 'this Nation seems generally averse to this incorporating Union', it was probable that the treaty would 'creat such dismall distractions and animosities amongst ourselves and such jealousies and mistakes betwixt us and our Neighbours as would involve these Nations into fatal breaches and confusions'.[88] Similarly, in a speech on 15 November, the duke of Hamilton spoke of his fears of domestic troubles and even civil war in the event of an incorporating union.[89] Referring to the locality addresses, he suggested the possibility of a freeholder rising: 'Shall we yield up the sovereignty and independency of the nation, when we are commanded by those we represent to preserve the same, and assured of their assistance to support us?'[90] Hamilton's draft act of settlement and national address warned that incorporation was more likely to divide than unite the two countries and his draft protest highlighted the 'threatning disorders and dangers' reflected in the many addresses against the treaty.[91]

Wielding the pressure of addresses and instructions, the Country party consistently argued that parliament could not approve the treaty without the consent of its constituents. After first demanding recesses for consultation and attempting to influence commissioners with instructions from the country, the party used addresses to prove a national aversion to the union. The party did its best to slow down parliamentary proceedings to allow sufficient time for the organisation of addresses from national and local bodies. Oppositional activists helped to secure addresses against the treaty from the Church and the Convention of Royal Burghs, providing a rhetorical framework for some localities to follow. A standard party text and the encouragement of local leaders further stimulated the production of addresses from shires, burghs and parishes. Though presented as the humble petitions of corporate bodies, these addresses raised the possibility of violent resistance to the treaty, shaking the confidence of some pro-unionists. On 14 November, Sir David Nairne, Secretary-Depute in London, wrote to the earl of Mar that 'coffee house company, begin to droop or dispond to hear of soe much doeing against the Union without doors and soe litle for it'. At the same time, Mar was finding that addressing was shaking the confidence of some of his followers in Edinburgh.[92] These aggressive expressions of opinion could not be ignored, but the extent to which they would influence proceedings would depend on how the Court responded to this popular challenge.

[88] NAS, PA 7/20/15; 'Scotland's ruine', 162–3.
[89] Manuscripts of the earl of Mar, 323.
[90] 'Scotland's ruine', 160.
[91] NAS, GD 406/1/7855; 'Scotland's ruine', 185, 191.
[92] Manuscripts of the earl of Mar, 320, 312.

Court management of addresses

Court party leaders took firm steps against the opposition's assertions of public opinion by attacking the constitutional legitimacy of instructions and addresses and discouraging participation in locality addressing. Pointing to the organisational efforts of Country leaders, Court speakers and writers disparaged the addresses as the product of disaffection rather than the 'sense of the nation'. The Court party also highlighted the risks of democratic disorder as it took repressive actions against crowds of petitioners in Edinburgh. Alongside these efforts to reject and control expressions of opinion, however, government ministers made selected concessions on petitioned grievances to satisfy their followers in parliament and reduce extra-parliamentary dissatisfaction. The combined strategy of suppression and conciliation succeeded in confirming the Court's parliamentary majority and reducing oppositional pressure in the short term.

Early in the session, the queen's officers and their followers condemned public instructions as an innovation in Scottish parliamentary practices. Though from Lockhart of Carnwath's perspective it appeared that freeholders were 'denied the liberty of giving instructions to their representatives', the Court's view was that instructions were 'not much regarded' because 'Precedents in like Cases would not support the Practice.'[93] Court pamphlets supported this view by attacking the Country notion of constituent sovereignty. These included an assertion of parliamentary sovereignty by the earl of Cromarty, who argued that commissioners for shires and burghs were 'not Delegates, but true integrent Parts of the Sovereign Constituted Body, on whom the Supreme Sovereign Power is (not Delegate) but Devolved'.[94] As such, commissioners were not subject to the instructions of their constituents. At an individual level, those supporting the treaty refused to accept instructions from their electors. As the duke of Hamilton lamented on 1 November, 'instructions are sent into the members of parliament but they Laugh at there constituents'.[95] Those laughing included George Baillie of Jerviswood, a prominent member of the *squadrone volante* and one of four members for Lanarkshire, who 'would receve noe instructions from his constituents'.[96]

When locality addresses first arrived in parliament, the queen's managers tried to block their presentation. The earl of Marchmont termed them 'seditious' and the duke of Argyll dismissed them as 'for no other use than to make kites'. Ministers eventually allowed them to be read when Sir James Foulis of Colinton, a commissioner for the shire of Edinburgh, declared that 'he did not doubt but those that subscribed them would come and own them at the

93 'Scotland's ruine', 147; Defoe, History of the union, 22.
94 [Mackenzie], Friendly return, 29.
95 NAS, GD 406/1/8104.
96 NAS, GD 406/1/5294.

door of the house, and crave liberty to deliver them out of their own hands'.[97] On 6 November the Court party, led by the earl of Marchmont, the marquis of Tweeddale and the earls of Rothes and Roxburgh, tried again to block addresses on the grounds that they were no longer relevant, the first article of the treaty having been approved. They did not succeed in preventing the presentation of the address of the Convention of Royal Burghs, but when Sir John Houstoun of Houstoun, commissioner for Renfrewshire, presented his shire's address, he was abused in 'gros & scandalous' terms. Intimidated by the debate, William Baillie of Lamington, one of the commissioners for Lanarkshire, refused to present any of the Lanarkshire parish petitions in his possession. The duke of Hamilton took the Hamilton parish petition from Baillie to present himself and the duke of Atholl presented the address of the burgh of Falkland, but few others had the courage to present addresses that day.[98]

Alongside these attempts to discourage the presentation of addresses, Court managers began to place limits on parliament's response. No formal reply was given to any anti-treaty petitions except the first address of the Commission of the General Assembly, which had been cleared with the queen's commissioner and chancellor in advance.[99] Parliamentary minutes and diaries reveal that only the first few addresses were debated, most being read at the start of a day's session with no subsequent discussion.[100] The Court's success in downplaying the addresses can be seen in the earl of Mar's comment after the 6 November session: '[the] force of adresses are now very near over'.[101]

Though the Court managed to curtail discussion of individual petitions, Country speeches still pointed to the addresses as evidence of a public consensus against the treaty. In response, Court speakers undermined the claim of the addresses to represent 'the sense of the nation', describing them as the product of faction and Jacobite intrigue. Issues of coverage were highlighted, as on 1 November when 'it was Noted, that the Address from Mid-Lothian was signed by not above Twelve of the Gentlemen, or thereabout, tho' there were above Two Hundred Gentlemen in that County; And that therefore it seemed the Argument, of its being the Sense of the Nation, must be very ill Grounded'.[102] Similarly, an address from Lanarkshire was attacked for presenting itself as the voice of 'wee the Heritors' rather than the subscribing heritors.[103] Lay elders characterised the commission's second address as 'but the deed of a pack't club and not the general sense of the church of Scot-

97 'Scotland's ruine', 150–1.
98 NAS, GD 406/1/6013, 8107; Manuscripts of the earl of Mar, 314; APS xi. 315–16. The only other address that day came from Fife and was probably presented by the duke of Atholl.
99 APS xi. 307; NAS, CH 1/3/8 (232, 234).
100 Hume of Crossrigg, Diary; Defoe, History of the union, minutes, 48, 52.
101 Manuscripts of the earl of Mar, 314.
102 Defoe, History of the union, minutes, 24.
103 NAS, GD 406/1/8122.

land', while the earl of Mar contended that the locality addresses had been 'procured by people mostlie disafected to the Government'.[104]

These attacks also appeared in supporting propaganda. In his London *Review*, Daniel Defoe sought to 'undeceive those People, who are impos'd upon, to think that the universal cry of the People of Scotland is against the Union'. Defoe claimed that 'Gentlemen Barons and Freeholders have in very few Places been concern'd' with the addresses; in particular, 'of three hundred Gentlemen of Quality and Estates in Louthian, I have not heard of above five, that have joyn'd with these Addresses'. To attack the address of the Convention of Royal Burghs, Defoe asserted that the burghs voting for the address at the Convention contributed just 14 per cent of the tax paid by the burgh estate. Therefore, he argued, though a majority of burghs attending the convention had voted for the address, they were actually a small, self-interested faction and not the sense of the trading part of the nation.[105] For other addresses he claimed that 'when the Names have been examined, [they] are found to be all Jacobites and Episcopal Dissenters'. He also alleged that some signatories were 'oblig'd to sign by Rabble and Tumult' or were duped into signing by the Jacobites, for 'the whole interest of the Party, by Books, Pamphlets, Rabbles, Speeches, Emissaries, and what not, has been employ'd to incense the poor unthinking People in the Country against their own Happiness, and bring them in to address against their Governours'.[106]

In parliamentary speeches, Court speakers rejected any suggestion that commissioners were required to follow the expressed opinion of their electors. They refuted the argument that parliament did not have the power to alienate its constituents' rights by declaring that members 'had ample commissions to do all things for the good of the country'.[107] More specifically, Court supporters pointed out that the current parliament had been elected in 1702 under a crown agenda that included a closer union. This countered Country arguments that 'the Parliament could not ratify ane Union unless called expressly for that effect'.[108] When the Country party began to demand an address to the queen, the earl of Mar contended that 'if the Parliament shoul'd address the Queen for a recess upon the addresses from the countrie ... this was makeing the addressers the Parliament's masters'. Rather than following the stated will of the addressers, it was the responsibility of parliament to determine 'whither the addresers were in the right or not; if in the right to be of their opinion, and if in the wrong it was their duety to bring them out of the mistake'.[109]

Defoe reinforced these arguments in his sixth essay with a restatement of traditional petitioning conventions of humility and deference. Defoe

104 Wodrow quarto lxxiii, fo. 271; *Manuscripts of the earl of Mar*, 323.
105 The same argument is noted by Lord Crossrigg: *Diary*, 180.
106 Daniel Defoe, *Review*, nos 141 (Tues. 26 Nov. 1706) and 147 (Tues. 10 Dec. 1706).
107 'Scotland's ruine', 142.
108 *Manuscripts of the earl of Mar*, 273.
109 Ibid. 324.

conceded 'the undoubted Right of the People ... to present their Grievances to their respective Authorities, be it King or Parliament' and allowed that representatives had a duty to consider these grievances. However, given that a 'Petition is in its Nature a Prayer, a Begging or Entreating' and that the Scottish addresses contained 'all manner of Insolencies, Scandals, Reproaches and unjust Assertions', he considered that the parliament had been 'over and above, regardful of their Duty, for that they have received such Addresses, containing such Insulting of their Authority'. Having read them, the parliament was under no obligation to agree with them – otherwise, 'it is no more an Address or Petition, but a Precept or Mandamus, the People signing it are no more Addressers, Petitioners or Desirers, but Directors and Preceptors, and the whole Scale of Order inverts to Democracy and Confusion'.[110]

When freeholders began to gather in Edinburgh to demand answers to their petitions, the Court party reasserted traditional restrictions on addressing to defuse this attempt to escalate the addressing campaign. A proclamation of 27 December 1706 denied that parliament had any obligation to reply to addresses and banned meetings of petitioners in Edinburgh. The proclamation declared that 'the good subjects of our ancient Kingdom ought to rest assured and contented That... our Estates of Parliament have and will proceed in that matter [of the union] with all due regaird and tenderness to the honour and interest of this our ancient Kingdom, both as to their civil and religious concerns'.[111]

Throughout the parliamentary session, Court discourse condemned the opposition's populist methods as dangerous and misleading. Addresses were portrayed as the product of 'underhand dealings... whereby the meaner sort were imposed upon and deluded'.[112] This stance reflected the Court party's ongoing rejection of popular participation in national affairs. As in earlier years, the party did not react to oppositional addresses with counter-addresses. In response to complaints from London on the lack of pro-treaty petitions, the earl of Mar stated that 'we thought it better to lett them allone'.[113] Pro-union addresses offered by expatriate Scots in London were rejected, though the earl of Mar thought that they might be useful in private discussions.[114] An isolated attempt to generate a petition from the burgh of Ayr showed the Court party that such efforts might do more damage than good as its small address was answered with an anti-treaty address signed by more than 1,000 merchants, tradesmen and inhabitants.[115]

Instead of generating counter-addresses, the Court party discouraged

[110] Defoe, *Two great questions considered*, 5, 7, 12.
[111] APS xi. 372.
[112] '*Scotland's ruine*', 147.
[113] *Manuscripts of the earl of Mar*, 328.
[114] Ibid. 312, 316, 320, 326, 330–1. A letter from London to the duke of Hamilton suggests that a pro-union address may have been published in London in the name of Scots residing in England and the English colonies: NAS, GD 406/1/11787.
[115] '*Scotland's ruine*', 148; NAS, PA 7/28/25 Ayr (2).

addressing from areas under its influence. In the Commission of the General Assembly, the efforts of pro-treaty elders and clergy resulted in a moderate first address accepted by Court managers as necessary to neutralise Presbyterian fears of union. Before submitting the commission's petition to parliament, William Carstares, the earls of Glasgow and Rothes and others delivered copies to the queen's commissioner, the duke of Queensberry, and her chancellor, the earl of Seafield. Both received the address 'very kindly and told them they did not doubt but what was therein Craven would be obtained'.[116]

Court party control of the Commission eroded in late October and early November as activist clergy and Country party elders pressed for further petitions to parliament. This included demands for a petition to parliament for a national fast on the union, which would have contributed to the Country party's efforts to organise addresses in the localities. A compromise for a day of prayer at the discretion of the presbyteries was secured at a very large meeting of the commission that included William Carstares, the earl of Marchmont, Lord President of the Court of Session Hew Dalrymple and Lord Justice Clerk Adam Cockburn of Ormiston.[117] Soon after, the Court party failed to stop a second, more assertive petition brought to parliament from the commission on 8 November.[118] To reduce the legitimacy of this address, Court elders protested against it in the commission and in parliament. These protesters included the earl of Marchmont, the earl of Rothes and George Baillie of Jerviswood.[119]

Court party supporters also worked to reduce local petitioning. In Glasgow, the provost refused to allow an address from the burgh but had to flee to Edinburgh when a crowd rose up to support an independent address organised by several deacons of trade. The earl of Mar recommended that the provost be compensated with £100 for his trouble.[120] The government was more successful in Edinburgh, where the town council set aside an address signed by 'many thousands' when the queen's ministers threatened to relocate parliament and the law courts to Stirling.[121] Similarly, the earls of Loudoun, Stair and Glasgow managed to prevent the submission of an address from the shire of Ayr.[122] Their influence appears to have overcome efforts by John Cochrane of Waterside in east Ayrshire to generate an address with the encouragement of the earl of Dundonald and John Brisbane the younger of Bishoptoun, an

---

116 NAS, CH 1/3/8 (232–4).
117 NAS, CH 1/3/8 (236–51); *Manuscripts of the earl of Mar*, 296–7.
118 NAS, CH 1/3/8(249).
119 Clerk of Penicuik, *History of the union*, 119; Defoe, *History of the union*, appendix, pt II, 16–17.
120 *Manuscripts of the earl of Mar*, 326.
121 'Scotland's ruine', 148; *Manuscripts of the earl of Mar*, 316.
122 'Scotland's ruine', 148.

anti-treaty commissioner for Ayrshire.[123] Persuasion by the dukes of Argyll and Queensberry, the earl of Seafield and others seems to have prevented addressing from the Highlands and limited it in Dumfriesshire, Galloway and the Borders.[124]

Though the court managed to reduce addressing from its areas of influence, enough addresses came to parliament to affect voting patterns. In early November, as the first wave of locality petitions arrived, the Court party lost several voters due to 'the addresses and the humour that's now in the country against the Union'.[125] This forced the queen's officers to recognise the need to grant concessions on selected grievances in order to win back followers and calm popular concerns. As the earl of Mar explained to Lord Halifax in England, 'we found it was impossible to carry it in Parliament without explanations'.[126] Along with an act for the security of the Church, amendments on trade and taxation were contemplated.[127]

Court leaders had already given an encouraging response to the first petition of the Commission of the General Assembly. In turn, parliament declared that 'before concluding the Union they would take the said Address to their consideration and would do every thing necessary for securing the true Protestant Religion and Church Government presently established by law in this kingdom'. On 4 November an overture for an Act for Security of the Protestant Religion was introduced after the first article of the treaty had been approved.[128] Though opponents pursued 'many additional clauses for its [the Church's] better security', they were blocked by 'the earl of Marchmont, the Justice Clerk, and others'.[129] The act's passage on 12 November satisfied the concerns of many Presbyterians and reduced clerical opposition at the parish level.[130] While many clerics thought that the Scots confession of faith allowed the Church to petition the state 'in cases extraordinary', some feared that continued petitioning by presbyteries would set a dangerous precedent for schismatic practices in the Church.[131] For moderate clergy, the Act for Security of the Protestant Religion sufficed as the government's response to the Church's humble petitions.[132]

In a similar fashion the address of the Convention of Royal Burghs, supported by other petitions as well as pamphlets and speeches, spurred the

---

[123] NAS, GD 406/1/5439, 5370.
[124] Exceptions include Roxburghshire, the burghs of Ayr, Kirkcudbright and New Galloway, four Glen Ken parishes in Galloway and the town of Maybole with several nearby parishes in Ayrshire.
[125] *Manuscripts of the earl of Mar*, 312.
[126] Ibid. 342.
[127] Clerk of Penicuik, *History of the union*, 118; *Manuscripts of the earl of Mar*, 330, 342.
[128] APS xi. 307, 315.
[129] 'Scotland's ruine', 163.
[130] Ibid. 155.
[131] Wodrow quarto xl, item 13.
[132] Defoe, *History of the union*, 53.

Court party to negotiate amendments on the treaty's trade and tax provisions. Widespread complaints about higher customs and excise taxes, backed by rioting in Edinburgh, led to temporary duty exemptions for domestic salt and malt and an adjustment to the excise on Scottish ale. The explanation on two-penny ale was expected to 'please the country here extreamly, and it was impossible to for us to carry this article without it'.[133] Amendments to protect grain producers included a premium on exported oatmeal and the continuation of Scottish prohibitions on the import of Irish victuals. Other issues raised by the burghs were also considered. Pressed by a petition from Bo'ness and proposals from the 'Committee of the Burrows', the specifications in article V with regard to ownership of British shipping were loosened.[134] In addition, article VIII was amended to include a drawback on the export of barrels of salted herring to accommodate higher duties on foreign salt.[135] Dunbar had addressed against these duties, asserting that the proposed rates would 'absolutely destroy the trade of fishing And particularlie the herring fishing, which is all the trade wee have'.[136] The town's address had been supported by a further petition from 'the salt owners, fishers of Herring & Whyte fish and others who make use of Scots salt'.[137]

Throughout the parliamentary debates of 1706–7, the Court party asserted the sovereignty of parliament over the people, arguing that parliamentarians should be trusted to protect Scottish interests. This rejection of the authority of public opinion, as represented by instructions and addresses, was consistent with the government's response to adversarial addressing from 1699. Disdaining popular participation in Scottish politics, Court managers discouraged addressing in the localities, dismissed it in parliament and argued against it in print. Nevertheless, the massive scale of the addressing campaign, in which dozens of locality addresses joined national petitions from the Church and the Convention of Royal Burghs, forced the Court to make key concessions on issues of religion and trade to buttress its majority and reduce public pressure on parliament.

---

[133] *Manuscripts of the earl of Mar*, 337.
[134] NAS, PA 7/28/27 Bo'ness; Hume of Crossrigg, *Diary*, 185; APS xi. 334–5.
[135] APS xi. 358–60.
[136] NAS, PA 7/28/20 Dunbar.
[137] APS xi. 359. The amendments can be seen in Whatley, *Bought and sold for English gold?*, appendix 6.

7

Crowds and Collective Resistance to the Treaty

Crowds, like the anti-incorporation addresses, have been interpreted since 1707 as either the voice of the people or as the product of elite, particularly Jacobite, manipulation.[1] This study has suggested that the role of the crowd in the early modern public sphere was more complex. Collective protests against national policy represented local opinion rooted in real grievances, shaped by political communications and often mobilised by party elites. In south-west Scotland a strong grass-roots Presbyterian culture created conditions for local action linked to national political affairs, while the availability of political information in and around Edinburgh made crowd activity in the capital more likely. Oppositional leaders tended to appropriate state rituals in organised protests to provide a form of legitimacy for these events, but more spontaneous rioting could erupt against those seen to threaten or betray local interests. Though the association of crowds with uncontrolled violence reduced their political legitimacy, protesting or rioting crowds could wield significant influence and force the government to make short-term concessions in the interests of stability.

Crowd activity in 1706–7 followed patterns seen in 1699–1705, but on a larger scale. From the summer of 1706, a wave of pamphlets, sermons, speeches and petitions brought awareness of the union treaty and its potential threat to particular interests to many ordinary subjects in the Lowlands. In response, anti-incorporation crowds appeared in Edinburgh, Glasgow, Stirling and Dumfries. In addition, Country party leaders in Edinburgh sought to organise collective action to support their attempts to defeat the treaty with negative public opinion. These included local musters of the Protestant militia, gatherings of petitioners in Edinburgh and initial moves towards an armed rising. Despite Country attempts to portray these mass actions as the voice of the people, Court party leaders were able to condemn and suppress most of these as illegal and dangerous. The ongoing threat of disorder, however, exerted pressure on the government and its following in parliament, encouraging modifications of the treaty to appease parliamentary and public concerns.

---

[1] 'Scotland's ruine', 143–4; Defoe, History of the union, 18, 21; Ferguson, Scotland's relations, 255; Riley, Union of England and Scotland, 226.

Riots and demonstrations

Crowd activities first emerged in Edinburgh in October as gatherings associated with the duke of Hamilton turned from demonstrations of popular support to open rioting against governmental figures. Riots and aggressive crowds continued to appear in Edinburgh through November in response to the progress of the treaty in parliament. Rioting also erupted in Glasgow in November when city leaders refused to petition parliament against the treaty. Deacons of trade in Glasgow organised a trades march against the treaty before rioting broke out; similarly, Cameronian leaders in the south-west organised an armed demonstration against the treaty in Dumfries and burgh magistrates were involved in a small demonstration against the treaty in Stirling. As well as magistrates, local clergy played a significant role in priming residents to act in defence of religious interests.

Crowds in Edinburgh displayed a close connection to national political discourse and events, aided by oppositional communication geared to all social levels. As Daniel Defoe explained, 'some Popular Speeches let fall by those Gentlemen who opposed the Treaty, and industriously spread about the Town' sought to convince the middling sorts that 'the Sovereignty of Scotland was to be Subjected to the English' while 'the poorer sort that understood less, had the same Thing in other Words. ... That the Crown of Scotland was Betray'd; That it was to be carryed to England, and never to be seen here more'.[2] The emotive idea that the crown of Scotland might be carried to England proved to be highly influential.[3] The duke of Hamilton, a key leader of the Country party, helped to spread this rumour: 'One night after the Parliament rose some boys got into the House [where the regalia was on display]. [Hamilton] call'd to make way for them to see the Crown, for perhaps they wou'd never see it more.'[4] Sermons also contributed, with one minister preaching on the text, 'Behold I Come quickly. Hold fast that which thou hast; let no man take thy Crown.'[5] Country communication also highlighted the higher cost of everyday commodities under English customs and excise duties. During the reading of the articles of union from 16 October, 'the People were made to believe, their Salt, their Malt, their Beer, their Fish, would all be loaded with insupportable Taxes, and their whole Trade would be ruin'd, their Houses plunder'd for Taxes, and their People starv'd'.[6] The earl of Mar reported to London that many believed that 'they were to loss the Crown and wou'd be taxt excessively'.[7]

Country party leaders encouraged the expression of anti-treaty sentiment

[2] Defoe, *History of the union*, 17, minutes, 10.
[3] Clerk of Penicuik, *History of the union*, 100.
[4] *Manuscripts of the earl of Mar*, 300.
[5] *Letters of Daniel Defoe*, 137.
[6] Defoe, *History of the union*, minutes, 10.
[7] *Manuscripts of the earl of Mar*, 298.

by crowds in Edinburgh during the parliamentary session. While the articles were read in October, the opposition 'sent messages to every shire in the kingdom, imploring the populace to provide whatever instant aid it could in the present crisis'. As a result, the 'buildings and streets around Parliament Hall were thronged'.[8] With the encouragement of the duke of Hamilton, a 'great number of apprentices and younger sort of people' escorted the duke from Parliament House to his lodgings every night.[9] Not long into the parliamentary session, the earl of Mar had come to expect rioting, reporting to London that oppositional leaders 'take themselves to the mob and cajol them all they can, in so much that they have got the mob and populace on their side intirely, and it is hardly to be doubted but before this affair end there will be some mobish affair'.[10]

Primed by the opposition, anti-incorporationists in Edinburgh only needed a trigger for action. This was provided by parliament's debates of 22 and 23 October on the Equivalent and customs and excise taxes. After escorting Hamilton home on 22 October, his supporters returned to the High Street, throwing stones and calling the treaty negotiators 'traitors'.[11] Some said that the crowds were encouraged that night with money distributed by 'two top peers', though the government lacked any direct evidence of this.[12] Towards the end of the day on 23 October, crowds pressed up to the doors of Parliament House, forcing the commissioner to adjourn. A large throng escorted Hamilton as he proceeded to the duke of Atholl's lodgings and his own lodgings in Holyrood Abbey. Some then converged on the home of Sir Patrick Johnston, a former provost of Edinburgh, one of the city's two parliamentary commissioners and a negotiator of the union treaty. The attackers shouted 'that they wou'd massacre him for being a betrayer and seller of his country'. Attention was also directed at two governmental officers who lived in the same building, though the local figure of Johnston attracted the most ire. After a detachment of town guards repelled the attack on Johnston's house, a crowd estimated at several thousand moved through the streets until at least midnight, throwing stones and beating drums to raise more supporters. The crowds dispersed early in the morning when the duke of Queensberry secured permission from the city magistrates to bring royal troops in through the Netherbow port to the High Street and Parliament Close.[13]

The deployment of troops in the city, with a permanent guard outside Parliament House, quieted the crowds for a time. However, violence broke out again on 1 November as parliament debated whether to begin voting on the articles or take a recess for members to consult their constituents. During

8 Clerk of Penicuik, *History of the union*, 97.
9 'Scotland's ruine', 143.
10 *Manuscripts of the earl of Mar*, 296.
11 *Letters of Daniel Defoe*, 133.
12 *Manuscripts of the earl of Mar*, 300.
13 Ibid. 298–9; *Letters of Daniel Defoe*, 135–6; Defoe, *History of the union*, 28–9; 'Scotland's ruine', 143; Clerk of Penicuik, *History of the union*, 101–3.

the session the 'Clamour without was so great That a Rabble was feared tho' the Guards are Numerous and were Drawn Out in Readyness'.[14] On 15 and 16 November, following Court victories on article II (the Hanoverian succession) and article III (the British parliament), stones were thrown at the duke of Queensberry's coach as it left Parliament Close for Holyrood Palace. Some stones came from windows on the High Street, indicating advance preparations. On both days parliament adjourned late in the evening, allowing the stone-throwers to act under cover of darkness. The uproar was greater on 16 November, when the rioters managed to injure one of the duke's servants and made his horses gallop off at an undignified speed.[15]

As in Edinburgh, Glasgow saw repeated rioting on the question of union with similar attacks on pro-incorporation town leaders. Local clergy drew public attention to the union question after an act passed by the synod of Glasgow and Ayr on 1 October called on ministers to 'excite themselves & one another & the people under their inspection and charge' to pray for divine guidance for parliament so that 'the rights & liberties of this Nationall church, now happily established by Law, may be confirmed & secured from danger'.[16] Another day of prayer, held in Glasgow on Sunday 3 November, allowed ministers to repeat this message.

Sometime before 7 November, members of the trades of Glasgow marched through town 'with this inscription on their hatts, No incorporating Union'. Though peaceful, the march had not been authorised by the burgh magistrates.[17] More violent activity began on 7 November as James Clark of the Tron church preached against the treaty. Clerk called on his parishioners to act to defend the city and the Church. That afternoon, drums called people out onto the streets in an initial show of force. The next day, a crowd accompanied several deacons of trade to the Council-House at the Tolbooth to demand that the provost address parliament against the union. When he refused 'the People fell a Shouting, and Raging, and Throwing Stones, and Raised a very great Uproar'. Like Sir Patrick Johnston in Edinburgh, John Aird, the provost of Glasgow, was a respected member of the local community, but his stance against addressing invited the retribution of the anti-incorporation crowd. The mob attacked the provost's house, taking away arms and goods, and broke the windows of the house of a local laird who had supported the provost in his refusal to address.[18]

Anti-union activity in Glasgow now turned to addressing. Over the next few days, local organisers solicited 380 signatures on an independent address to parliament against the treaty from the 'Merchants and Trades of the City

---

14 *Letters of Daniel Defoe*, 142.
15 *Manuscripts of the earl of Mar*, 326–7; *Letters of Daniel Defoe*, 151; Clerk of Penicuik, *History of the union*, 132.
16 NAS, CH 2/464/2 (103–5).
17 *Manuscripts of the earl of Mar*, 318.
18 Defoe, *History of the union*, 59–61.

of Glasgow'.[19] While many signatures were given freely, letters to government ministers from some Glasgow residents accused organisers of pressuring
them to sign under threat of violence.[20] The Glasgow address was conveyed
to Edinburgh by the deacons of the tailors and the shoemakers and presented
to parliament on 15 November.[21]

News from Edinburgh of the approval on 12 November of the Act of
Security for the Church sparked another brief outburst in Glasgow to protest
against parliament's failure to address key issues raised by the second petition
of the Commission of the General Assembly.[22] A larger altercation began on
Saturday 23 November when a crowd tried to free a tobacco spinner named
Parker who had been imprisoned for selling goods taken from the provost's
house during the 8 November riot. This new crowd was led by a former sergeant
from a Scottish regiment serving in Flanders named George Finlay, allegedly
a Jacobite. The crowd entered the Tolbooth to demand a bond that had been
prepared for Parker's release. Though the magistrates handed it over, Parker's
supporters still attacked the provost with stones and curses as he made his way
home. A loosely organised crowd then searched for weapons in the homes of
other town officers who had failed to oppose the treaty. They also accosted
passers-by with the threatening question, 'Are you for the Union?' Later that
night, a large crowd returned to the Tolbooth but was repelled by a select
party of the town guard. The opposition of many in the trades had weakened
the town guard, which relied on artisans for its soldiers and junior officers,
forcing town magistrates to hand-pick those willing to resist the rioters.[23]

In the ensuing week, reports came to town of a planned rendezvous at
Hamilton of armed men from Stirling, Angus, Galloway and Lanarkshire,
with the intent of descending on Edinburgh to raise parliament. On Friday
29 November Finlay and an armed following marched from Glasgow towards
Hamilton. Though initially reported in Edinburgh as a hundred men, Finlay's
group appears to have numbered between forty-five and fifty. Though Finlay
was said be a Jacobite, his followers indicated Presbyterian sympathies in
declaring their determination to 'never part with the Religion, Liberty, independency: and Crown' of Scotland.[24]

Finlay's departure from Glasgow did not stop the tumults in the town.
On Monday 2 December, a Proclamation against Unlawful Convocations of
29 November and an Act against Musters of 30 November arrived in Glasgow
and were read out at the Tolbooth before a 'vast Multitude'. Stone-throwing

19 NAS, PA 7/28/34 Glasgow.
20 Letters of Daniel Defoe, 150.
21 Defoe, History of the union, 62.
22 Letters of Daniel Defoe, 148; Manuscripts of the earl of Mar, 322.
23 Defoe, History of the union, 62–6. In 1704 the captains of the guard companies included
one hammerman, four maltmen, two cordiners, one weaver, one tailor, one heftmaker, one
mealman and a dyster: Glasgow burgh extracts, 374.
24 Letters of Daniel Defoe, 163; Manuscripts of the earl of Mar, 339; Defoe, History of the
union, 66; NAS, GD 406/1/5383.

by the crowd led to an altercation with the town guard. The rioters subdued and disarmed the guard, aided by the desertion of some tradesmen from the trained bands. Arms were seized from the Tolbooth and houses again searched for arms and plunder.[25]

Finding no supporters at Hamilton, Finlay and his small army returned to Glasgow on Wednesday 4 December and handed over their weapons to the deacons of trade on the following day. Soon after, royal dragoons entered Glasgow and arrested Finlay and one follower, a man called Montgomery. Unauthorised drums beat briefly on their arrival and a few stones were thrown as they left, but no other resistance was shown. On the troops' departure, however, 'the Rabble Rose again and Took all the Magistrates prisoners and Declared that if their Two men were not Restored and sent home Again they would Treat the Magistrates just in the same Manner as they should be Treated'. As Finlay had agreed a 'Cessation of Arms' with the magistrates, his supporters judged his arrest to have betrayed this agreement. Unable to quell the crowd, two deacons of trade and two baillies set off for Edinburgh to negotiate with the government.[26] Separately, when the prisoners arrived in Edinburgh, an unidentified group led by a hat-maker's servant attempted to free them, but was repelled by the prisoners' guard.[27]

The Glasgow riots reflected a fundamental split in the community over the treaty. Magistrates in Glasgow had to remember that they 'depend[ed] upon their friends that are in court for good offices to the Town'.[28] Moreover, the treaty's offer of free trade attracted some Glasgow merchants 'who promise themselves vast wealth by liberty of Trading in the West Indies'.[29] Merchants already trading illicitly with the English North American colonies had an interest in regularising their activities.[30] Others, however, saw danger in the union, particularly to the Presbyterian Church. While the burgh's provost refused to support an address, the burgh's parliamentary commissioner, Hugh Montgomery, usually a Court party supporter, voted against the treaty.

Though many Presbyterians objected to the treaty, the rioting, and Finlay's march to Hamilton, 'divided the honest party' in the town, some rejecting armed or violent resistance.[31] After the tumults in Glasgow, a cleric described the rioters as 'a Rabble of whores & scumm' and 'a pack of graceless Rakes whom noe man of Religion can own'.[32] Though deacons of trade organised the peaceful march against incorporation and an independent address,

[25] Defoe, *History of the union*, 67–8.
[26] Ibid. 70–1; *Letters of Daniel Defoe*, 166–8; NAS, PC 1/53 (492); *Post Man* (Thurs. 12 Dec.–Sat. 14 Dec. 1706).
[27] *Manuscripts of the earl of Mar*, 350.
[28] Wodrow quarto xl, item 12.
[29] NAS, GD 406/1/9747.
[30] T. C. Smout, 'The Glasgow merchant community in the seventeenth century', *SHR* xlvii (1968), 56, 64–5.
[31] Wodrow quarto xl, item 8.
[32] Ibid.

they did not support the subsequent riots, agreeing measures with the town council on 18 November to prevent further disturbances. These included a daily mustering of the town guard and a curfew for 'all women, boys, young men, and servants' (though the deacons were not willing to take personal responsibility for the good behaviour of their households).[33]

Local protests against the treaty were also seen in Dumfries, encouraged by Presbyterian clergy and organised by anti-incorporation heritors and Cameronians. On 10 October the synod of Dumfries followed the example of the synod of Glasgow and Ayr in ordering its clergy to encourage parishioners to pray for divine guidance in parliament's consideration of the treaty. As in 1703–4, when the synod ordered parishioners to be stirred up against Catholics, in 1706 its clergy sought to 'stir up the godly within their bounds, to a just Concern, in their Prayers to God, for the Interest of the Church and Nation, in this present Juncture'.[34] Capitalising on high levels of popular awareness of the treaty, local leaders began to organise demonstrations in opposition to the proposed union. On 29 October a group of thirty-one freeholders subscribed a set of instructions to their commissioners requiring them not to vote for any treaty articles that threatened their interests in 'Our Church Government by Law Established, Our Liberty, and our Trade'.[35] In November leaders of the separatist Cameronians met near Sanquhar and resolved to organise a public protest against the treaty of union.[36] On 20 November a large crowd, reported between 200 and 3,000, gathered at the market cross in Dumfries as an armed contingent of Cameronians burned the treaty of union. According to an account published by the protesters, 'double Squadrons of Foot and Horse, in Martial Order' surrounded the fire, accompanied by trumpets and drums. The burning articles were held up on a pike 'to the view of all the People', who indicated their approval 'by Huzza's and Chearful Acclamations'. The minutes of the treaty negotiations and a list of the negotiators were also burned.[37]

Following this symbolic rejection of the treaty, the Cameronians posted a declaration against the ratification of the articles of union. This paper described the treaty as 'utterly destructive' of 'this nation's independency, crown rights and our constitute laws, both sacred and civil' and declared that parliament could not take away the nation's fundamental rights without the people's permission. The writers intended their paper to act as a form of legal protest against the treaty, asserting that 'whatever ratification of the foresaid union may pass in Parliament, contrary to our fundamental laws, liberties and priviledges concerning church and state, may not be binding upon the nation now, nor at any time to come'. They sent their statement to Edinburgh 'to

---

33 *Glasgow burgh extracts*, 399–402; NAS, PC 1/53(492).
34 NAS, CH 2/98/1(252–3).
35 *Instructions for the commissioners of the sheriffdom of Dumfreis*, [Edinburgh 1706].
36 John Ker of Kersland, *The memoirs of John Ker of Kersland*, London 1726, 34.
37 Anon, *An account of the burning of the articles of the union at Dumfries*, [Edinburgh] 1706; Defoe, *History of the union*, 41–2; 'Scotland's ruine', 177–9.

be Printed and kept in Record' as 'the Testimony of the South part of this Nation'.[38]

A smaller burning of the articles of union occurred in Stirling where the town's magistrates, like those in Glasgow, disagreed over the degree to which the town would protest against the treaty. Stirling's commissioner to parliament, Lt Col. John Erskine, deputy governor of Stirling Castle, found himself caught between local opposition to the treaty and his obligations to the queen as an army officer and to his relative the earl of Mar as governor of Stirling Castle. Erskine played a double game, voting for the union in parliament but opposing it through addresses from the Convention of Royal Burghs and the burgh of Stirling.[39] On 16 November Stirling's town council ordered an address against the union to be signed by 'the council and communitie'. The council mustered 'the haill inhabitantis within this burgh and territories thereof, betuixt sixtie and sixtine yearis' on Monday 18 November to sign the address, with a penalty of £5 for anyone not appearing. Erskine presented the address to the assembled inhabitants, 'and with his sword Drawn in One hand, and his pen in the Other, signd it, and made the Rest do so also'.[40]

Stirling's official resistance, however, did not extend to crowd disorder. A burning of the articles of union was organised by Patrick Stivinson, a former treasurer of Stirling, on Wednesday 4 December, with the apparent cooperation of members of the town guard. As Captain William Holburn of the queen's forces at Stirling Castle reported to Erskine in Edinburgh, 'This day at twelve a'clock I was standing near the cross at Stirlin, and ther cam some ruffians out from a sham gward the toun keeps since the dragouns went from this and brought the articles of the Treatie of Union to the cross, kindled a fire and threw the articles in it with severall huzas.' In addition, a declaration against the union was posted to the market cross, as in Dumfries. According to Holburn, the town was full of 'seditious people', with the guard 'good for nothing but to raise tumults'.[41] The council, however, denied any involvement of town magistrates in the burning, disowned the event in the council records and blamed it on 'some drunken people and boyes ... who wer lykewayes ignorant of the late act of parliament against tumultuarie and irregular meetings and convocations of the leidges, the same never having been proclaimed here'. To protect themselves, the town sent a baillie to Edinburgh with letters to the duke of Queensberry and Erskine providing their version of events and asking for advice on how to proceed.[42]

The events in Stirling, Dumfries, Glasgow and Edinburgh demonstrate the willingness of many ordinary subjects, especially committed Presbyterians, to

---

[38] Anon., *An account of the burning*; '*Scotland's ruine*', 177–9.
[39] *Royal burghs extracts*, 399–400.
[40] *Stirling burgh extracts*, 109; *Letters of Daniel Defoe*, 153.
[41] *Manuscripts of the earl of Mar*, 347, 353.
[42] *Stirling burgh extracts*, 110.

take action against incorporation through crowd activities. Country party publications, clerical sermons and the leadership of magistrates and heritors provided encouragement and coordination for these activities. Retributive riots also boiled up as angry crowds sought to punish local treaty supporters. These events sent strong messages to the centre about the risks of popular disorder: crowds in Edinburgh presented an immediate threat to the safety of parliament, while Finlay's march to Hamilton and the appearance in Dumfries of hundreds of armed Cameronians suggested open rebellion. Though the turn towards violence and disorder alienated some supporters, the effect of these crowd events on the union debates was significant in combination with further collective activities organised by Country party leaders from Edinburgh.

Country party collective activity

While protests and disturbances took place in Edinburgh, Glasgow, Dumfries and Stirling, Country party operatives working from Edinburgh attempted to organise mass actions to reinforce their efforts to defeat the treaty with negative public opinion. As Charles Hamilton, earl of Selkirk and brother to the duke of Hamilton, wrote to his mother Anne, duchess of Hamilton, 'the breaking of the glase windous does no good and their must be more then that to fright the Court'.[43] Party measures included musters of the Protestant militia, a gathering of petitioners in Edinburgh, attempts at an armed march on parliament and a desertion of parliament by oppositional members. Where possible, these activities used standing law, recent precedent and the Claim of Right to justify aggressive mass actions designed to disrupt the passage of the treaty in parliament with the threat of popular resistance and open rebellion.

The 1704 Act of Security provided a legal basis for musters of armed men in its order 'that the whole Protestant Heretors and all the Burghs within the same [kingdom] shall furthwith provide themselves with fire arms for all the fencible men who are Protestants within their respective bounds' and 'to Discipline and Exercise their said fencible men once in the moneth at least'.[44] A February 1705 newsletter reported that 'people are very busy in arming themselves throughout Scotland', while a 1726 memoir indicated that at least some Lowland parishes and burghs established regular musters of armed citizens and renewed this practice in 1706.[45] The synod of Glasgow and Ayr recommended 'frequent rendezvous and exercises of the fencible men through all the Burghs and paroches of this countrey, that in case their service and assistance shall be required for the defence and maintenance of

---

[43] NAS, GD 406/1/8122.
[44] APS xi. 137.
[45] *Portland manuscripts*, iv. 164; Ker of Kersland, *Memoirs*, 23, 28.

the liberties and rights of the church and Nation they may be in all suitable readiness to answer the call'.[46] Stirling called a muster of its fencible men to sign the burgh's address against the treaty and musters took place in Lanarkshire around the Hamilton area with the support of Duchess Anne. Writing on 29 November she reported to her son that 'We have frequent Rendevouz here, and as long as we have Law for it, Lett them say what they will of me, I will encourage them.'[47]

Militia musters offered the opposition a legal way to intimidate the Court party with a show of force. In contrast, plans for a joint rising of Cameronians and Jacobites offered significant leverage to the Country opposition but little legitimacy. A number of Jacobite nobles and gentlemen, including the duke of Hamilton, had discussed a possible rising with a French envoy in 1705.[48] French aid on behalf of the exiled Stewarts in St Germains was not forthcoming, leading some Jacobites to seek joint action with Covenanting Presbyterians in 1706–7. In November a Presbyterian cleric reported that 'the Jacobites (if we may believe them) swear that if the Presbyterians stand fast nou to the Liberties and sovereignty of the Kingdome, for ever they shall be for presbitry'.[49] Rumours circulated of a landing of James Stewart and claims 'that he had turn'd Protestant, and offers not only to establish and confirm Presbitry, but the Solemn League and Covenant'.[50] The notion of Presbyterian–Jacobite cooperation drew on existing discourse suggesting the possibility of a Protestant Stewart restoration. In 1702 John Spottiswoode, an advocate and baron of Berwickshire, proposed that the Stewart heirs be invited to live in Scotland and take instruction in religion, with the aim of restoring them if they turned Protestant.[51] Similarly, another 1702 proposal hoped that 'James VIII and III' would convert to Protestantism to secure his crown. The author recommended that Queen Anne marry him into the Hanover family and declare him heir when 'the people be convinced that he is a true protestant'.[52]

The idea of an armed Presbyterian–Jacobite march on Edinburgh to raise parliament was developed by a coalition of shire commissioners: George Lockhart of Carnwath (a commissioner for Midlothian) and William Cochrane of Kilmaronock (a commissioner for Dumbartonshire), both Jacobites, and John Brisbane the younger of Bishoptoun, one of Ayrshire's representatives. Lockhart, Cochrane and Brisbane encouraged James Cunningham of Aiket, a Presbyterian, laird from Ayrshire, former army major and survivor of Darien, to recruit Presbyterians in the south-west to rendezvous at Hamilton for a march on Edinburgh. Lockhart secured a degree of support from the duke of

---

[46] Wodrow quarto lxxiii, fo. 271.
[47] NAS, GD 406/1/9734.
[48] Gibson, *Playing the Scottish card*, chs ii, iii.
[49] Wodrow quarto xl, item 8.
[50] *Manuscripts of the earl of Mar*, 340.
[51] [Spottiswoode], *Speech of one of the barons*, 5–6.
[52] *Report on the Laing manuscripts*, ed. Henry Paton, London 1925, ii. 543.

Hamilton for the plan, while Cochrane gained the more ready approval of the duke of Atholl. Cunningham was assured that Atholl Highlanders would secure the pass at Stirling as part of the plan.[53]

The project advanced to the point of a call to arms, with Finlay's small band marching from Glasgow on 29 November in expectation of joining an army of many thousands at Hamilton. Preparations for a march were reported in Hamilton, Dumfries, Annandale, Galloway and Stirling. Robert Wylie called on his parishioners to join the rising and the parish's second minister offered to captain them.[54] Wylie's papers from this period include a manifesto to be read on the occasion of an insurrection. This justified a rising as 'called of God' to stop those who would betray 'the known mind of the nation their constituents'.[55] At the final hour, the duke of Hamilton cancelled the expedition, writing letters to halt any moves towards Edinburgh. Though he had promised to support the plan with 'everything that an honest man could desire', no doubt in hopes that the rumour of a rising would intimidate the Court party, he was not willing to allow resistance to exceed legal limits.[56]

With the collapse of the November rising, some clergy still looked to a Presbyterian insurrection to rescue the Church. As one minister saw it in early December, 'There is no other way left to break the project but the appearance of the country. ... Addresses and Representations being slighted there seems noe other way left but armes.' English forces were known to be at the borders and the leadership of the opposition by Atholl and Hamilton had been weakened by disagreements. Nevertheless, there seemed 'noe way left but the honest party to rise without the Influence any of the sides and to chuse ane honest leader, and come in, and these 2 D[uke]s and others from the parties to joyn them without any of their men when they come near the toun'.[57] Events reveal, however, that such ideas remained at the level of speculation as no independent rising of Presbyterians appeared.

While rebellion was being planned in November, operatives in Edinburgh sought to weaken the government's ability to control open resistance. As part of the Country party's petitioning activities, regiments in the royal forces were encouraged to address against the union. Anticipating difficulty in getting the queen's officers to address against the government, organisers prepared a petition for rank and file soldiers to submit to their officers. This asserted their dislike of the treaty and their unwillingness to fight their fellow subjects to enforce the union. In addition, soldiers were warned that 'if this union go on, they will certainly be carried abroad and will never be trusted in their own dissatisfied country'.[58] This subversion programme seems to have

53 'Scotland's ruine', 179–82.
54 Manuscripts of the earl of Mar, 337; Letters of Daniel Defoe, 163.
55 Wodrow quarto lxxiii, fos 283–7.
56 'Scotland's ruine', 182–4; Manuscripts of the earl of Mar, 180–3.
57 Wodrow quarto xl, item 8.
58 Ibid. quarto lxxiii, fos 280–1.

had an effect by mid-November, when some in Edinburgh had deep concerns about the reliability of the forces. Daniel Defoe reported to Robert Harley that 'The few Troops They have here are Not to be Depended Upon – I have this Confesst by Men of the best Judgement – The officers are good but Even the Officers Own They Dare Not Answer for Their Men.'[59]

After the cancellation of the Presbyterian–Jacobite rising, party organisers turned to a gathering of petitioners in Edinburgh to reinforce their addresses. This idea had been raised earlier in the session, but a meeting of addressers now gained acceptance as a legitimate alternative to open resistance. This was based on precedents for the attendance of barons in person at parliament and the idea that petitioners had a right to hear answers to their petitions.[60] The duke of Atholl and Andrew Fletcher of Saltoun advanced this measure, with the duke of Hamilton agreeing to support it. The petitioners were to 'second' their addresses in person, asking the duke of Queensberry to stop the union or recommend new elections to the queen.[61] The addressers would also sign a national address to the queen asking her to drop the treaty and call a new parliament and a General Assembly.[62]

Letters from the duke of Atholl produced a flow of Highlanders to Edinburgh, including known Catholics and Jacobites.[63] The duke asked his mother-in-law, the duchess of Hamilton, to organise attendance from the west with all to be in Edinburgh by 20 December. In response, Andrew Hay of Craignethan, Anne's sheriff-depute for Lanarkshire, sent out a circular letter to a reported sixty-nine local heritors.[64] Separately, Cameronian leaders made their way to Edinburgh 'with a very serious Intention to come into any honest Measures against the Union'.[65] With several hundred petitioners in town, the project stalled when the duke of Hamilton demanded that the national address include a statement in favour of the Hanoverian succession. With the duke of Atholl opposed to any support for the house of Hanover, organisers bickered for several days until a proclamation forced the collected heritors to disperse.[66]

In early January, as debates began on article XXII (Scottish representation in the British parliament), Hamilton proposed that his party submit an overture to settle the succession on the Hanoverian heir, though with limitations. This would be followed by a formal protest, an exodus of oppositional members and a national address to the queen if the act of settlement were refused. Like the gathering of petitioners, the idea of a walkout had been in circulation earlier in the session, with the passage of article XXII noted

[59] *Letters of Daniel Defoe*, 147.
[60] Wodrow quarto lxxiii, fo. 276; [Ridpath], *Considerations*, 58–9.
[61] 'Scotland's ruine', 184; NAS, GD 406/1/7851.
[62] 'Scotland's ruine', 185–6.
[63] *Letters of Daniel Defoe*, 182; NAS, PC 1/53 (493).
[64] *Letters of Daniel Defoe*, 184; *Manuscripts of the earl of Mar*, 363.
[65] Ker of Kersland, *Memoirs*, 36; NAS, GD 406/1/8074.
[66] 'Scotland's ruine', 186; *Letters of Daniel Defoe*, 188.

as the deadline for such an event. Though Atholl again refused to participate in a plan involving the Hanoverian succession, Hamilton's followers
prepared themselves for a walkout. On the designated day, however, the duke
of Hamilton refused to take the lead, causing the plan to collapse.[67]

The failure of the walkout scheme marked the end of organised activities against the treaty. Various Country party elements had hoped to pressure parliament through collective action in musters, a rising, a gathering
of freeholders and a walkout. These added an edge to the party's pamphlets,
addresses and instructions against the union by indicating the possibility of
armed resistance. Oppositional leaders displayed a lack of unity on these
activities, the duke of Hamilton seeking to limit his involvement in illegal
activities and disagreeing with the duke of Atholl over proposals to replace
the treaty with the Hanoverian succession. The effectiveness of these measures, however, was not only restricted by internal dissent but by strong steps
taken by the Court party to reduce the challenge presented by oppositional
shows of force.

Court management of crowds and collective actions

More than any other expression of collective opinion, the impact of anti-
incorporation crowds depended on intimidation and the threat of violence.
In Scotland at this time, the association of crowds with Covenanting rebellion or Jacobite counter-revolution increased the perceived menace, and thus
potential influence, of collective action. At the same time, however, it also
increased the government's ability to draw on standing law and precedent to
reduce the danger of disorder and rebellion. Nevertheless, though the government had grounds on which to act against crowds and restore order, it had
to make some concessions to the disaffection expressed in such gatherings in
order to reduce extra-parliamentary pressure on its supporters.

Rioting in Edinburgh was contained by the combined use of troops and
new proclamations against disorder, bringing together precedents employed
since 1699 in the control of Edinburgh mobs. The scale of the riot in Edinburgh on 23 October 1706, and the inability of the town guard to stop it,
allowed the government to bring in royal troops to restore the peace, as they
had in June 1700.[68] Regiments entered with a deliberate show of strength and
a demonstration of the support of the burgh magistrates for this exercise of
royal authority:

> about Midnight A body of the Guards besides those posted at the Cannon
> Gate Entred the City, Drums beating, March't up the High street to the
> Parliament Close, and His Grace the Duke of Argyll Mounted at the head

[67] NAS, GD 406/1/7855; Wodrow quarto lxxiii, fo. 276; 'Scotland's ruine', 188–96.
[68] Manuscripts of the earl of Mar, 299; Defoe, History of the union, 29.

of the Horse Guards to have seconded them. After the foot Came my Ld
Provost, the Bayliffs and Magistrates.[69]

After the riot, the privy council issued a proclamation requiring the town to
prevent further disturbances. Echoing the terms of earlier proclamations in
1700 and 1705, this 'Proclamation against Tumults and Rables' condemned
the crowd's attacks on government figures. The council ordered the town
magistrates to ensure that householders control their servants and the masters
of Edinburgh University their students and required burgh residents to assist
in repressing any future tumults. In addition, soldiers were indemnified from
any 'slaughter, Mutilation wounds Blood or Bruises' inflicted while bringing
crowds under control.[70] The town council reinforced this proclamation
with a set of orders on 24 October, including a requirement that landlords
hand in lists of lodgers in the city, a measure that had been recommended in
June 1700.[71]

A majority in parliament confirmed the illegitimacy of political riot with
a vote of thanks to the privy council on 24 October, defeating oppositional
arguments against the deployment of troops around Parliament House.[72] From
this point, two regiments of foot contributed to a distinct lessening of crowd
disturbances in Edinburgh. After disorders broke out again in mid-November,
parliament reaffirmed the need for control by empowering one of its committees to investigate the latest tumult and take steps to prevent further disorders.[73] Reports of organised resistance outside Edinburgh led the privy council
to turn to parliament yet again on 29 November to authorise suppression.
Ministers reported 'irregular and tumultuary meetings by some people of
the common & meanest degree in armes' and 'papers dropt inviting people
to take up armes & to provide ammunition & provision in order to their
marching to disturb the Parliament'. Few in parliament could argue publicly
against measures to prevent armed revolt, with only four votes opposing the
Proclamation against Unlawful Convocations of 29 November. This banned
organised protests, associations and armed risings, authorised the use of troops
to enforce the proclamation and pardoned in advance any injuries or deaths
caused by the forces. In addition, the Act against all Musters of 30 November
suspended the clauses in the Act of Security authorising musters.[74]

These measures gave the government firm grounds on which to require
burghs to maintain the peace. On 30 November, the privy council sent the
new proclamation and act to the town councils of Glasgow and Dumfries for
local publication, demanding that they restore order in their burghs.[75] With

[69] *Letters of Daniel Defoe*, 136.
[70] NAS, PC 13/3/1706 (24 Oct.).
[71] *Edinburgh burgh extracts, 1701–1718*, 128.
[72] APS xi. 309.
[73] APS xi. 331.
[74] APS xi. 341–4.
[75] NAS, PC 1/53 (491–2).

rioting continuing in Glasgow, the council ordered the magistrates to secure guarantees from their householders for the good behaviour of their dependants. They also called the masters of Glasgow University to Edinburgh to demand that they maintain better control of their students.[76] At the request of the Glasgow magistrates, troops arrived in Glasgow to arrest Finlay on 5 December.[77] Around 14 December a 'Detachment of Foot and Dragoons' was quartered in the city.[78]

The government's ability to send forces to Glasgow was supported by the movement of five regiments of English troops to Northern Ireland and three to the English border in late November, with more horse troops sent to the border in early December.[79] This gave the queen's ministers the confidence to send Scottish troops away from Edinburgh, while news of the English troops dissuaded some from further resistance.[80] The voting of cess in early November guaranteed funds for overdue army salaries, improving the loyalty of the Scottish troops.[81] In addition, the earl of Leven, commander of the queen's forces in Scotland, convened the troops to assure them that they would not be sent abroad after the union.[82]

The repression of risings was aided by the government's use of secret agents. In addition to providing information to the queen's ministers on oppositional plans, agents capitalised on the inherent incompatibility of Jacobites and Covenanters to dissuade the latter from joining with the Jacobites in a rising. Major James Cunningham of Aiket, sent by the Country party to coordinate a rising in the Presbyterian south-west, may have been a double agent, though the point at which he switched sides is unclear. In his memoirs, George Lockhart of Carnwath expressed his confidence in Cunningham's sincerity despite his association 'with some of the leading men of the Court' during the parliamentary session and his receiving a company of foot after the union.[83] Nevertheless, the memoirs of Sir John Clerk of Penicuik describe him as an agent of the duke of Queensberry and Cunningham received a payment of £100 sterling from a secret £20,000 provided by the English treasury to help secure the passage of the treaty.[84] Cunningham had longstanding arrears of pay from his service as an officer in the army, totalling £270 sterling in 1705.[85]

The duke of Queensberry also won over John Ker of Kersland, a supporter

---

76 *Manuscripts of the earl of Mar*, 353; NAS, PC 1/53 (492–3).
77 *Letters of Daniel Defoe*, 165.
78 Ibid. 172.
79 *Manuscripts of the earl of Mar*, 336, 353.
80 'Scotland's ruine', 183.
81 *Manuscripts of the earl of Mar*, 317.
82 *Letters of Daniel Defoe*, 142.
83 'Scotland's ruine', 180–1.
84 Clerk of Penicuik, *History of the union*, 144 n. 1; 'Scotland's ruine', 257. Lockhart's biographer has suggested that Cunningham went over to the Court after the failure of his rising: Szechi, *George Lockhart*, 67.
85 APS xi. 285–6.

of the Revolution settlement with links to the Cameronians through his wife's family. In this case the duke secured his agent well before trouble developed. Ker reports in his memoirs that Queensberry convinced him that if the Cameronians rebelled, 'the French King would improve the Opportunity, by sending over Troops to that Country, by which Britain would become a Field of Blood, and not only the Protestant Religion, but even the Liberties of Europe would be in Danger'. Ker says that he used his influence with the Cameronians to convince their leaders not to rise with the Jacobites, limiting their resistance to the burning of the treaty at Dumfries and joining the gathering of freeholders in Edinburgh in December.[86]

A third agent, John Pierce, persuaded John Hepburn, the Hebronite leader, not to rise with the Jacobites. An associate of Daniel Defoe, Pierce was an English Whig who fled to Scotland in 1704 after publishing a mock address to the House of Lords considered seditious by the London government. Like Defoe, Pierce seems to have eschewed his populist Whig sentiments to secure protection from prosecution through government employment.[87] Having sent Pierce to Galloway, by late December Defoe could report to Robert Harley that Pierce had 'Opened [Hepburn's] Eyes in Severall things … and he Authorizes me to assure you there is No Danger from him.'[88] The Hebronites took no direct action against the treaty other than sending a petition to parliament.[89]

It was difficult for the opposition to keep its collective activities secret, allowing rumours and insider reports to aid the government's efforts to contain resistance. Notified of preparations for a rising, the queen's ministers readied the Proclamation against Unlawful Convocations and Act against Musters in late November. The duke of Queensberry learned of subsequent plans for a gathering of freeholders in Edinburgh when a Lanarkshire heritor turned in a copy of a circular letter inviting addressers to Edinburgh.[90] This intelligence allowed the government to introduce a proclamation on 27 December against meetings of petitioners, taking the opposition by surprise.[91] Declaring the attempts to call addressers to Edinburgh 'unwarrantable & seditious', the proclamation threatened to prosecute 'illegal convocations'.[92] In addition, as petitioners poured into Edinburgh in December, the privy council required the city magistrates to seize arms and any horses over the value of 100 merks belonging to persons who had not taken the oaths of allegiance. The council also renewed earlier orders for the provision of lists of strangers lodging in the

---

[86] Ker of Kersland, *Memoirs*, 28–36.
[87] Owens and Furbank, 'New light', 134–43.
[88] *Letters of Daniel Defoe*, 180–1.
[89] 'Scotland's ruine', 182; NAS, PA 7/28/22.
[90] 'Scotland's ruine', 187.
[91] *Manuscripts of the earl of Mar*, 364.
[92] APS xi. 369–72.

town and ordered the magistrates of Stirling, Leith and Queensferry to notify them of travellers moving through their towns towards Edinburgh.[93]

In managing open opposition, the Court party relied on the Church to calm popular anger in the localities. The government had little direct control over individual clergy, but could influence some on the Commission of the General Assembly.[94] Led by William Carstares, the commission voted on 6 December to send a letter to the presbyteries recommending 'to all our Brethren' that they 'Discountenance and Discourage all Irregularities and Tumults'.[95] In turn, printed sermons by William Wisheart, the commission's moderator, urged 'all sober and well-meaning People' to prevent 'great Confusions in this Nation' by avoiding crowd activities and trusting in parliament to resolve the union issue.[96]

The commission's move against popular disorder did not just reflect Court party influence among its leadership. Many ministers in the Church were uncomfortable with uncontrolled rioting. Though Covenanting political thought contained strong justifications for popular defence of the Presbyterian Church, many clergy remained unsure about the legitimacy of rabbles. In 1703, when Presbyterians in Glasgow attacked an unauthorised episcopalian meeting house, Robert Wodrow was able to justify this:

> I am as much as any against rabbles and risings without countenance of laufull authority, yet it seems to me reasonable that quhen inferior officers of justice are out of the road of their deuty and slack in the execution of laues, its private persons deuty to remonstrate and seek for redresse, and quhen none can be had, I cannot see but the pouer of defending themselves, their libertyes, property, religion, and the standing laues of the realme devolves itself naturally on private persons, or the people.

Wodrow, however, made a clear distinction between what he saw as the mindless violence of lesser persons and the actions of 'the reflecting part'.[97] For Wodrow, the 1706 rioting in Glasgow went too far: 'I love no such methods, I would have all order preserved.'[98] Some clergy also opposed rioting on pragmatic grounds, the Glasgow tumults having become 'one of the Best handles ever the court had under the collour of Lau and Reason to crush all opposite measures to the union'.[99]

With anti-union clergy questioning the appropriateness of rioting, the Court party had little difficulty in justifying repressive action against collective action taken to intimidate the parliament. The risk of disorder seemed clear: opponents of union, the earl of Mar reported, 'stick not to say that the

93 NAS, PC 1/53 (493–4).
94 *Manuscripts of the earl of Mar*, 340.
95 Defoe, *History of the union*, appendix, 25; NAS, CH 1/3/9 (60–1).
96 Wisheart, *Two sermons*, 9, 11, 12.
97 *Wodrow letters*, 260–1.
98 Wodrow quarto xl, item 12.
99 Ibid. item 8.

Parliament will be rais'd by force' and that 'the Commissioner will never live to touch this Act'.[100] Rumour magnified the peril of popular resistance as talk of an association oath sworn by 50,000 and a rising of 15,000 circulated in Edinburgh in early November.[101] These accounts joined stories of 'a great Muster of severall parishes at the Kirk of Shotts and of intimations made to them to repair to Edinburgh with ten dayes provisions and also of another such meeting at Lesmahagow'.[102]

Reports of the Glasgow riots and their association with the Jacobite Finlay further justified control measures and contributed to the cooling of resistance among some Presbyterians. Defoe reported on 22 November that 'The Eyes of the people begin a little to Open and I had the honour to hear an [Commission of the General] Assembly man tell me yesterday he was afraid Some were gone too far and that they were to be onley the Cats foot [for the Jacobites].'[103] Defoe did his best to encourage this shift through his propaganda, accusing the Jacobites of inciting riots and urging his Presbyterian readers to see the treaty as the only way to block the Catholic Stewarts from the throne. His *Letter to the Glasgow men* (1706) warned Presbyterians in Glasgow that they were acting as stooges for the Jacobites. Defoe made a point of distributing this letter in the south-west, printing around 2,500 copies to send to Glasgow, Lanark, Hamilton, Stirling and Dumfries.[104]

In parliament, most votes on crowd control drew large majorities against popular resistance. After the 23 October riot in Edinburgh, some claimed that the mobs represented 'the true spirit of this country', renewing this contention in November during debates on the proclamation and act against convocations and musters.[105] Despite this, only the government's attempt to ban meetings of freeholders in December attracted a significant number of negative votes. With forty-four adherents, George Lockhart of Carnwath led a protest in defence of the rights of freeholders to assemble, but the chancellor's argument that 'Such riotous gatherings were … bound to lead to acts of violence and public disorder' convinced a majority of parliamentarians to support the restrictions.[106]

In one way the Court party's ability to contain violent extra-parliamentary resistance to the treaty in 1706 was aided by the development of opinion politics in parliament. Though ideological divisions made parliament difficult to manage, the institutionalisation of the Country opposition gave its leaders reasons to refrain from open rebellion. In particular, with the development of the public sphere from 1699, the duke of Hamilton's power and standing

---

[100] *Manuscripts of the earl of Mar*, 310, 313.
[101] *Letters of Daniel Defoe*, 140, 150.
[102] Wodrow quarto lxxiii, fo. 282.
[103] *Letters of Daniel Defoe*, 153.
[104] Ibid. 170.
[105] *Manuscripts of the earl of Mar*, 299–300, 339.
[106] APS xi. 369, 371; Clerk of Penicuik, *History of the union*, 152.

became linked to his ability to marshal country opinion.[107] Though Hamilton drew on the threat of popular disorder to put pressure on the government, open revolt would turn his opposition into sedition and threaten his position as a potential minister with a large following. As a result, Hamilton had to judge the potential success of a rising in 1706 against the possibilities of office in post-union Britain. After meetings in August 1705 with a French emissary, Hamilton knew that France would only fund a Scottish rising as a short-term diversion to force the English to end their war for the Spanish succession.[108] Rebellion in 1706 was likely to result in eventual English conquest of Scotland and the loss of Hamilton's political role, his lucrative Lancashire estates and possibly his life. Though Hamilton's private letters show that he did not wish for union, he chose to quash the attempted rising of Cameronians and Jacobites while evading any blame for the appearance of Finlay and his followers in Hamilton.[109]

For her part, Anne, duchess of Hamilton, a staunch Presbyterian and Revolution supporter, seems never to have contemplated illegal action, having had no part in her son's Jacobite plotting. On receiving the proclamation against musters, Duchess Anne ordered all Hamilton musters to end, threatening her tenants with dispossession if they appeared in arms.[110] Similarly, when Finlay's small army arrived in Hamilton, the duchess informed the government and took measures to maintain order.[111] Anne consistently encouraged her son to resist the union 'in a Lawfull way'. This included, in her view, the desertion of parliament and she wished her son had led the opposition out long before January 1707.[112] The duke's refusal to lead the Country party walkout in January indicates the degree to which he was unwilling to risk his political standing by open resistance by this point. Having been in contact with Lord Treasurer Godolphin in London during the debates, Hamilton understood that his political future was at stake.[113]

Similarly, the duke of Atholl had to think of his political position. Though Atholl promised support to the planned rising, and Lockhart of Carnwath claimed in his memoirs that it had the restoration of the Stewarts as its ultimate aim, it is notable that the rising consisted of a Presbyterian march on Edinburgh, with Atholl only promising to hold the pass at Stirling.[114] Though Jacobite lairds like Lockhart of Carnwath were willing to organise a rising,

---

107 Gibson, *Playing the Scottish card*, 47.
108 Ibid. ch. iii.
109 *Letters of Daniel Defoe*, 184; *Manuscripts of the earl of Mar*, 337; NAS, GD 406/1/8074, 9738.
110 *Letters of Daniel Defoe*, 165.
111 NAS, GD 406/1/5383, 8075.
112 NAS, GD 406/1/9740.
113 NAS, GD 406/1/7895.
114 'Scotland's ruine', 181.

Scottish Jacobite nobles were not prepared to lead a rebellion in 1706 without French assistance.[115]

Though oppositional nobles hesitated to lead an open insurrection against the treaty, the apparent threat of collective action gave the government grounds on which to repress disorderly activity. Nevertheless, public resistance, both real and rumoured, still had a significant impact on the making of the union. Protests and riots gave weight to concerns published in addresses, pamphlets and speeches, causing some Court party followers to reconsider their support for the treaty. Under this combined assault, the government began to consider amendments to the treaty. While the queen's ministers in London warned against changes, the earl of Mar and his colleagues argued that some were necessary, or 'the whole affair will faill'.[116] As the parliamentary debates proceeded, ministers negotiated limited changes to quell popular resistance and reassure pro-treaty voters.

During November and December concessions were negotiated, in response to widespread complaints, on the security of the Church, the burden of taxation under union and the loss of the Scottish crown. These included an act to secure the Presbyterian Church in union, debated after the first Edinburgh riots and as locality addresses and rumours of musters and Cameronian risings began to arrive in Edinburgh. With the act's passage on 12 November, the earl of Mar expressed the government's hope that 'the ministers and populace will be pleased and the humor against the Union abate'.[117] In his memoirs Sir John Clerk of Penicuik reports that the act 'did something to calm the outcries of the mob and the fears of the clergy'.[118] Rioting, combined with petitions, also led to concessions on taxation, trade and the honours of Scotland.[119] Amendments were negotiated on certain articles, including an adjustment to the excise on Scots ale and tax exemptions for domestic salt and malt in response to popular concerns for the cost of these commodities. In January parliament approved an amendment to article XXIV requiring that the Scottish crown, sceptre and sword of state be kept in Scotland after the union.[120] More than any other amendment, this change reflected the pressure of crowds, as the idea that the Scottish crown would go to London had greatly agitated many in Edinburgh. Clerk of Penicuik's memoirs confirm that these concessions helped to reduce popular objections to the treaty in the short term.[121]

Although pursued as unlawful, collective resistance succeeded in reinforcing oppositional opinion expressed in pamphlets, petitions and speeches. Oppositional leaders encouraged demonstrations of popular support to reinforce its efforts to defeat the treaty with negative public opinion while violent

[115] Gibson, *Playing the Scottish card*, ch. iii.
[116] *Manuscripts of the earl of Mar*, 329–30.
[117] Ibid. 319.
[118] Clerk of Penicuik, *History of the union*, 121.
[119] *Letters of Daniel Defoe*, 172; Whatley, 'Economic causes', 160–2.
[120] APS xi. 401.
[121] Clerk of Penicuik, *History of the union*, 144.

protests emerged in Edinburgh and other localities as anti-incorporationists turned against local union supporters. Crowds around Parliament House, plus reports of riots, musters, demonstrations and a possible rising, placed significant pressure on parliamentarians and the government. Violent resistance, however, divided the opposition, with some rejecting mobbish disorders and open insurrection. The perceived threat of Covenanting and Jacobite rebellion allowed the queen's ministers to employ a range of measures to restore order while negotiating selected amendments to the treaty to address popular concerns.

Conclusion
Public Opinion and the Making of
the Union of 1707

Although dominant accounts of the making of the union characterise it as a 'political job', this view does not take adequate account of the role played by opinion politics in the union crisis. The political job perspective rests on a number of assumptions about public opinion in early modern Scotland: that expressions of public opinion against the union were spontaneous and represented a popular consensus against the union; that the opposition in 1706–7 failed to capitalise on popular anti-treaty opinion; and that public opinion had no effect on the outcome of the union crisis. In simple terms, public opinion was irrelevant because a corrupt parliament betrayed the will of the people. This interpretation has little in common with the dynamics of the early modern public sphere as revealed in this study. Those who see the union simply as a political job have accepted expressions of oppositional opinion at face value without recognising their constructed nature or acknowledging the extent of their power and influence within the political process. By assessing the development and role of public opinion in the union crisis, this book has shown that the politics of opinion shaped and influenced the crisis from beginning to end.

Historians agree that the post-Revolution crown's inability to manage Scottish politics led to crown proposals for incorporation from 1700, while the refusal of the Scottish parliament to accept the Protestant succession in 1703–4 caused English ministers to support incorporation from 1705. Narrow interpretations of these events have attributed the intransigence of the Scottish parliament to the self-interested strategies of Scottish magnates who engaged in oppositional antics in order to secure power and ministerial posts. Politics, in this view, is a game played by magnates and ministers with no role for public opinion. Consistent with this interpretive framework, the passage of the treaty of union through the Scottish parliament has been attributed to secret dealings by the Court party with the *squadrone volante* (the New Party of 1704), by means of which promises of power in post-union Britain and unofficial cash payments created a pro-union majority.[1]

Magnate strategies, coalition politics and secret payments are all important to any understanding of the union, but do not provide a sufficient explana-

---

[1] Ferguson, 'Making of the treaty of union'; Riley, *Union of England and Scotland*, and *King William*; Ferguson, *Scotland's relations*, chs x–xiv.

tion for the passage of the union treaty in the Scottish parliament of 1706–7. This book has sought to offer a broader perspective on the Scottish political environment of 1699–1707 by integrating public and popular politics and the activities of elite leaders. This study shows that public opinion was not just the rhetorical window-dressing of self-serving magnates: it existed as the actual opinions of those Scots connected with national politics through interpersonal, institutional and print communications; and as the represented opinions of those involved in an aggressively populist Country party opposition. Public opinion helped to create the union crisis, for it was the destabilising effect of adversarial opinion politics operating from 1699 onwards that pushed the crown and the English ministry towards a policy of incorporating union. Public opinion also shaped the union crisis, for the crown and its Scottish ministers could not pass an act for treaty negotiations in 1705 or union in 1706–7 without taking account of 'country' opinion on union.

The economic effects of the Nine Years War, crop failures and the crown's lack of support for the African Company and its Darien colony had, by 1699, produced a deep pool of discontent among many Scottish elites and middling sorts. The duke of Hamilton and other noble leaders marshalled this discontent in a series of petitions calling for a meeting of the Scottish parliament to resolve the nation's grievances, capitalising on the 1689 Claim of Right's protection of a subject's liberty to petition. Though the crown countered with a proclamation forbidding repeated petitioning on Darien, the Country party delivered a total of three national addresses and twenty-six petitions from burghs and shires. Print and manuscript pamphlets supported the petitioning campaigns, outlining a platform of demands to be pursued in parliament. Crowds in Edinburgh indicated their espousal of a Country stance in a June 1700 riot instigated by party organisers. In calling the first national petition a 'nationall covenant', Archibald Pitcairn recognised parallels between 1699–1700 and 1637–8, a period of similarly populist oppositional activity organised by Scottish nobles leading to Scottish rebellion, British civil war and the execution of the king.[2] As in 1637–8, the Country opposition claimed to represent a Scottish national interest against an absentee king and his ministry, blaming Scotland's economic problems on Anglocentric crown policy.

By 1700, therefore, the crown faced a challenge not just from Machiavellian magnates but from those heritors and burgesses whose distress at Scotland's appalling economic situation had been solicited by the Country party's pamphlets and petitions and embodied in the Edinburgh riot. Though the crown clawed back votes in the 1700–1 parliament through a combination of personal persuasion, patronage and policy concessions, the level of resources required by the ministry to regain its majority could not be sustained on an

---

2   NAS, PC 1/52(67).

ongoing basis. With guarantees for regular meetings and open debate secured for parliament in the 1689 Claim of Right, and with conflicts of interest between Scotland and England likely to recur, the cost of managing country opinion in Scotland would be high. The development of opinion politics during the Darien crisis thus contributed to the crown's shift towards a policy of incorporating union from 1700. Since 1603 crown proposals for closer union had been met with resistance from both England and Scotland; nevertheless, from 1700 incorporation became the policy of King William and his successor, Queen Anne.

With its abandonment of Anne's 1702 parliament and subsequent boycott of the cess, the Country party maintained pressure on the crown with expressions of oppositional opinion. Anne pursued a closer union in her 1702 parliament, securing an act authorising union talks from the remaining rump of Court adherents. Despite an attempt by her secretary, Viscount Tarbat, to develop English as well as Scottish support for incorporation with his 1702 tract *Parainesis pacifica*, English ministers remained uninterested in closer union. English representatives reluctantly conceded free trade to the Scots in Anne's first union talks, but negotiations collapsed when the English proved unwilling to reimburse the losses of the African Company or compensate Scotland for the higher costs of English customs rates in an economic union.

English interest in a closer union, and the necessary concessions to secure it, increased in 1703–4 as the Country party, now containing the newly elected Jacobite Cavalier faction, resisted the settlement of the Scottish succession. Though the English parliament had settled the crown on the Protestant Sophia of Hanover in 1701, the failure of the 1702 union talks meant that in Scotland the succession remained open. Seeking to capitalise on this, the Country party demanded modifications to the union of crowns before Sophia of Hanover could be accepted. Country pamphlets and speeches promoted a reform platform including limitations on the monarch to shift decision-making powers from London to Edinburgh and a free trade agreement to give the Scots access to English markets and capital. With James Hodges's popular notion of a federal union countering crown pressure for incorporation, Country discourse provided a vision of a federal union under a shared Protestant successor with the Scottish parliament acting as the guardian of Scottish liberties. At the same time, a public battle over proposals for toleration for Episcopalian dissent raised fears for the safety of the Scottish Church in the Anglo-Scottish union.

In 1703 and 1704 the Country party proposed overtures to force concessions from the crown before settling the succession. By passing the Act of Security in both sessions, the opposition demonstrated to English ministers the difficulty of managing oppositional opinion in Scotland. A Country majority defeated in turn the crown's premier manager, the duke of Queensberry, in 1703 and the New Party ministry, recruited from the marquis of Tweeddale's Country Whig faction, in 1704. The Country party's success in 1704 relied in part on the movement of Queensberry's followers to the opposition to ensure the failure of Tweeddale's rival ministry; but it also reflected strong and wide-spread discontent over the union of crowns, fuelled by Country pamphlets and speeches.

Public expressions of disaffection reached new heights in the spring of 1705 with a reopening of African Company wounds. Many in and around Edin-burgh followed the trial of the crew of the *Worcester*, accused of pirating an African Company ship. A rumour of a crown reprieve for the convicted pirates sparked a mob attack on Chancellor Seafield on the day of the executions, but the privy council had already decided to maintain the favour of country opinion in parliament by allowing the first three hangings to proceed. Soon after, the Scottish parliament met to consider the Alien Act, the response of the English parliament to the Act of Security. This demanded that the Scot-tish parliament settle the succession, or pass an act authorising negotiations for a treaty of union, or face economic sanctions. English Whig ministers had concluded with the crown that if the Scottish parliament continued to refuse to settle the succession, incorporation was needed to reduce the influ-ence of the Scottish opposition in British politics. Though the Alien Act and the *Worcester* case sparked an outburst of anti-English publications in Scotland, the Country party's continuing emphasis on economic grievances created a window of opportunity for the Court party. Now led by the duke of Argyll, the Court party appealed to Country interest in a treaty for free trade to construct a parliamentary majority for an act for a treaty of union. Signifi-cantly, the act excluded consideration of church matters and did not specify an incorporating union.

The Scottish Court party remained attuned to country opinion in 1706, with its negotiators initially proposing a more palatable federal union. Though this exceeded what the English were willing to concede to secure union, the Scottish delegation did gain an agreement for Scottish access to English markets. This required the application of higher and more exten-sive English customs and excise duties to Scotland but negotiators secured an 'Equivalent' for those customs duties allocated to the repayment of pre-union English national debt. The first claimants on this lump sum of nearly £400,000 sterling were to be African Company shareholders whose investments would be bought out with interest. Negotiators in 1706 thus secured critical conces-sions designed to answer economic grievances raised in Country discourse since 1699.

The treaty did not, however, satisfy other Country concerns. From the summer of 1706 party leaders worked to defeat the treaty using public opinion. Pamphlets by leading writers asserted the sovereignty of parliamentary elec-tors and the people in general, demanding that parliament vote according to the expressed wishes of their constituents. These and other publications presented a range of arguments against the treaty to develop popular opinion against incorporation. Wrapped in patriotic calls for the continuing exist-ence of the ancient kingdom of Scotland, these focused on the insecurity of Scotland's religious and trading interests under the jurisdiction of a British parliament. The appeal of free trade was countered by complaints about the burden of English customs and excise duties, with an emphasis on the cost to consumers of higher taxes on salt, malt and ale.

These mainstream appeals spoke to a wide opinion base against incorporation created by Country discourse since 1699. The party mobilised its supporters through a series of petitions to parliament from national and local bodies. Country leaders and lieutenants organised the signing of petitions against incorporation from their areas of influence, particularly lands held by members of the Hamilton family. Clergy contributed to the organising of petitions from parishes and a few presbyteries, following the lead of the Commission of the General Assembly. In the commission's meetings early in the parliamentary session, a Court party majority produced a moderate address asking for a confirmation of the establishment of the Presbyterian Church in union. The arrival of more Country-minded ministers produced a more aggressive second representation in early November. This Court–Country divide in the commission was also seen in the Convention of Royal Burghs and the African Company, both of which voted by a narrow margin to petition against the treaty. Alongside petitions from these national institutions, a total of 116 shires, burghs, parishes and presbyteries submitted seventy-nine addresses. More than 20,000 ordinary subjects signed the locality petitions, far exceeding the degree of popular participation generated by the Country party in 1699–1701.

In parliament, the Country party used the petitions to reinforce their assertion of the authority of constituent opinion. In October the party demanded a parliamentary recess so that electors might be consulted and encouraged the production of instructions from shires and burghs to members. As Country party members presented locality petitions to parliament from early November, speakers claimed an overwhelming national consensus against the union, demanding new elections for a more representative parliament.

The party also encouraged out-of-doors expressions of opinion to demonstrate the extent of their popular support. Large crowds escorted the duke of Hamilton to and from parliament during the session and gathered at the doors of Parliament House during key debates. Many were alerted to the potential dangers of popular political engagement when rioting against pro-union figures began in Edinburgh in late October. There were also riots in Glasgow in response to the provost's refusal to allow the city to petition parliament. Repeated incidents in Glasgow led to the burgh virtually being taken over by an armed faction captained by a reputed Jacobite, who led a detachment of followers to rendezvous at Hamilton for a planned march on Edinburgh.

The raising of parliament by force had been considered by some within the Country party, with several Jacobite lairds working in November to trigger action by Covenanters in the south-west. Interest in active resistance among hardline Presbyterians was suggested by the burning of the articles of union at Dumfries by the Cameronians and the expression of Covenanting objections to the treaty in petitions from the Hebronites and a number of parishes. The

Country party also sought to intimidate parliament by means of a gathering of hundreds of armed petitioners in Edinburgh in December, by a planned walk-out of parliament, and by a national address to the queen in January.

Conflict between Jacobite and Revolution interests in the Country coalition contributed to the failure of these attempts, as did the duke of Hamilton's desire to preserve his standing in British politics by avoiding open rebellion. Hamilton's performance has attracted particular censure, in combination with accusations of parliamentary corruption.[3] Nevertheless, the Court party's active development of ideological support for the treaty should also be recognised. The Court first achieved a majority in the 1705 parliament on the promise of a treaty with England and it built a majority again in 1706–7 on the promise of the Hanoverian succession, security for the Presbyterian Church, a communication of trade and the reimbursement of African Company shareholders. Positive propaganda for incorporation and concessions on key objections produced an amended treaty that a majority in parliament could accept. Crown management measures also included assertive responses to oppositional attempts to generate anti-treaty addresses and pressure parliament with collective action.

Before 1706 few in government had supported the publication of positive propaganda for incorporation. From the summer of 1706 the output of Daniel Defoe joined that of Scottish writers to provide an ongoing stream of unionist pamphlets during the parliamentary session. In these, the opposition's assertions of freeholder and popular sovereignty were rejected in favour of parliamentary sovereignty to provide a constitutional justification for any member voting against the wishes of constituents as expressed in addresses and instructions. To influence opinion on the treaty, unionist tracts argued that incorporation would produce a peaceful, prosperous, Protestant Britain and attacked the anti-unionists as dangerous and irrational.

While on the one hand contributing to pro-union discourse, the Court party also made every effort to minimise the effects of anti-union discourse. Party leaders could not stop the presentation of petitions to parliament, but they highlighted their radical nature to undermine their legitimacy. Specific concerns raised by the petitions and echoed privately by members of the Court majority were met with calculated concessions. A carefully choreographed response to the first petition on union from the Commission of the General Assembly led to an act securing the Presbyterian Church in union, while the queen's ministers also allowed the negotiation of amendments to the treaty to resolve a number of economic concerns.

In addition, Country party attempts to back up their petitions with collective action were quashed. After repressing the Edinburgh riots with a full

---

[3] Ferguson, 'Making of the treaty of union', 109, and *Scotland's relations*, 267; '*Scotland's ruine*', 106–7.

exercise of governmental authority, the Court party secured new proclamations and acts against further action. These measures took advantage of conventional fears of the mindless mob, as well as more specific concerns for Covenanting unrest and a Jacobite counter-revolution. The deployment of Scottish troops in Edinburgh and Glasgow, the movement of English troops to the borders and Northern Ireland, the banning of musters of the Protestant militia and the outlawing of gatherings of petitioners together secured parliament from the threat of a violent end to its session. In addition, the government capitalised on Presbyterian concerns about the security of the Revolution to undermine the resistance of Covenanters in the south-west, using secret agents to win over local leaders.

In building a majority coalition, the Court party appealed to the desire of the Whig *squadrone volante* for the Hanoverian succession, securing the support of its leaders with promises of political advantage in post-union Britain and payments from an unrecorded £20,000 sterling sent up from the English Treasury to pay arrears of salary owed to office-holders. Though over £12,000 of the £20,000 was paid to the duke of Queensberry for his expenses, £2,854 went to five nobles in the *squadrone* and £3,251 to seventeen members of the Court party.[4] Despite claims that a 'hucksters' mood' prevailed in the 1706–7 parliament, the court's pro-union coalition was not made with the outright purchase of oppositional votes.[5] Of the £20,000, only £1,150 went to three members of the opposition, of whom two voted in favour of the union.[6] Though George Lockhart of Carnwath claimed that the Equivalent represented 'the cleanliest way of bribing a nation', those opposing the union in 1706–7 included many with significant investments in the African Company.[7] While the Equivalent provided financial incentives to some members of parliament, the Court party also drew on interest in the Protestant succession and free trade and fears of mobs, Covenanters and Jacobites to build support for incorporation.

Across the divided terrain of Scottish politics there were grounds for support for, as well as resistance to, incorporation. Expediency and personal interest determined the positions of some, but many held views shaped by experience, ideology and public debates. The development of a public critique of the union of crowns, proposals for a reformed, federal union and attacks on the dangers of closer union influenced many against incorporation before 1706. Recognising this, in 1706–7 the government went to great lengths to provide an alternative view of incorporation as the path to peaceful prosperity under a Protestant monarch. At the same time, anti-union discourse turned increas-

4 'Scotland's ruine', 257. In one case, a payment went to a relative of a member.
5 Ferguson, 'Making of the treaty of union', 108.
6 'Scotland's ruine', 257.
7 Ibid. 172. A recent analysis has found no significant link between ownership of African Company shares and pro-union voting: McLean and McMillan, *State of the union*, 43–5.

ingly radical as tracts asserted popular sovereignty, revived Covenanting rhetoric and advocated open resistance to parliament. Aggressive attempts to influence parliament with expressions of negative opinion spilled over into riots as rumours of a rising spread through Edinburgh. Drawing attention to the destabilising potential of anti-unionism, Court propaganda portrayed the opposition as a danger to all settled authority and called on subjects to support parliament in their lawful deliberations.

Under these conditions, some Scots accepted incorporation, if reluctantly, as the best option under the circumstances. Backing for the treaty, or a disinclination to oppose it, can be seen in the narrowness of the majorities in favour of the petitions from the Convention of Royal Burghs, the African Company and the Commission of the General Assembly. A handful of pamphlets published late in the session indicate the emergence of support for an amended treaty to secure the Protestant succession. Even Covenanted Presbyterians could accept incorporation under the right circumstances, as indicated by the views of Jonet Fergusone, a godly woman from Glasgow. In October 1706 Jonet wrote to the duke of Hamilton to urge him to ensure that the Covenants were renewed in the union. Though she did not like the union, to her it was more important that Scotland's covenanted Church be maintained than its kingdom.[8] Trade also provided reasons to support the treaty, as seen in a letter from the burgh of Montrose to its parliamentary commissioner indicating the town council's expectation of the 'many and great' advantages to be gained from the union and its fear that rejection of the treaty would lead England to impose new economic sanctions.[9]

Opinion in Scotland divided on the union, though the development of adversarial opinion politics in the union crisis produced far more evidence of opposition to incorporation than support for it. Such was the nature of the early modern public sphere: those excluded from political decision-making by fundamental ideological differences attempted to build a power base by claiming to represent the public interest. The nature of the union of crowns, with its absentee king, meant that the opposition in Scotland could claim to represent not just a public but a national and patriotic interest. Using publications to develop and inform support in the shires and burghs, oppositional leaders drew on traditional patterns of consultation between the government and its subjects to bring the pressure of public opinion to bear upon government.

The Country party's failure in its attempts to use public opinion to defeat the treaty of union reveals the limitations of opinion politics in the early modern period. Since representations of opinion had legitimacy only as a means of consultation, petitions and instructions could not force members to vote against the treaty. To increase their limited leverage, Country discourse

8   NAS, GD 406/1/5230.
9   Smout, 'The burgh of Montrose, 182–4.

made radical claims for constituent and even popular sovereignty and relied heavily on mass engagement in petitions and crowd actions to back up its representations. Yet the very aggression of these tactics made them likely to provoke state repression. Public opinion claimed a moral authority as the voice of the commonweal, but the state contested the legitimacy of these oppositional representations. To the crown, opinion politics only mattered insofar as it threatened central control of politics and policy. The Country party's assertive opposition to the treaty resulted in a shift of support away from the Court party in early November 1706, spurring ministers to crack down on disorder while offering concessions to relieve the pressure on its coalition. The politics of opinion in 1706–7 therefore ended in compromise and concession, the typical response of early modern authorities to petitioned grievances. Though the Country party could not defeat the enactment of the treaty, opinion politics succeeded in producing a treaty which had been modified in response to public objections.

The union crisis thus provides key insights into the workings of the early modern public sphere. During this era, censorship and conventional limitations on the public nature of politics restricted the involvement of subjects in political discourse and activity, creating a sharply limited public sphere largely existing in personal communication in oral or written forms. During crisis periods, however, involvement expanded as oppositional leaders sponsored mass communications and mobilised disaffected opinion to influence the crown. This study has outlined the preconditions in the public sphere in rising literacy, expanding communication networks and regular meetings of political bodies; and in the ideological divisions that fuelled political disagreements and contributed to the development of a permanent opposition in institutional politics. In Scotland these ideological divisions included the political dichotomy of supporters of the Whig Revolution and Jacobites, and the religious dichotomy of Presbyterians and Episcopalians, with each group containing conformists and extremists. In addition, Scotland's union of crowns and absentee monarch created Anglo-Scottish conflicts of interest and gave extra weight to oppositional claims to represent a national interest. Conditions of censorship and the book trade made the pamphlet a key form of political communication in early eighteenth-century Scotland; and conventions of humble entreaty made the petition the primary means by which adversarial opinion was expressed. Crowds also played a role in opinion politics as organisers sought to reinforce their demands with demonstrations of popular support, though collective action did not always remain within the parameters set by elite leaders.

In a crisis, the shaping and mobilising of oppositional opinion gave power to leaders seeking to change national policy. Oppositional magnates in Scotland may have mobilised public opinion to build their personal standing and power as party leaders, but their activities rested on real disaffection rooted in individual experience of crown policy and deeply held ideological commitments. By influencing local opinion with pamphlets, and encouraging its

167

expression in petitions, party leaders accused the government of failing to serve the commonweal. The implicit threat of disorder suggested by aggressive, mass representations of opinion could secure concessions from the state; but, if pushed too far, it could backfire on the organisers by raising fears of disorder and democratic anarchy.

As long as the state could contain opinion politics with private management and affordable concessions, it did not need to make its own public appeals to opinion. During the union crisis, the Scottish public sphere was dominated by oppositional voices until 1706. Supporters of the government produced only a handful of pamphlets, driven by a need to court English opinion in London as much as Scottish opinion. Only in 1706, when the experience of an unmanageable Scottish opposition had convinced crown and ministry alike of the need to reduce Scotland's political independence through incorporation, did the Court party devote significant resources to wooing Scottish opinion.

Though the product of crisis, opinion politics contributed to stability in Scotland by giving an institutional voice to discontent and forcing the crown to make concessions in response to oppositional grievances. After the union of 1707, Scottish representatives were absorbed into the Whig–Tory dynamic operating in the British parliament, removing an independent Scottish Country interest from British politics.[10] In the first decades after union, pamphlets and printed petitions brought some complaints from Scotland into the British public sphere, but it became more likely that discontent in Scotland would emerge in forms of open revolt.[11] This can be seen not just in the Jacobite rebellions, but in ongoing local resistance to changes arising from the union, including smuggling and rioting in reaction to new customs exactions, tumults in 1720 over an increase in grain exports encouraged by treaty drawbacks, and rioting in 1725 over an attempt to impose a malt tax in Scotland.[12] It can also be seen in parish-level resistance to unwanted ministers after the reimposition of patronage in 1712 and the refusal of hardline clerics to take the 1712 abjuration oath because of its incompatability with

---

10 Shaw, *Eighteenth-century Scotland*, ch. ii.

11 Anon., *Reasons against passing the bill to prevent carrying forreign goods from Scotland to England, after the union*, London 1707; *The case of the towns of Glasgow, Aberdeen, Dumfries and others praying a redress of the present manner of assessing the royal boroughs of Scotland*, [London 1711]; [Edinburgh magistrates], *A defence of the magistrates of Edinburgh, and Lords of the Session, against the appeal and complaint of Mr. James Greenshields*, [Edinburgh? 1711]; [William Carstares], *The case of the Church of Scotland, with relation to the bill for a toleration*, London [1712]; *To the queens most excellent majesty, the most humble representation and petition of the Commission of the General Assembly*, [Edinburgh?] 1712; Anon., *Advice to all Scots electors, by a burges of Edinburgh*, [Edinburgh 1713/14?].

12 Christopher A. Whatley, The union of 1707, integration and the Scottish burghs: the case of the 1720 food riots', *SHR* lxxviii (Oct. 1999), 192–218

Presbyterian principles.[13] This post-union dynamic reminds us that public opinion begins with real differences and grievances at the local level; the public sphere provides a means by which these can be framed, mobilised and heard.

---

[13] Callum G. Brown, 'Protest in the pews: interpreting Presbyterianism and society in fracture during the Scottish economic revolution', in T. M. Devine (ed.), *Conflict and stability in Scottish society, 1700–1850*, Edinburgh 1990, 97–9; Anon., *Information for Mr. Colin Campbell moderator of the presbytery of Aberdeen*, [Edinburgh?] 1714; Anon., *A letter from a gentleman in Edinburgh to his friend in the country concerning the way and manner in which the abjuration oath was sworn by the ministers in the shire of Edinburgh*, [Edinburgh] 1712; *Act and recommendation of the Commission of the General Assembly for preserving the unity and peace of the Church*, [Edinburgh] 1712.

Bibliography

Unpublished primary sources

Dumfries Archive Centre
A   2/8 (7)
RB   2/2/10
G   2/6/17

Edinburgh, National Archives of Scotland
Church of Scotland papers
CH 1/2/4/1, 1/2/5/1, 1/2/5/3, 1/2/22/2, 1/2/22/3, 1/3/8, 1/3/9, 2/98/1, 2/464/2, 8/184

Dukes of Hamilton and Brandon papers
GD 406/1/4368, 4444, 4813, 4815, 4830, 4900, 4910, 4927, 4944, 4948, 4976, 5004, 5100, 5116, 5118, 5119, 5181, 5195, 5230, 5294, 5297, 5321, 5343, 5370, 5383, 5439, 6013, 7077, 7091, 7098, 7127, 7138, 7851, 7854–5, 7895, 8025, 8074–5, 8104, 8107, 8122, 9731, 9734, 9738, 9740, 9744, 9747, 10926, 11787

Justiciary Court records
JC 26/81/31

Parliamentary papers
PA 7/17/21A, 7/20, 7/28

Privy council records
PC 1/52, 1/53, 13/3/1706

Edinburgh, National Library of Scotland
Wodrow quartos
vols xxviii, xxx, xl, lxxiii

Advocates MS
'Heads of things fit to be granted and done in the ensuing session of parliament' (1700)
'Resolution of some doubts, with relation to the publick debts of Scotland, as stated in the 15 article of the Treaty of Union' (3 Feb. 1707)

Glasgow University, Department of Special Collections
A. M., 'A short conference ... anent the union of the two kingdoms', London 1703

Motherwell, North Lanarkshire Council Archives, Motherwell Heritage Centre
Hamilton of Dalzell papers USC 052

Published primary sources

Official documents and publications
Acts of the parliaments of Scotland, ed. Thomas Thomson, [Edinburgh] 1824–70, v–xi

The statutes at large, ed. Owen Ruffhead, London 1769, iv

Newspapers and periodicals
Edinburgh Courant
Edinburgh Gazette
Flying Post
Post Man
Review

Contemporary books and articles
[Patrick Abercromby], The advantages of the Act of Security, compar'd with these of the intended union: founded on the revolution-principles publish'd by Mr. Daniel De Foe, [Edinburgh] 1707

Act and recommendation of the Commission of the General Assembly for preserving the unity and peace of the Church, [Edinburgh] 1712

Analecta scotica, ed. J. Maidment, Edinburgh 1834, i, ii

Anderson, James, An historical essay, shewing that the crown and kingdom of Scotland, is imperial and independent, Edinburgh 1705

Anon., A letter, giving a description of the Isthmus of Darian [sic], Edinburgh 1699

Anon., A short and impartial view of the manner and occasion of the Scots colony's coming away from Darien, [Edinburgh] 1699

Anon., The people of Scotland's groans and lamentable complaints, pour'd out before the high court of parliament, [Edinburgh 1700]

Anon., A memorial briefly pointing at some advantages of the union of the two kingdoms, London 1702

Anon., Draught of an act for toleration with a few short remarks thereupon, [Edinburgh 1703]

Anon., A letter to a member of parliament, occasioned, by the growing poverty of the nation, [Edinburgh 1703?]

Anon., A plea against pamphlets in a letter from a gentleman in the countrey to his correspondent in Edinburgh, Edinburgh 1703

Anon., A seasonable alarm for Scotland ... concerning the present danger of the kingdom, and of the Protestant religion, [Edinburgh] 1703

Anon., *A speech in parliament touching the freedom and frequency of parliament*, [Edinburgh 1703]

Anon., *A three-fold cord for ensuring and securing of Presbytery in Scotland*, [Edinburgh 1703]

Anon., *A panegyrick on a noble peer and worthy patriot*, [Edinburgh 1703/4?]

Anon., *The Act of Security is the only rational method of procuring Scotland a happy constitution, free from the illegal invasions of its liberties and laws, and the base usurpation of its ancient sovereignty*, [Edinburgh] 1704

Anon., *A discourse of present importance*, [Edinburgh] 1704

Anon., *An essay, shewing, that there is no probability of there being so much French interest, as it's certain there's English influence in our present parliament of Scotland*, [Edinburgh] 1704

Anon., *The great danger to Scotland as to all its sacred and civil concerns, from these, who are commonly known by the name of Jacobites*, [Edinburgh] 1704

Anon., *Hereditary succession in the Protestant line, unalterable: in answer to the Scots Bill of Security*, London 1704

Anon., *A manifesto, asserting and clearing the legal right of the Princess Sophia, and her issue, the Serene House of Hanover, to the succession of Scotland*, Edinburgh 1704

Anon., *Scotland's interest: or, the great benefit and necessity of a communication of trade with England*, [Edinburgh] 1704

Anon., *The sin and shame of Scotland*, Edinburgh 1704

Anon., *A watch-word to Scotland in perillous times*, [Edinburgh] 1704

Anon., *An essay for promoting of trade, and increasing the coin of the nation, in a letter from a gentleman in the country to his friend at Edinburgh, a member of parliament*, Edinburgh 1705

Anon., *An essay upon the union of the kingdoms of England and Scotland*, [London] 1705

Anon., *Great Britain's union, and the security of the Hanover succession, consider'd*, London 1705

Anon., *The horrid murther committed by Captain Green and his crue, on Captain Drummond and his whole men*, [Edinburgh 1705]

Anon., *The merits of piracie, or a new song on Captain Green and his bloody crue*, [Edinburgh 1705]

Anon., *Observator or a dialogue between a country man and a landwart school-master*, nos 1–8, [Edinburgh] 1705

Anon., *A seasonable advice to all who encline to go in pirrating*, [Edinburgh 1705]

Anon., *Some weighty considerations, why Scotland should stipulate terms of an union with England: by a letter from the country to his friend in parliament*, [Edinburgh 1705]

Anon., *A speech concerning a treaty of union with England*, [Edinburgh 1705]

Anon., *An account of the burning of the articles of the union at Dumfries*, [Edinburgh] 1706

Anon., *An answer to some queries, &c. relative to the union: in a conference betwixt a coffee-master, and a countrey-farmer*, [Edinburgh] 1706

Anon., *A copy of a letter from a country farmer to his laird, a member of parliament*, [Edinburgh 1706]

Anon., *Counter quiries to the quiries burnt at the cross of Edinburgh*, [Edinburgh] 1706

Anon., *A discourse concerning the union*, [Edinburgh 1706]

Anon., *The equivalent explain'd*, [Edinburgh 1706]

Anon., *A letter to Sir J. P. Bart.* [Sir John Pakington] *a member for the ensuing parliament, relating to the union of England and Scotland*, [London? 1706?]

Anon., *To the loyal and religious hearts in parliament, some few effects of the union, proposed between Scotland and England*, [Edinburgh 1706]

Anon., *Remarks for the salt-masters, fishers of salmond, herrings and white-fish, and others who make use of Scots salt, humbly offered upon the eighth article of the Treaty of Union*, [Edinburgh 1706]

Anon., *The smoaking flax unquenchable*, [Edinburgh] 1706

Anon., *A speech in season against the union*, [Edinburgh 1706]

Anon., *State of the controversy betwixt united and separate parliaments*, [Edinburgh] 1706

Anon., *We heard that the parliament is sitting at Edinburgh ... A word to the Unioners and their confederats thee parliamenters*, [Edinburgh 1706]

Anon., *Reasons against passing the bill to prevent carrying forreign goods from Scotland to England, after the union*, London 1707

Anon., *The Scotch echo to the English legion*, [Edinburgh] 1707

Anon., *A true and exact list of the whole kings of Scotland since Fergus the First*, Edinburgh 1707

Anon., *A letter from a gentleman in Edinburgh to his friend in the country concerning the way and manner in which the abjuration oath was sworn by the ministers in the shire of Edinburgh*, [Edinburgh] 1712

Anon., *Advice to all Scots electors, by a burges of Edinburgh*, [Edinburgh 1713/14?]

Anon., *Information for Mr. Colin Campbell moderator of the presbytery of Aberdeen*, [Edinburgh] 1714

[John Arbuthnot], *A sermon preach'd to the people, at the mercat cross of Edinburgh: on the subject of the union*, [Edinburgh?] 1706

[William Atwood], *The superiority and direct dominion of the imperial crown of England, over the crown and kingdom of Scotland*, London 1704

[William Atwood], *The Scotch patriot unmask'd*, London 1705

Bacon, Sir Francis, *A brief discourse of the happy union betwixt the two kingdoms of Scotland and England*, [Edinburgh? 1702]

[John Bannatyne], *A letter from a Presbyterian minister in the countrey, to a member of parliament and also the Commission of the Church concerning toleration and patronages*, [Edinburgh] 1703

[John Bannatyne], *Some queries proposed to consideration, relative to the union now intended*, [Edinburgh 1706]

Beeston, Sir William, *By the honourable Sir William Beeston Kt his majesties lieutenant governor*, Edinburgh 1699

[William Black], *Some considerations in relation to trade*, [Edinburgh] 1706

[Andrew Brown], *Some very weighty and seasonable considerations tending to dispose, excite and qualify the nation, for the more effectual treating with England in relation to an union of confederacy*, [Edinburgh] 1703

[Andrew Brown], *A scheme proposing a true touch-stone for the due trial of a proper union betwixt Scotland & England*, Edinburgh 1706

[Sir Alexander Bruce of Broomhill], *A speech in the parliament of Scotland, in relation to presbyterian government*, [Edinburgh 1702]

Burnet, Gilbert, *History of my own time*, ed. M. J. Routh, Oxford 1833

[Robert Calder], *Reasons for a toleration to the episcopal clergy*, Edinburgh 1703

[Andrew Cant], *A sermon preached on the XXX day of January 1702/3 at Edinburgh*, Edinburgh 1703

[William Carstares], *The case of the Church of Scotland, with relation to the bill for a toleration*, [London 1712]

The case of the towns of Glasgow, Aberdeen, Dumfries and others praying a redress of the present manner of assessing the royal boroughs of Scotland, [London 1711]

Charters, writs and public documents of the royal burgh of Dundee, 1292–1880, ed. William Hay, Dundee 1880

[James Clark], *Scotland's speech to her sons*, [Edinburgh 1706]

Clerk of Penicuik, Sir John, *History of the union of Scotland & England*, ed. Douglas Duncan, Edinburgh 1993

[John Clerk of Penicuik], *A letter to a friend, giving an account how the treaty of union has been received here*, [Edinburgh] 1706

Company of Scotland Trading to Africa and the Indies, *A full and exact collection of all the considerable addresses…and other publick papers relating to the Company of Scotland trading to Africa and the Indies*, Edinburgh 1700

———— *Scotland's right to Caledonia (formerly called Darien) and the legality of its settlement, asserted*, [Edinburgh] 1700

———— *The humble representation of the council-general of the Company of Scotland trading to Africa and the Indies*, Edinburgh 1706

'Correspondence between George Ridpath and the Reverend Robert Wodrow', ed. James Maidment, *Miscellany of the Abbotsford Club*, Edinburgh 1837, i

Correspondence of George Baillie of Jerviswood MDCCII–MDCCVIII, ed. Gilbert Eliot-Murray-Kynynmound, 2nd earl of Minto, Edinburgh 1842

The Darien papers, ed. John Hill Burton, Edinburgh 1849

[Daniel Defoe], 'A memorial from the gentlemen, freeholders, and inhabitants of the counties of _____ in behalf of themselves and many thousands of the good people of England' (1701), in *The works of Daniel Defoe*, ed. William Hazlitt, London 1843, iii. 3–5

[Daniel Defoe], 'The original power of the collective body of the people of England, examined and asserted' (1701), in *A true collection*, i. 133–66

[Daniel Defoe], *A true collection of the writings of the author of the true-born Englishman*, London 1705

[Daniel Defoe], *An essay at removing national prejudices, against a union with England, part III*, [Edinburgh] 1706

[Daniel Defoe], *A letter concerning trade, from several Scots gentlemen that are merchants in England, to their country-men that are merchants in Scotland*, [Edinburgh] 1706

[Daniel Defoe], *A letter from Mr. Reason, to the high and mighty prince the mob*, [Edinburgh 1706]

[Daniel Defoe], *Observations on the fifth article of the treaty of union, humbly offered to the consideration of the parliament, relating to foreign ships*, [Edinburgh] 1706

[Daniel Defoe], *The rabbler convicted*, [Edinburgh] 1706

[Daniel Defoe], *A seasonable warning or the pope and king of France unmasked*, [Edinburgh] 1706

[Daniel Defoe], *A short letter to the Glasgow-men*, [Edinburgh 1706]

[Daniel Defoe], *The state of the excise after the union, compared with what it is now*, [Edinburgh] 1706

[Daniel Defoe], A fifth essay, at removing national prejudices, [Edinburgh] 1707

[Daniel Defoe], Two great questions considered, I: What is the obligation of parliaments to the addresses or petitions of the people, and what the duty of the addressers?; II: Whether the obligation of the Covenant or the other national engagements, is concern'd in the Treaty of Union? Being a sixth essay at removing national prejudices against the union, [Edinburgh] 1707

Defoe, Daniel, The history of the union of Great Britain, Edinburgh 1709

[James Donaldson], A letter to a member of parliament, from a wel-wisher of his country, [Edinburgh 1705]

Drake, James, Historia anglo-scotica, London 1703

Dumbarton burgh records, 1627–1746, Dumbarton 1860

Dundas, John, The method of procedure by presbyteries in setting of schools in every parish, Edinburgh 1709

Early letters of Robert Wodrow, 1698–1709, ed. L.W. Sharp, Edinburgh 1937

[Edinburgh magistrates], A defence of the magistrates of Edinburgh, and Lords of the Session, against the appeal and complaint of Mr James Greenshields, [Edinburgh? 1711]

Extracts from the records of the burgh of Edinburgh, 1689–1701, ed. Helen Armet, Edinburgh 1962

Extracts from the records of the burgh of Edinburgh, 1701–1718, ed. Helen Armet, Edinburgh 1967

Extracts from the records of the burgh of Glasgow, ed. Sir James D. Marwick, Glasgow 1908

Extracts from the records of the Convention of the Royal Burghs of Scotland, Edinburgh 1880

Extracts from the records of the royal burgh of Lanark, ed. Robert Renwick, Glasgow 1893, iv

Extracts from the records of the royal burgh of Stirling, 1667–1752, ed. Robert Renwick, Glasgow 1889, ii

[Blackerby Fairfax], A discourse upon the uniting Scotland with England, London 1702

[Robert Ferguson], A just and modest vindication of the Scots design, for the having established a colony at Darien, [Edinburgh] 1699

Fletcher, Andrew, 'Two discourses concerning the affairs of Scotland' (1698), in Political works, 83–117

[Andrew Fletcher], Overture for limitations on the successors of Her Majesty ... who shall be likewise kings of England, [Edinburgh 1703]

[Andrew Fletcher], Speeches, by a member of the parliament, which began at Edinburgh, the 6th of May 1703, [Edinburgh] 1703

Fletcher, Andrew, Political works, ed. John Robertson, Cambridge 1997

[William Forbes], A pil for pork eaters, or a Scots lancet for an English swelling, [Edinburgh] 1705

[Archibald Foyer], Scotland's present duty, [Edinburgh] 1700

[Archibald Foyer], Queries to the Presbyterian noblemen, barons, burgesses, ministers and commoners in Scotland who are for the scheme of an incorporating union, [Edinburgh 1706]

[George Garden], A letter to the episcopal clergy in Scotland, Edinburgh 1703

[Francis Grant], An essay for peace, Edinburgh 1703

[Francis Grant], *The patriot resolved, in a letter to an addresser, from his friend,* [Edinburgh] 1707

[James Hadow], *A survey of the case of the Episcopal clergy,* Edinburgh 1703

[John Hamilton, Lord Belhaven], *A speech in parliament, by the Lord Belhaven; upon the Act for Security of the Kingdom,* Edinburgh 1703

——— *The Lord Belhaven's speech in parliament, the 17th of July 1705,* [Edinburgh] 1705

——— *The Lord Belhaven's speech in parliament the 15th day of November 1706,* [Edinburgh] 1706

——— *The Lord Belhaven's speech in parliament the second day of November 1706,* [Edinburgh 1706]

Her Majesties most gracious letter to the parliament of Scotland: together with His Grace the Lord Commissioner, and the Lord High Chancellor their speeches, Edinburgh 1704

Her Majesties most gracious letter to the privy council of Scotland, Edinburgh 1703

[James Hodges], *The rights and interests of the two British monarchies, inquir'd into, and clear'd; with a special respect to an united or separate state: treatise I,* London 1703

[James Hodges], *That part of a late book which relates to a general fast and humiliation,* [Edinburgh] 1706

[James Hodges], *The rights and interests of the two British monarchies inquir'd into and cleared: with a special respect to an united or separate state: treatise III,* London 1706

The humble representation of the commission of the late General Assembly, [Edinburgh 1703]

Hume of Crossrigg, Sir David, *A diary of the proceedings of the parliament and privy council of Scotland, May 21, 1700–March 7,1707,* Edinburgh 1823

[John Humfrey], *A draught for a national church accommodation; whereby the subjects of England and Scotland, however different in their judgements concerning episcopacy and presbytery, may yet be united… in one Church and kingdom of Great Britain,* London 1705

Instructions by the magistrates and town council of the burgh of Lauder, to their commissioner in parliament, Edinburgh [1706]

Instructions for the commissioners of the sheriffdom of Dumfries, [Edinburgh 1706]

It is resolved, that the parliament shall consider an act… and therefore, prop. The Act for Peace and War is altogether useless, [Edinburgh 1703]

[James Johnston], *Reflections on a late speech by the Lord Haversham, in so far as it relates to the affairs of Scotland,* London 1704

Ker of Kersland, John, *The memoirs of John Ker of Kersland,* London 1726

A lady of honour, *The golden island or the Darian [sic] song: in commendation of all concerned in that noble enterprize of the valiant Scots,* Edinburgh 1699

Leslie, John, earl of Rothes, *A relation of proceedings concerning the affairs of the Kirk of Scotland, from August 1637 to July 1638,* Edinburgh 1830

Letter in 1320 to Pope John declaring for Robert the Bruce, [Edinburgh] 1706

The letters of Daniel Defoe, ed. George Harris Healey, Oxford 1955

Leven and Melville papers: letters and state papers chiefly addressed to George earl of Melville secretary of state for Scotland, 1689–91, ed. William H. L. Melville, Edinburgh 1843

The Lochmaben court and council book, 1612–1721, ed. John B. Wilson, Edinburgh 2001

Logan, John, *A sermon preached before… the honourable estates of parliament in the New-Church of Edinburgh upon the 27 of October 1706*, Edinburgh 1706

[George Mackenzie, earl of Cromarty], *A continuation of a few brief and modest reflexions*, [Edinburgh 1703]

[George Mackenzie, earl of Cromarty], *A few brief and modest reflexions, perswading a just indulgence to be granted to the episcopal clergy and people in Scotland*, [Edinburgh] 1703

[George Mackenzie, earl of Cromarty], *A friendly return to a letter concerning Sir George Mackenzie's and Sir John Nisbet's observation*, [Edinburgh] 1706

[George Mackenzie, earl of Cromarty], *Trialogus: a conference betwixt Mr. Con, Mr. Pro and Mr. Indifferent, concerning the union: second conversation*, [Edinburgh] 1706

[George Mackenzie, earl of Cromarty], *Two letters concerning the present union, from a peer in Scotland to a peer in England*, [Edinburgh] 1706

[George Mackenzie, Viscount Tarbat], *Parainesis pacifica*, Edinburgh–London 1702

[George Mackenzie, Viscount Tarbat], *Speech in the parliament of Scotland upon the union and upon limitations*, [Edinburgh 1702]

The manuscripts of the duke of Hamilton, ed. W. Fraser, London 1887

The manuscripts of his grace the duke of Portland, London 1897, iv

[Gavin Mitchell], *Humble pleadings*, [Edinburgh?] 1713

[William Paterson], *An inquiry into the reasonableness and consequences of an union*, London 1706

[Peter Paxton], *A scheme of union between England and Scotland, with advantages to both kingdoms*, London 1705

Philo-Britan [Walter Harris], *The defence of the Scots settlement at Darien, answered*, London 1699

Philo-Caledon, *A defence of the Scots settlement at Darien*, [Edinburgh] 1699

[James Ramsey], *A letter from a gentleman to a member of parliament concerning toleration*, Edinburgh 1703

Report on the Laing manuscripts, ed. Henry Paton, London 1925, ii

Report on the manuscripts of the earl of Mar and Kellie, ed. Henry Paton, London 1904

[George Ridpath], *An enquiry into the causes of the miscarriage of the Scots colony at Darien*, Glasgow 1700

[George Ridpath], *Scotland's grievances relating to Darien*, [Edinburgh] 1700

[George Ridpath], *A discourse upon the union of Scotland and England*, [Edinburgh?] 1702

George Ridpath], *An historical account of the antient rights and power of the parliament of Scotland*, [Edinburgh] 1703

[George Ridpath], *The proceedings of the parliament of Scotland begun at Edinburgh, 6th May 1703*, [Edinburgh?] 1704

[George Ridpath], *The reducing of Scotland by arms … considered*, London 1705

[George Ridpath], *Considerations upon the union of the two kingdoms*, [Edinburgh?] 1706

R. S., *Some neutral considerations, with relation to two printed papers, which are cry'd about the streets*, [Edinburgh 1707]

'Scotland's ruine': Lockhart of Carnwath's memoirs of the union, ed. Daniel Szechi, Aberdeen 1995

Seafield correspondence from 1685 to 1708, ed. James Grant, Edinburgh 1912

A selection from the papers of the earl of Marchmont, 1685–1750, ed. G. H. Rose, London 1831

[William Seton of Pitmedden], The interest of Scotland, in three essays, Edinburgh 1700

[William Seton of Pitmedden], Memorial to the members of parliament of the Court party, [Edinburgh 1700]

[William Seton of Pitmedden], A short speech prepared to be spoken, by a worthy member in parliament, concerning the present state of the nation, [Edinburgh] 1700

[William Seton of Pitmedden], Some thoughts, on ways and means for making this nation a gainer in foreign commerce, Edinburgh 1705

[William Seton of Pitmedden], Scotland's great advantages by an union with England: showen in a letter from the country, to a member of parliament, [Edinburgh] 1706

Seton of Pitmedden, William, A speech in the parliament of Scotland, the second day of November, 1706 on the first article of the treaty of union, London 1706

[Robert Sibbald], The liberty and independency of the kingdom and Church of Scotland asserted. to which is added, a speech at the proclamation of K. James VI concerning the succession to the crown of England, Edinburgh 1703

[Sir Archibald Sinclair], Some thoughts on the present state of affairs, [Edinburgh] 1703

[Thomas Spence], The testamentary duty of the parliament of Scotland, [Edinburgh] 1707

[John Spottiswoode], A speech of one of the barons of the shire of B—— [Berwick] at a meeting of the barons and freeholders of that shire, [Edinburgh] 1702

[John Spottiswoode], The trimmer: or, some necessary cautions, concerning the union of the kingdoms of Scotland and England; with an answer to some of the chief objections against an incorporating union, [Edinburgh] 1706

J[ohn] S[preull], An accompt current betwixt Scotland and England balanced, [Edinburgh?] 1705

State-papers and letters addressed to William Carstares, ed. Joseph McCormick, Edinburgh 1774

Stewart of Goodtrees, James, Jus populi vindicatum, n.p. 1669

Taylor, Joseph, A journey to Edenborough in Scotland, ed. William Cowan, Edinburgh 1903

Ta hir grace her majesties high commissioner, an te honourable estates of parliament; te address far te fishers on te Highland coasts, an all uthers inhapiting te Highlands, [Edinburgh 1706]

To his grace her majesties high commissioner and the honourable estates of parliament: the heemble petition of the peer shank workers and fingren spinners of Aberdeen, and places, thereabout, [Edinburgh 1706]

To his grace, her majesties high commissioner, and honourable estates of parliament, the humble address of a considerable body of people in the south and western shires, [Edinburgh 1706]

To his grace, her majesty's high commissioner, and the right honourable, the estates of *parliament, the address of the commissioners to the general Convention of the Royal Burrows*, [Edinburgh 1706]

To his grace his majesties high commissioner, and the right honourable the estates of parliament: the humble petition of the council-general of the Company of Scotland trading to Africa and the Indies, [Edinburgh] 1698

To the queen's most excellent majestie, the humble address and supplication of the suffering episcopal clergy in the kingdom of Scotland, [Edinburgh] 1703

To the queens most excellent majesty, the most humble representation and petition of the commission of the General Assembly, [Edinburgh?] 1712

Unto his grace, her majesties high commissioner and the right honourable the estates of parliament, the humble address of the presbytry of Hamilton, [Edinburgh 1706]

[James Webster], *An essay upon toleration by a sincere lover of the Church and State*, [Edinburgh] 1703

[James Webster?], *A letter from one of the Country party to his friend of the Court party*, [Edinburgh 1704]

[James Webster], *Lawful prejudices against an incorporating union with England*, Edinburgh 1707

Williamson, David, *A sermon preached in Edinburgh at the opening of the General Assembly*, Edinburgh 1703

Wilson, John, *An essay on enthusiasm*, Edinburgh 1706

Wisheart, William, *A sermon preached before the synod of Lothian and Tweeddale*, Edinburgh 1703

——— *Two sermons on Jeremiah 30.7*, Edinburgh 1707

[Robert Wylie], *A letter from a gentleman in the city, to a minister in the countrey*, [Edinburgh 1703]

[Robert Wylie], *A speech without doors concerning toleration*, [Edinburgh] 1703

[Robert Wylie], *The insecurity of a printed overture for an act for the Church's security*, [Edinburgh] 1706

[Robert Wylie], *A letter concerning the union, with Sir George Mackenzie's observations and Sir John Nisbet's opinion upon the same subject*, [Edinburgh] 1706

Secondary sources

Backscheider, Paula R., *Defoe: ambition & innovation*, Lexington 1986

——— *Daniel Defoe: his life*, Baltimore 1989

Baldwin, Geoff, 'The "public" as a rhetorical community in early modern England', in Alexandra Shepard and Phil Withington (eds), *Communities in early modern England*, Manchester 2000, 199–215

Baron, Sabrina A., 'The guises of dissemination in early seventeenth-century England: news in manuscript and print', in Dooley and Baron, *Politics of information*, 41–56.

Beik, William, *Urban protest in seventeenth-century France*, Cambridge 1997

Brake, Wayne te, *Shaping history: ordinary people in European politics, 1500–1700*, Berkeley 1998

Brown, Callum G., 'Protest in the pews: interpreting Presbyterianism and society in fracture during the Scottish economic revolution', in T. M. Devine (ed.), *Conflict and stability in Scottish society, 1700–1850*, Edinburgh 1990, 83–105.

Cogswell, Thomas, Richard Cust and Peter Lake (eds), *Politics, religion and popularity in early Stuart Britain*, Cambridge 2002

Colley, Linda, *Britons: forging the nation, 1707–1837*, New Haven 1992

Couper, W. J., *The Edinburgh periodical press*, Stirling 1908, i

Cowan, Edward J., *'For freedom alone': the Declaration of Arbroath, 1320*, East Linton 2003

Cowans, Jon, 'Habermas and French history: the public sphere and the problem of political legitimacy', *French History* xiii/2 (June 1999), 134–60

Cressy, David, *Bonfires and bells: national memory and the Protestant calendar in Elizabethan and Stuart England*, London 1989

Croft, Pauline, 'The reputation of Robert Cecil: libels, political opinion and popular awareness in the early seventeenth century', *Transactions of the Royal Historical Society* 6th ser. i (1991), 43–69

——— 'Libels, popular literacy and public opinion in early modern England', *Historical Research* lxviii (1995), 266–85

Cust, Richard, 'News and politics in early seventeenth-century England', *P&P* cxii (1986), 60–90

——— 'Charles I and popularity', in Cogswell, Cust and Lake, *Politics, religion and popularity*, 235–58

Davis, Natalie Zemon, 'The rites of violence', in her *Society and culture in early modern France*, London 1975, 152–87

DeKrey, Gary S., *A fractured society: the politics of London in the first age of party, 1689–1715*, Oxford 1985

——— *London and the Restoration, 1659–1683*, Cambridge 2005

Devine, T. M. and J. R. Young (eds), *Eighteenth-century Scotland: new perspectives*, East Linton 1999

Donaldson, Gordon, *Scotland: James V to James VII*, Edinburgh 1971

Dooley, Brendan, 'The public sphere and the organisation of knowledge', in John Marino (ed.), *Early modern Italy, 1550–1796*, Oxford 2002, 209–28

——— and Sabrina A. Baron (eds), *The politics of information in early modern Europe*, London 2001

Downie, J. A., *Robert Harley and the press: propaganda and public opinion in the age of Swift and Defoe*, Cambridge 1979

——— 'The development of the political press', in Clyve Jones (ed.), *Britain in the first age of party*, London 1987, 111–28

Dunlop, A. Ian, *William Carstares and the Kirk by law established*, Edinburgh 1964

Ferguson, William, 'The making of the treaty of union of 1707', *SHR* xliii (Oct. 1964), 89–110

——— 'Recent interpretations of the making of the treaty of union of 1707', *Scottish Tradition* vii/viii (1977–8), 95–114

——— *Scotland's relations with England: a survey to 1707*, Edinburgh 1994

Fox, Adam, 'Rumour, news and popular political opinion in Elizabethan and early Stuart England', *HJ* xl (1997), 597–620

Gibson, John, *Playing the Scottish card: the Franco-Jacobite invasion of 1708*, Edinburgh 1988

Goldie, Mark, 'Divergence and union: Scotland and England, 1660–1707', in Brendan Bradshaw and John Morrill (eds), *The British problem, c. 1534–1707: state formation in the Atlantic archipelago*, Basingstoke 1996, 220–45

———— 'The unacknowledged republic: office holding in early modern England', in Harris, *Politics of the excluded*, 153–94

Gunn, J. A. W., *Politics and the public interest in the seventeenth century*, London 1969

———— *Queen of the world: opinion in the public life of France from the Renaissance to the Revolution*, Oxford 1995

Habermas, Jürgen, *The structural transformation of the public sphere*, trans. Thomas Burger and Frederick Lawrence, Cambridge MA 1989

Haldane, A. R. B., *Three centuries of Scottish posts: an historical survey to 1836*, Edinburgh 1971

Halliday, Paul D., *Dismembering the body politic: partisan politics in England's towns, 1650–1730*, Cambridge 1998

Hanagan, Michael P., Leslie Page Moch and Wayne te Brake, *Challenging authority: the historical study of contentious politics*, Minneapolis 1998

Harris, Bob, *Politics and the rise of the press: Britain and France, 1620–1800*, London 1996

———— 'Historians, public opinion and the "public sphere"', *Journal of Early Modern History* i (1997), 369–77

———— 'Scotland's herring fisheries and the prosperity of the nation, c. 1600–1760', *SHR* lxxix (Apr. 2000), 39–60

———— 'Scotland's newspapers, the French Revolution and domestic radicalism (c. 1789–1794)', *SHR* lxxxiv (Apr. 2005), 38–62

Harris, Tim, *London crowds in the reign of Charles II: propaganda and politics from the Restoration until the Exclusion Crisis*, Cambridge 1987

———— 'London crowds and the revolution of 1688', in Eveline Cruickshanks (ed.), *By force or by default? The revolution of 1688–1689*, Edinburgh 1989, 44–64

———— 'The problem of "popular political culture"', *History of European Ideas* x (1989), 43–58

———— '"Venerating the honesty of a tinker": the king's friends and the battle for the allegiance of the common people in Restoration England', in Harris, *Politics of the excluded*, 195–232

———— *Restoration: Charles II and his kingdoms, 1660–1685*, London, 2005.

———— (ed.), *The politics of the excluded, c. 1500–1800*, Basingstoke 2001

Hindle, Steve, 'The political culture of the middling sort in English rural communities, c. 1550–1700', in Harris, *Politics of the excluded*, 125–52

Holmes, Geoffrey, *The making of a great power: late Stuart and early Georgian Britain*, London 1993

Houston, R. A., *Scottish literacy and Scottish identity: illiteracy and society in Scotland and northern England, 1600–1800*, Cambridge 1985

Insh, George P., *The Company of Scotland*, London 1932

Jackson, Clare, *Restoration Scotland, 1660–1690: royalist politics, religion and ideas*, Woodbridge 2003

Jones, Clyve (ed.), *Party and management in parliament, 1660–1784*, Leicester 1984

Jouhaud, Christian, 'Readability and persuasion: political handbills', in Roger Chartier (ed.), *The culture of print: power and the uses of print in early modern Europe*, Cambridge 1989, 235–60

Kelly, Paul, 'Constituents' instructions to members of parliament in the eighteenth century', in Jones, *Party and management*, 169–89

Kidd, Colin, *Subverting Scotland's past: Scottish Whig historians and the creation of an Anglo-British identity, 1689–c.1830*, Cambridge 1993

————— 'Religious realignment between the Revolution and the union', in Robertson, *Union for empire*, 145–68

Kishlansky, Mark, 'The emergence of adversary politics in the Long Parliament', *JMH* xlix (Dec. 1977), 617–40

Knights, Mark, *Politics and opinion in crisis, 1678–81*, Cambridge 1994

Koziol, Geoffrey, *Begging pardon and favor: ritual and political order in early medieval France*, Ithaca 1992

Lake, Peter, 'Puritans, popularity and petitions: local politics in national context, Cheshire, 1641', in Cogswell, Cust and Lake, *Politics, religion and popularity*, 259–89

Law, Alexander, *Education in Edinburgh in the eighteenth century*, London 1965

Leneman, Leah, *Living in Atholl: a social history of the estates, 1685–1785*, Edinburgh 1986

Levy, F. J., 'How information spread among the gentry, 1550–1640', *Journal of British Studies* xxi/2 (1982), 11–34

Love, Harold, *Scribal publication in seventeenth-century England*, Oxford 1993

Lynch, Michael, 'Urbanisation and urban networks in seventeenth-century Scotland: some further thoughts', *Scottish Economic and Social History* xii (1992), 24–41

Macinnes, Allan I., 'Influencing the vote: the Scottish estates and the treaty of union, 1706–7', *History Microcomputer Review* (Fall 1990), 11–25

————— *Charles I and the making of the Covenanting movement, 1625–1641*, Edinburgh 1991

————— 'Politically reactionary Brits? The promotion of Anglo-Scottish union, 1603–1707', in S. J. Connolly (ed.), *Great Britain and Ireland since 1500*, Dublin 1999, 43–55

McLean, Iain and Alistair McMillan, *State of the union*, Oxford 2005

McLeod, W. R. and V. B. McLeod, *Anglo-Scottish tracts, 1701–1714*, Lawrence 1979

McMillan, William, *John Hepburn and the Hebronites*, London 1934

Mann, Alastair J., *The Scottish book trade, 1500–1720: print commerce and print control in early modern Scotland*, East Linton 2000

Mason, Roger A. (ed.), *Scotland and England, 1286–1815*, Edinburgh 1987

Miller, John, 'Public opinion in Charles II's England', *History* lxxx (1995), 359–81

Monod, Paul, 'The Jacobite press and English censorship, 1689–95', in Eveline Cruickshanks and Edward Corp (eds), *The Stuart court in exile and the Jacobites*, London 1995, 125–42

Owens, W. R. and P. N. Furbank, 'New light on John Pierce, Defoe's agent in Scotland', *Transactions of the Edinburgh Bibliographical Society* vi/4 (1998), 134–43

Pagan, Theodora, *The Convention of the Royal Burghs of Scotland*, Glasgow 1926

Paul, James Balfour, *The Scots peerage*, Edinburgh 1904

Penovich, Katherine R., 'From "revolution principles" to union: Daniel Defoe's intervention in the Scottish debate', in Robertson, *Union for empire*, 228–42

Pincus, Steve, '"Coffee politicians does create": coffeehouses and Restoration political culture', *JMH* lxvii (Dec. 1995), 807–34

Raymond, Joad, *The invention of the newspaper: English newsbooks, 1641–1649*, Oxford 1996

Riley, P. W. J., *The union of England and Scotland: a study in Anglo-Scottish politics of the eighteenth century*, Manchester 1978

——— *King William and the Scottish politicians*, Edinburgh 1979

Robertson, John, 'Andrew Fletcher's vision of union', in Mason, *Scotland and England*, 203–25

——— 'An elusive sovereignty: the course of the union debate in Scotland, 1698–1707', in Robertson, *Union for empire*, 198–227

——— (ed.), *A union for empire: political thought and the British union of 1707*, Cambridge 1995

Rogers, Nicholas, 'Riot and popular Jacobitism in early Hanoverian England', in Eveline Cruickshanks (ed.), *Ideology and conspiracy: aspects of Jacobitism, 1689–1759*, Edinburgh 1982, 70–88

——— *Whigs and cities: popular politics in the age of Walpole and Pitt*, Oxford 1989

Russell, James Anderson, *History of education in the stewartry of Kirkcudbright*, Newton-Stewart 1951

Sawyer, Jeffrey K., *Printed poison: pamphlet propaganda, faction politics, and the public sphere in early seventeenth-century France*, Berkeley 1990

Schwoerer, Lois G., *'No standing armies'! The anti-army ideology in seventeenth-century England*, Baltimore 1974

Scotland, James, *The history of Scottish education*, London 1969, i

Scott, Paul H, '"Bought and sold for English gold"', *Chapman* lxix–lxx (Autumn 1992), 161–6

——— *Andrew Fletcher and the treaty of union*, Edinburgh 1994

——— 'Defoe in Edinburgh', in *Defoe in Edinburgh and other papers*, East Linton 1995, 3–17

Shaw, John Stuart, *The political history of eighteenth-century Scotland*, Basingstoke 1999

Smout, T. C., *Scottish trade on the eve of union, 1660–1707*, Edinburgh 1963

——— 'The Anglo-Scottish union of 1707: the economic background', *Economic History Review* xvi (1963–4), 455–67

——— 'The Glasgow merchant community in the seventeenth century', *SHR* xlvii (1968), 53–71

——— 'The road to union', in Geoffrey Holmes (ed.), *Britain after the Glorious Revolution*, London 1969, 176–96

——— 'The burgh of Montrose and the union of 1707: a document', *SHR* lxvi (Oct. 1987), 182–4

Smyth, Jim, *The making of the United Kingdom, 1660–1800*, Harlow 2001

Somers, Margaret R., 'Citizenship and the place of the public sphere: law, community and political culture in the transition to democracy', *American Sociological Review* lviii (1993), 587–620

Speck, W. A., *The birth of Britain: a new nation, 1700–1710*, Oxford 1994

Speier, Hans, 'The rise of public opinion', in Robert Jackall (ed.), *Propaganda*, Basingstoke 1995, 26–46

Stephen, Jeffrey, 'The Kirk and the union, 1706–07: a reappraisal', *Records of the Scottish Church History Society* xxxi (2002), 68–96

Stevenson, David, 'A revolutionary regime and the press: the Scottish Covenanters and their press, 1638–51', *The Library* vii (1985), 315–37

——— 'The early Covenanters and the federal union of Britain', in Mason, *Scotland and England*, 163–81

Suzuki, Mihoko, *Subordinate subjects: gender, the political nation, and literary form in England, 1588–1688*, Aldershot 2003.

Szechi, Daniel, 'Defending the true faith: Kirk, State and Catholic missioners in Scotland, 1653–1755', *Catholic Historical Review* lxxxii (1996), 397–411

——— *George Lockhart of Carnwath, 1689–1727: a study in Jacobitism*, East Linton 2002

Temple, Richard Carnac, *New light on the mysterious tragedy of the 'Worcester', 1704–5*, London 1930

Thompson, E. P., 'The moral economy of the English crowd in the eighteenth century', *P&P* 1 (1971), 76–136

Walter, John, *Understanding popular violence in the English revolution: the Colchester plunderers*, Cambridge 1999

Watt, Tessa, *Cheap print and popular piety, 1550–1640*, Cambridge 1991

Whatley, Christopher A., 'Salt, coal and the union of 1707: a revision article', *SHR* lxvi (Apr. 1987), 26–45

——— 'Economic causes and consequences of the union of 1707: a survey', *SHR* lxviii (1989), 150–81

——— 'Scotland, England and "the golden ball": putting economics back into the union of 1707', *Historian* li (Autumn 1996), 9–13

——— 'The union of 1707, integration and the Scottish burghs: the case of the 1720 food riots', *SHR* lxxviii (Oct. 1999), 192–218

——— *Bought and sold for English gold? Explaining the union of 1707*, East Linton 2001

Whyte, Ian D., 'Urbanisation in eighteenth-century Scotland', in Devine and Young, *Eighteenth-century Scotland*, 176–94

Wood, Andy, *Riot, rebellion and popular politics in early modern England*, Basingstoke 2002

Wrightson, Keith, 'The politics of the parish in early modern England', in Paul Griffiths, Adam Fox and Steve Hindle (eds), *The experience of authority in early modern England*, Basingstoke 1996, 10–46

Young, J. R., 'The parliamentary incorporating union of 1707: political management, anti-unionism and foreign policy', in Devine and Young, *Eighteenth-century Scotland*, 24–52

Zaret, David, *Origins of democratic culture: printing, petitions and the public sphere in early modern England*, Princeton 2000

Unpublished theses

Birkeland, Mairianna, 'Politics and society in Glasgow, c. 1680–c. 1740', PhD diss. Glasgow 1999

Bowie, Karin, 'Scottish public opinion and the making of the union of 1707', PhD diss. Glasgow 2004

Clarke, T. N., 'The Scottish Episcopalians, 1688–1720', PhD diss. Edinburgh 1987

Ferguson, William, 'Electoral law and procedure in eighteenth- and early nineteenth-century Scotland', PhD diss. Glasgow 1957

Patrick, Derek John, 'People and parliament in Scotland, 1689–1702', PhD diss. St Andrews 2002

Index

Abercromby, Patrick, 102

Act anent Peace and War (1703), 53, 78

Act for a Treaty with England (1705), 81, 87, 91, 97, 160, 162

Act for Security of the Protestant Religion (1707), 107, 113–14, 125, 136, 142, 157, 164

Act of Security (1704), 25, 53, 73–4, 85, 89–90, 146, 151, 161–2

addresses, *see* petitions and addresses

adversarial politics, 4–5, 13, 54, 57, 160, 166–7

African Company: attack on director, 34; buyout in 1706 treaty, 96 n. 20, 97, 106, 162, 164; establishment, 17, 27–9; involvement in *Worcester* case, 10, 41, 162; petitions, 28–9, 30, 32, 58–9, 97, 115, 163, 166. *See also* Darien colony

Aird, John, provost of Glasgow, 141

Alien Act (1705), 41, 43, 79, 81, 90, 161

Anderson, James, 53, 89

Annandale, marquis of, *see* Johnstone, William, 1st marquis of Annandale

Anne, queen of Scotland and England: accession (1702), 35, 36, 45, 46, 82; and Church of Scotland, 40, 47, 85, 112, 118, 125; and Episcopalians, 16, 36–8; interest in closer union, 67, 69, 73–4, 82–3, 159, 161; and Jacobites, 16, 36, 147; loyalty to, 46–7, 83, 145; petitions to, 35, 59–60, 81, 99, 128–9, 149, 164; and political communications, 45, 53, 64, 81, 82–3, 85, 87, 90, 112, 118; 1702 parliament, 9, 27, 35, 161; and *Worcester* trial, 42

Arbuthnot, John, physician to Queen Anne, 106–7

Argyll, duke of, *see* Campbell, Archibald, 1st duke of Argyll; Campbell, John, 2nd duke of Argyll

Articles of Grievances (1689), 18

Atholl, duke of, *see* Murray, John, 1st earl of Tullibardine and 1st duke of Atholl

Atwood, William, 52, 89

Baillie, George, of Jerviswood, 42, 124, 131, 135

Bannatyne, John, minister of Lanark parish, 68, 76, 99, 109, 118, 124

Black, William, 96, 107

book trade and print market, 9, 19, 21–3, 167; booksellers and printers, 20, 21–3, 25, 33, 49–52, 76, 87, 89. *See also* newspapers; pamphlets

Boyle, David, 1st earl of Glasgow, 118, 135

bribery, *see* Court party

bribery and corruption, 8, 70–2, 90, 97–8, 152, 159, 165

Brisbane, John, younger, of Bishoptoun, 122, 135, 147

Brown, Andrew, 76

Bruce, Sir Alexander, of Broomhill, 4th earl of Kincardine, 37, 51, 85

Burnet, Gilbert, bishop of Salisbury, 82

Campbell, Archibald, 1st duke of Argyll, 16, 48, 51

Campbell, John, 2nd duke of Argyll, 16, 42, 81, 131, 136, 150, 162

Carstares, William, principal of Edinburgh University, 47, 112–13, 118, 135, 154

Cavaliers, *see* Jacobites

Cameronians, *see* Presbyterians

censorship, 45, 49–53, 55, 88–9, 92, 100, 127, 167

Charles I, king of Scotland and England, 57–8, 84

Church of Scotland: and book licensing, 49; insecurity of Church in union: (1699–1705), 68, 77, 82, 86–91; (1706–7), 93–4, 98, 112, 114, 117, 118–21, 124–7, 136, 141–4, 157, 161–3; security of Church in union, 85, 104, 106–7, 109, 111–14, 136, 154–5, 157, 164, 166. *See also* Presbyterians

Church of Scotland, General Assembly and Commission of the General Assembly: and Catholicism, 39–40, 63; and crowds, 113, 154–5; and Darien colony, 31–2, 71; and instructions, 18, 47, 116; meetings, 18; and petitions,